LEADING SECTORS
AND WORLD POWERS

STUDIES IN INTERNATIONAL RELATIONS
Charles W. Kegley, Jr., and Donald J. Puchala,
General Editors

LEADING SECTORS
AND WORLD POWERS
The Coevolution of Global Politics and Economics

George Modelski and William R. Thompson

University of South Carolina Press

Published in Columbia, South Carolina, by the
University of South Carolina Press

Manufactured in the United States of America

00 99 98 97 96   5 4 3 2 1

Library of Congress Cataloging-in-Publication Data

Modelski, George.
    Leading sectors and world powers : the coevolution of global
economics and politics / George Modelski and William R. Thompson.
        p.   cm. — (Studies in international relations)
    Includes bibliographical references and index.
    ISBN 1-57003-054-5
    1. Long waves (Economics)   2. International economic relations.
3. World politics.   I. Thompson, William R.   II. Title.
III. Series: Studies in international relations (Columbia, S.C.)
HB3729.M63   1996
337—dc20   95-4372

CONTENTS

Part Five: Looking Ahead

TABLES

FIGURES

PREFACE

The global economy has risen over the past millennium through a succession of leading sectors; the waxing and waning of these sectors, moreover, synchronized closely with the ascent and decline of the world powers. That is the thesis our work presents and defends, and in this new perspective the two key processes of global politics and global economics, known as long cycles and K-waves stand revealed as having an evolutionary and, even more significantly perhaps, a "coevolutionary" character. This thesis has been tested with remarkably good results against empirical and quantitative data, and that in itself makes another compelling story: the clarification and ordering of what has hitherto been thought of as belonging in the realms of anarchy and impenetrable chaos.

The present work is part of the long-cycles research program that we have been pursuing since the late 1970s, and it breaks new ground in several respects. In the first place, it extends and broadens the empirical study of the rise and decline of world powers, and complements it with an empirical and statistical account of the strategic sectors of the global economy. Our first large empirical project was a time series of seapower concentration over the last five centuries, which documented five surges, at regular intervals, in the degree to which one power held sway over the world's oceans—thus showing the existence of long cycles. We now document the existence of a comparable sequence of surges in global economic activity over an even longer period, and define the conditions in which spurts in crucial economic sectors serve as leading indicators of changes in global political leadership.

In the second place, the work presented here breaks new ground by extending the temporal scope of our global analysis, beyond what recently was regarded as the conventional limit of 1500, to cover the entire millennium that is now coming to a close. The relevant experience, we maintain, began about one thousand years ago and centered on Sung China; the experience prompted far-reaching Mongol experiments with world empire, and then moved to renaissance Italy, and onward to Western Europe, until the onset of full globalization in the last century. We propose that meaningful generalizations about global politics not only need to be tested against the entire experience with global-level interactions, but must also account for the profound transformations that have occurred in global political and economic organization in that time span.

Thirdly, we now locate our work within an evolutionary paradigm that enlarges the explanatory power and scope of our propositions to include the workings of dynamic systems at the global level. We propose that the long cycles of the rise and decline of world powers, and the K-waves of the movement of leading sectors, are both nonlinear processes that might best be understood as instances of evolutionary learning. The coevolution of these two processes, moreover, shapes the global political economy. In our view, an evolutionary paradigm offers explanations of structural change in international affairs that are superior to those of neorealism.

Close observers of the long-cycles program might note that we have now adopted a numbering system for the processes we are studying. We have identified ten long cycles, and to each correspond two K-waves of leading sectors; the global system is now experiencing LC10 (long cycle number ten), and the nineteenth K-wave. We believe that such a systematization, linked to a standard dating scheme, might facilitate research and communication. We also make allowance for the fact that the two global processes we have singled out for analysis are nested within larger world system evolutionary movements.

For those who wonder about the relevance of all this we might point out that our work interprets the recent dislocations in the global economy as manifestations of a transition crisis to a sociotechnical paradigm; that new paradigm is now generating emerging sectors in the information industries. Leadership in respect to such strategic portions of the global economy will be a leading indicator of character of changes in global structures and institutions in the next century.

Our interest in the interaction of politics and economics at the global level goes right back to the beginning of our research program. But it was not until the mid-1980s that one of the coauthors undertook empirical studies of leading sectors after 1500. In fact, the paper written jointly for the Moscow Kondratieff Centenary Conference in March 1992 produced the first full-scale version of our argument. That same paper was also presented at the annual convention of the International Studies Association in Atlanta later that month, and at ISMEA (Institut des Sciences Mathematiques et Economiques Appliquee) in

Paris in June 1993. We are indebted for valued comments received on each of these occasions.

Some readers might wonder why we do not present our findings in strict chronological order—beginning with China, and then moving on to Italy and Western Europe. The answer is that we have been making our way slowly by gradually reaching further and further back into the past. The conventional starting point was the set of five waves since the Industrial Revolution that were closely identified with Kondratieff. This point proved inadequate, and led to an extension of research back to about 1500. After the Moscow conference, we found that China and Italy needed to be given the full treatment as well. The results of that work are found in chapters 9 and 10 in greater detail than the earlier sections because we could take less prior knowledge for granted. In our view, no well-rounded student of international affairs will in the future be able to plead ignorance of the role played by these earlier developments in the molding of the global system.

We extend our special thanks to those who commented on chapter 9 on Sung China—including Hok-lam Chan, Andre Gunder Frank, Nicholas Lardy, Feng-hwa Mah, and James Townsend. Andrew Bosworth's research on the world city system proved suggestive for some of our formulations in chapters 8 and 9.

Finally, we wish to offer our warm thanks to the special panel of the International Studies Association's Annual Meeting in Washington, D.C. (April 1994), consisting of Terry Boswell, Christopher Chase-Dunn, Andre Gunder Frank, Jacek Kugler, and chair Robert Denemark, who patiently read a draft of the final work and were generous with their extended comments. We are also indebted to the following publishers for permission to adapt previously published maps for our own purposes: figure 6.3 is based on a figure in Dan Sleigh, *Jan Compagnie: The World of the Dutch East India Company* (Sleigh 1980, 29); figure 10.3 is adapted from a map in Janet L. Abu-Lughod, *Before European Hegemony: The World System* (Abu-Lughod 1989, 123, fig. 4: "Mediterranean Routes of Genoa and Venice in the Middle Ages"); and figure 10.4 is a slight modification of one originally published in Frederic C. Lane, *Venice: The Maritime Republic*. We are especially grateful to Suzanne Hull, graphic services manager, at the Indiana University Center for Media and Teaching Resources for technical assistance in the development of several maps utilized in this study.

LEADING SECTORS
AND WORLD POWERS

Part One

INTRODUCTION

Chapter One

Problem and Premises

The long-term relationship between world economic and world political structures and processes has received considerable attention in the past decade or so.[1] On the economic side of the ledger, much of the attention has been focused on price fluctuations and, to a lesser extent, on output. On the political side attention has been focused on fluctuations in systemic warfare and on phases of global leadership. It might be fair to add that more of this literature has tended to be empirically inductive rather than theoretically sanctioned— even though the important variables have not commonly been treated simultaneously. Some analysts have preferred to place the primary focus on economic processes while others have stressed power concentration and bloodshed. Not surprisingly, the basic relationships among economic growth, global leadership, and warfare remain disputed.

We propose a solution to this problem of structural coordination. Working within the parameters of the theory of long cycles of global politics, we argue that the rise and decline of leading sectors in the global economy (the Kondratieff process or K-wave) are coordinate with the rise and decline of world powers (the long cycle of global politics) in such a fashion that one long cycle (one period of ascendancy) is associated with two K-waves organized around innovative sectors in world commerce and industry.

The paired processes are thus interrelated in several respects. The processes have, of course, a common spatial base and are temporally adjacent. Moreover, the innovations of the first wave shape the developments of the second wave, and tend to reinforce it. The first wave also generates the financial and economic resources needed to put together a winning coalition and a strategy in the ensuing global war. Victory in global war, furthermore, paves the way for the second growth spurt just as participation in the war effort may have significant effect on the creation of new markets, products, and technologies. We develop our theoretical argument more fully in chapter 4. Concrete hypotheses on the sequential timing of new leading sectors, leadership, and global war may be derived from the theoretical framework. To test these hypotheses, we utilize a data base on leading sector spurts in the global political economy from the fifteenth century onward. With only minor exceptions, the hypotheses are strongly supported by the data analysis conducted in chapter 7. More broadly, we might interpret the K-waves that activate successive leading commercial/industrial sectors in conjunction with long cycles as forming one segment of the evolution of the global system over the past millennium, and in particular, as marking successive phases in the emergence of the global economy and in the rise of global politics.

THE PREMISES

The two major premises of this analysis are the existence both of the Kondratieff wave, and of the long cycle. Scholarly opinion is by no means unanimous on these points—our purpose here is not to continue discussion of that question, but rather to proceed to the next: how do those two processes interact?

K-Waves

A significant body of scholarship now converges on the view that long Kondratieff waves (or K-waves) do exist. The first to make this point in a major way was Nikolai D. Kondratieff (1892–1938). Writing between 1922 and 1928 Kondratieff assembled statistical material and an array of arguments to demonstrate the regularity of fifty- to sixty-year-long fluctuations in the world capitalist system; the time series of prices and output he assembled concerned mostly Britain, and the United States.[2] The principal conclusion of Kondratieff's analysis (1984, 89) is that "on the basis of available data, it may be assumed that the existence of long cycles in economic conditions is very probable."

Kondratieff's work was prominently taken up by Joseph Schumpeter whose major study, *Business Cycles* (1939), not only named this phenomenon the Kondratieff, but also linked it in an imaginative way to Kondratieff's theory of innovation. When concern over the long-run economic issues revived again in the 1970s, Walt Rostow's *The World Economy* (1979) revived this question by providing both new arguments and a wealth of empirical material (especially on new industrial sectors) spanning more than two centuries. Gerhard Mensch (1979) proposed a metamorphosis model of industrial evolution to represent both the growth spurts that he saw as the result of the bunching of basic innovations and the stagnation, or the technology stalemate, which follows when growth ends—as it did after the oil shock of 1973–1974. Giovanni Dosi (1983, 78–101) and others have recognized each such bunching of basic innovations to constitute a new "technological (or sociotechnical) paradigm." J. J. van Duijn's *The Long Wave in Economic Life* (1983) summarized the state of the debate, reviewed the empirical evidence, and produced a synthesis that can serve as a baseline for the present discussion.

The synthetic view emerging from this literature (see, in particular, van Duijn 1983, chap. 8; W. R. Thompson 1990, 1992a) converges on a common dating scheme, at least for the last five K-waves, and has the following other attributes:

1. K-waves in the first place concern output, rather than prices, and sectoral output growth and infrastructural investment in the global economy rather than the general macroeconomic performance of individual countries (as might be indicated by gross domestic product measures for national economies).
2. K-waves arise from the bunching of basic innovations that set in motion technological revolutions that create lead industrial sectors; basic innovations respond to unmet needs and market demand and must therefore be regarded as activating growth processes that are in part endogenous.
3. K-waves unfold as (four-phased) industry and product life cycles that imply *S*-shaped growth curves (rather than sine-waves with their upswings and downswings).
4. K-waves are an international phenomenon more visible in international production data than in those of individual countries (van Duijn 1983, 143); they are processes of a lead national economy (such as that of the United States), and of world trade in products and services of leading sectors, hence of the global economy.

We can now define K-waves as processes of rise and decline of leading sectors or, for short, as structural changes in the global economy. Fundamental to these changes are clusters of basic innovations that are broadly defined, as in Joseph Schumpeter's (1934, 66) classic formulation, as new products and methods of production, opening of new markets and sources of raw materials, and the pioneering of new forms of business (or commercial) organization. In the chapters that follow we shall have occasion to show that K-waves have fielded growth spurts in each of these classes of economic innovation.

One might have thought that the study of K-waves would represent one of the central concerns of economists, both theoretical and applied. That has not been so. Standard textbooks assign a rather limited place to long-range growth processes. In the eleventh edition of his influential manual, Paul Samuelson (1980, 241) refers only in a footnote to so-called Kondratieffs as the "alleged very long waves'' and comments ''whether these long waves are simply historical accidents, due to chance gold discoveries, inventions, and political wars, it is still too soon to say.''

This comment is illustrative of the gap that has for so long separated neoclassical economic theory, and efforts to understand long-term structural change. Neoclassical theory has treated both innovations (gold discoveries, too, are innovations in Joseph Schumpeter's meaning of the term), and political processes (wars) as historical accidents—that is, as exogenous to the problem under study. This is the heart of the theory (as formulated by Robert Solow, among others): the output of an economy, defined by its production function, depends only on the amount of capital and labor employed. Yet statistical tests of this conception (R. H. Solow 1957) have also found that capital and labor alone account for maybe one-half of the growth in output—the residual being attributed to technical progress. In other words, the Solowian tradition regards technological progress as an exogenous and fortuitous process—some sort of manna from heaven that now and then rains upon the fortunate ones—that does not feature in the theory. Current developments, however, influenced by the obvious demonstration effect of Pacific Rim growth, are causing some basic rethinking. Paul Romer (1990), among others, argues that technological change lies at the heart of economic growth, because technological change is endogenous and propelled by markets (contradicted by Robert Solow), and that it is a factor of production with special characteristics (nonrivalry and partial excludability) that gives the change a separate place in the production function among the basic inputs of the economy.[3]

The economic profession might be on its way toward incorporating innovation, and perhaps K-waves, into regular economic theory. But there are some other questions arising from the van Duijn synthesis that need to be resolved: why is the conventional treatment of K-waves generally restricted to the period since the Industrial Revolution? While it is true that some scholars, such as Fernand Braudel (1984, 73), have argued the applicability of this conception as far back as the sixteenth century, these scholars have not pursued this matter to any great extent. Surely innovations have been known to occur before the invention of the steam engine. Secondly, some other matters of interest to political scientists remain to be clarified: how do we explain the observed fact that the prominent bunching of innovations in the last four K-waves occurred, earlier, in Britain and, lately, in the United States? Is this merely a matter of historical accident, or ''manna from heaven'' calling for no explanation? And what is the role of war in all this? Is war merely a dependent variable as van Duijn (1983, 12) seems to imply, and are all wars equal in this respect? These, and other questions, bring us to our second major premise.

Long Cycles

The existence of long (leadership) cycles in global politics is the second premise of this analysis. We can define long cycles as instances of structural change because they are processes that in recent centuries have periodically rearranged the structure of global political arrangements and given rise to the phenomenon of world powers. Students of the subject since Kondratieff have generally taken it for granted that, for instance, Britain, widely recognized as a world power, should also have been the locus of the first industrial K-waves, and the United States should have been the locus of those that followed. That is, both countries were prominent not only in their economic leadership, but also in their political leadership.

While the precise characteristics of the process remain a matter of continuing debate, the existence of a sequence of leading powers itself is increasingly taken for granted. The list differs in particulars, especially for the earlier cases, and explanations vary, but as William R. Thompson (1988, 34) has argued, the similarities on the basic question of a pattern seem greater than the differences. Scholars such as Robert Gilpin (1981), Immanuel Wallerstein (1984), Paul Kennedy (1988), and Joshua Goldstein (1988) converge on a list that constitutes such a sequence.

We shall refer to the variant of structural political change employed in this analysis as the theory of long cycles (see Modelski 1978, 1987, 1990; W. R. Thompson 1988). We see long cycles as having marked the rise and decline of world powers. Table 1.1 shows the powers that have participated in that process in a global leadership function since the fifteenth century and the dating scheme that provides our temporal framework.

We show each successive long cycle, focused on one world power, to be a four-phased process; a long-cycle phase is a unit of our analysis.[4] The table might be read two ways. When we wish to focus on the rise of a power, we analyze its progress in its learning mode via the phases of agenda-setting, coalition-building, macrodecision, and execution.[5] When we wish to focus on decline, we observe that the phases of global war, and world power are the high points of the leadership process, which then moves (on the next line) through the phase of delegitimation, to deconcentration. We note, too, that the West European powers form one four-cycle bloc in this table, and that the U.S. cycle is the first in a new such (post-European) bloc. We are not forecasting a global war for 2030, but we do infer that a macrodecision phase is due—which in the past has taken that form, but in the future might assume other forms.

The long cycle might thus be viewed as the output of a political production function whose product is global leadership—that is coping with, and

Table 1.1
Long Cycles in Global Politics: Learning and Leadership Patterns

Long-Cycle Mode	Phases			
Learning ("Rise")	Agenda-setting	Coalition-building	Macrodecision	Execution
Leadership ("Decline")	Delegitimation	Deconcentration	Global War	World Power
	Starting In			
	(Chinese/Italian Renaissance)*			
	930			
	(West European)			
Portugal	1430	1460	1494	1516
Dutch Republic	1540	1560	1580	1609
Britain I	1640	1660	1688	1714
Britain II	1740	1763	1792	1815
	(post-European)			
United States	1850	1873	1914	1945
	1973	2000	2030	2050

*The Chinese/Italian renaissance periods are discussed in chapters 9 and 10.

producing solutions for, global problems. A production function lays out the set of possibilities that define what can be produced and how. The factors (or inputs) that go toward creating a global leadership production function are forces of global reach (advantaged by insularity), a lead economy, an open society, and responsiveness to global demand (problems) via innovation (see, for example, Modelski 1987, 220–28). Or else the long cycle appears as a learning process whose four phases successively optimize the utilization of each of these factors, even though all factors are present and essential throughout (Modelski 1990). Thus the phase of macrodecision/global war requires that maximum emphasis be placed on forces of global reach. The phase of execution/world power puts the spotlight on the lead economy and its place in the global economic order. Agenda setting/delegitimation highlights innovative potential and flexibility in confronting new problems. Coalition-building/ deconcentration draws upon the resources of an open society.

Structural Similarities

We have earlier defined K-waves as the rise and decline of leading sectors, and we now recognize long cycles as the rise and decline of world powers. This makes it clear that we have two parallel processes of structural change. That is, the K-wave, as a long-term economic process, interacts not with random historical accidents but with an equally well-structured political process that accounts for changes in the global political order, and the part that (global) wars have played in it.

Our analysis of K-waves centers not on prices or macroeconomic quantities, but on (globally) leading commercial and industrial sectors in the economies originating them. In the same way, the analysis of long cycles does not concern nation-states in general, but those states that have filled the role of global leadership, or those of challengers. K-waves direct attention to clusters of (endogenous) basic innovations, and the processes by which such innovations diffuse and transform major sectors of the global economy. Long cycles explain the rise of each world power as the emergence of a structure that in itself is a major (endogenous) institutional innovation, and one that is a response to (partly endogenous) priority global problems. A K-wave has been represented as a four-phase life cycle, and so has the long cycle when viewed as a learning (or leadership) process. Finally, if the K-wave is an evolutionary process of the global economy, so the long cycle is a process of the global political system.

There is one other similarity that we need to note. Both processes are subject to instability in the course of transition (or metamorphosis) from one period to the next. The march of economic innovation has been marked, in Joseph Schumpeter's famous phrase, by "creative gales of destruction," bringing with it the decline of some industries, massive unemployment, and distress to large areas. The long cycle of global politics has been paced by periods of generation-long warfare. In the twentieth century, moreover, the instabilities attendant upon these two processes seemed to have become particularly damaging—bringing the Great Depression in the transition from the first to the second U.S. K-wave, and the two world wars in the transition from British to U.S. global leadership.

We do not see these similarities as coincidental. The similarities exist because the K-wave and the long cycle of global politics are interdependent processes. Elaborating and testing the nature of this interdependency is what we propose as the focus of this analysis.

The subsequent chapters are grouped in four clusters. The first cluster—chapters 2, 3, and 4—establishes our theoretical foundation. We first review earlier examinations linking long-term economic growth and warfare. As many as fourteen types of interpretation are described in chapter 2. But each one comes with different types of analytical handicaps. Reviewing the multiple interpretations en masse facilitates the development of seven criteria in chapter 3 that can be used to evaluate the various arguments. The criteria are presented in the form of questions that a viable argument linking long-term economic growth, global politics, and war should be able to answer. While most of the fourteen approaches may be able to answer some of the seven critical questions, only one argument in our estimation is able to deal with all seven. In chapter 4, we discuss precisely how our leadership/long-cycle argument treats each criteria.

Chapters 5, 6, and 7 are devoted to testing some of the implications of the leadership/long-cycle interpretation. Chapter 5 develops several explicit hypotheses on the timing of leading sector growth spurts, global war, political leadership, and innovation. These variables are operationalized in chapter 6 with appropriate data from the fifteenth century to the present. Chapter 7 reports the empirical outcome of the hypothesis testing. Given the difficulties of developing pertinent indicators over a five-hundred-year span, the hypotheses prove to be quite successful in specifying the sequential timing of important structural changes.

The last two groups of chapters seek to extend the interpretation backwards and forwards in time. Chapter 8 develops reasons why this temporal extension is conceivable. Chapter 9 then demonstrates how our argument can be applied to developments in tenth-century Sung China. The point is not merely that developments in the tenth century paralleled later developments, but that the rhythms of modern or post-fifteenth-century, long-term, economic growth can be linked directly to economic growth in the tenth and ensuing centuries. While chapter 9 focuses on the nature of K-waves in China between the tenth and thirteenth centuries, chapter 10 examines the diffusion of long-term economic growth from the east to the west and its manifestation in Italian (especially Genoese and Venetian) economic activities of the thirteenth through fifteenth centuries. In both chapters an attempt is made to continue the commitment made in earlier chapters toward seeking empirical support for the Chinese and Italian generalizations.

Our last chapter focuses on the present and near-future. We are currently in the midst of an uncomfortable transition from one K-wave to the next. While it is one thing to identify the forms taken by earlier K-waves, it is quite another to specify what form the next one is likely to take. Nevertheless, we are not without clues that permit us to forecast some of the likely carriers of the next wave. Another question that deserves discussion is whether global war is likely to continue to play its traditional role in the sequencing of long-term economic growth. The past may be useful in predicting the future but it need not determine just what that future will be. Nevertheless, the regularities of the past are impressive. For the role of global war to diminish in these processes, some specific changes in international political behavior will be essential.

Part Two

THE STATE OF THE FIELD

Chapter Two

The Confused State
of the Literature

I have always heard it said that peace brings riches; riches bring pride; pride brings anger;
anger brings war; war brings poverty; poverty brings humanity; humanity brings peace, as
I have said, brings riches, and so the world's affairs go around.

Luigi da Porto, 1509 (Blainey 1973, 87)

The commencement of . . . peace after a long war, generally produces considerable distress in trade. It changes in a great degree the nature of the employments to which the
respective capitals of countries were before devoted.

David Ricardo, 1817 (Rostow 1990, 84–85)

Wars and revolutions do not come out of the clear sky. . . . They originated from real,
especially economic circumstances . . . solely during the upswing of long waves . . . wars
originate in the acceleration of the pace and increased tension of economic life.

Kondratieff, 1935

Some people want war, not because they enjoy mass murder, not because the mass hysteria
of war times is an antidote for boredom, not because an ambitious king, dictator, or president selfishly desires to be a hero in history, but because they think it is a good way to end
a business depression.

F. G. Dickinson, 1940 (326)

We can draw the conclusion that it is the frequency of wars—i.e., a political phenomenon—that introduces the periodical element in the secular economic changes. The
enigma of long waves in econometrics is thus in a first approximation nothing but a mirror
of the enigma of the periodicity of wars.

J. Aakerman, 1944 (Soderstrom 1982, 28)

Many historians and political scientists (and even some economists) would like to believe
that wars and the economy behave according to some inexorable, interrelated, wave-like
cycle. While such notions have a romantic appeal to our need to search out the driving

13

forces of history, the reality is, alas, much more mundane. . . . The intensity of war over time is a simple random walk, and prices are a first order moving average. . . . Since war is a random walk, one may say that there is a permanent level of war in the international system. This being the case, one should not expect to find wars driving fluctuations in the price level, as many cycle theorists believe.

J. A. C. Conybeare, 1990 (336–37).

These quotations testify to persistent beliefs about the relationship between war and long-term economic growth. While the contemporary majority opinion on the question tends to dismiss war as a temporary nuisance to the normal course of economic progress, throughout the twentieth century, and longer, a few observers have maintained that war cannot be dismissed as an exogenous aberration in the growth process. Instead, our contention is that global war and long-run economic growth processes are reciprocally interdependent. For better or worse, and arguments exist that portray the relationship as either beneficial or dysfunctional, to understand one process we must also come to terms with what the other process represents and how the two processes interact.

The goal of this chapter is to review the pertinent literature on the war/long-term growth connection—a larger, richer, and more complicated literature than is often realized. As many as fourteen different approaches to the relationship can be isolated.

FOURTEEN APPROACHES TO THE WAR/LONG-TERM ECONOMIC GROWTH RELATIONSHIP

Table 2.1 identifies fourteen clusters of explanatory approaches to the question of how war and economic growth processes interact in the long run. The focus in table 2.1 is placed entirely on long-term growth processes. There is another, more general, literature on how war impacts economic systems (Rasler and Thompson 1992) that has been ignored if its emphasis is on relatively short-term economic processes and impacts. All of the fourteen approaches in table 2.1, although some of the examples discussed are not always as clear as they might be on this subject, explicitly refer to long waves of economic expansion and contraction before and/or after wars. At the same time, one should note that a large portion of the long-wave literature does not appear in the table. The reason is simple. Most long-wave analyses do not give war a prominent role. There is also no mention of analyses of war cycles (see W. R. Thompson 1985; Thompson and Rasler 1988; among others) that are not interrelated with economic cycles. Thus table 2.1 is the outcome of applying two filters. Both long economic waves and war must be addressed in some fashion to qualify for table 2.1.

We emphasize that table 2.1 is not intended to be comprehensive in its coverage of representative authors. The works listed under each approach are meant to illustrate and elaborate how the war-growth relationship is seen as functioning. Authors who are especially vague (a possible fifteenth approach) include Wright (1942/1965) and Toynbee (1954)—both of whom raised the possibility of a relationship between long-term economic fluctuations and war without much specification of what they had in mind—are excluded from the table.

The principal distinguishing feature of most of these approaches is the sequential pattern of upswing, downswing, and war. Three emphases begin with upswings, three with war, and three with downswings. Once someone begins with one of the three parts of the puzzle, there are only so many ways to mix the remaining two parts. Nevertheless, some approaches defy this seemingly safe generalization by repeating one of the three variables. In addition, there are five other approaches that are difficult to identify in terms of the variable sequence, either because the variable sequence is not clear, not important, or not consistent.

One other interesting facet of these clusters of explanatory emphasis is the timing of their appearance. With some exceptions, this literature's chronology is markedly bimodal. Most of the literature either emerged between the end of World War I and the beginning of World War II or after the middle to late 1970s. This facet is not coincidental nor is it difficult to explain. Interest in long waves, in general, is most likely in downturns of the economy and least likely in upturns. In addition, several of the explanatory clusters are closely connected to the dramatic impacts of World War I, like so many of our theoretical explanations of international relations. The more recent output moreover reflects, in part, a renewed concern for theorizing about and testing the interrelationships among economic and political processes.

Realistically, there are only so many features of the literature that can be identified usefully in the abstract. Particularly since this literature does not appear to be all that familiar to many readers, it seems advisable to first let the literature "speak" for itself. This can be done by briefly describing each of the fourteen approaches. After establishing this information base, we can return to more general questions in the second section of this chapter.

One awkward element in this presentation is the matter of spatiotemporal parameters. Authors usually have more or less specific times and places in mind when they have advanced their various arguments. We need to alert the reader to what these qualifications might be, or what we infer them to be, be-

Table 2.1

Fourteen Clusters in the Literature on War
and Long-term Cycles of Economic Growth

U → W	U → W → D	U → W/D → U
Kondratieff (1935/1984)	Hansen (1932)	Modelski (1981, 1982)
Macfie (1938)	Davis (1941)	
Blainey (1973)	Bernstein (1941)	
Schuman and Rosenau (1972)	Dickinson (1941)	
Doran (1983)	Imbert (1959)	
Mansfield (1988)	Goldstein (1988, 1991a)	
	Boswell and Sweat (1991)	

W → D	W → D → U	W → U → D
Ricardo (1817)	Aakerman (1932, 1944)	Rostow (1980)
	Rose (1941)	Thompson and Zuk (1982)
	Silberling (1943)	Craig and Watt (1985)

D → W	D → W → U	D → W → D
Frank (1978)	Bergesen (1985)	Mensch (1979)
Russett (1983)		

Hegemonic Phase Dependent	Evolving Relationship	Intermittent Reinforcement
Research Working Group (1979)	Williams, McGinnis and Thomas (1992)	Trotsky (1923)
Hopkins, Wallerstein et al. (1982)	Williams (1993)	Hansen (1964)
		Liska (1990)

Differential Outcomes	No Relationship
Keynes (1919)	Schumpeter (1939)
Angell (1933)	Conybeare (1990)
Organski and Kugler (1980)	
Olson (1982)	
Brenner (1985)	

W = war, U = economic upswing, D = economic downswing

cause, otherwise, the presumption may be that the generalizations apply everywhere and for all times. That type of argument in fact is rarely encountered. However, there is no need to devote a great deal of space to boundary delineations in this chapter since we will return to this issue in chapters 3 and 4. It should suffice if we give some brief warning about spatiotemporal qualifications early on in each description of the arguments.

The order of presentation is somewhat arbitrary. We begin with approaches that commence with upswings because they are the most common in the literature. A second and probably not unrelated reason is that Kondratieff (1935), although he neither initiated long-wave analysis nor was the first to make a connection between war and long waves, nonetheless must be considered as the progenitor or patriarch of war/long-wave hypotheses. His early hypothesis clearly linked wars to upswings and this is as good a reason as any to begin with upswing-driven interpretations.

Upswing-War Relationship

The Kondratieff Interpretation

Kondratieff's work in the 1920s (spatiotemporal boundaries: industrialized states in the late eighteenth to early twentieth centuries) was responsible for stimulating an intense debate among Soviet economists about the future of the capitalist system. Later, western analysts interested in long-wave analysis usually begin with those conducted by Kondratieff. In the process of listing a number of regularities associated with upswings and downswings, Kondratieff (1935) observed that wars were more likely to occur on the long upswing than on the downswing due to the increased tensions associated with economic competition on upswings. In this early argument, wars were only a by-product of the long wave and not an integral component of the economic fluctuations.

The Macfie-Blainey Interpretation

Macfie (1938) and Blainey (1973) may not genuinely belong in this survey because their references to an upswing-war relationship do not always explicitly differentiate between long-term and short-term phases of prosperity. Nevertheless, the logic of their argument (spatiotemporal boundaries: industrialized states in the nineteenth to twentieth centuries) should hold equally well in the long as in the short run.[1] Their argument is of interest as well for its specification of the relationship as a post–1815 phenomenon.

The argument is simple: a period of economic recovery affects moods and expectations. Individuals become more optimistic about the future and their sense that they can control their environment. Consumers and producers are affected equally, as are governmental decision makers. In particular, governmental revenues are rising while social problems are declining. The reverse

Assume scredit constraint? Has phenomenon changed over Time as gov't finance has changed

situation holds in economic downturns in which governments are more apt to be either cautious or apprehensive.

An economic upswing is neither a necessary nor a sufficient cause of war. Wars occur in both good and poor economic phases. But they are more likely to occur on the upswing and when they do occur, they are more likely to be long wars. Moreover, these generalizations (Blainey 1973, 92) are thought to be more applicable to the post-Napoleonic period than to the pre-nineteenth-century era for two reasons. Economic moods were increasingly likely to be shared by a number of states after 1815. The oscillations between pessimism and optimism also became sharper in an age of industrialization.

Other Relevant Observations

Shuman and Rosenau (1972, 76) state that there ''seems to be no rational basis for the upswing of the long wave any more than there is for the down-swing.'' Thus, the upswing is important for starting wars—trough wars begin after the trough and peak wars before the peak, so both types of war are located on the upswing. Peak wars have important economic and other types of impact, but they are not given any systematic credit for driving the economic cycle upwards or downwards.

Mansfield (1988) found a statistically significant tendency for the number of wars to be higher in upswings than in downswings, but this finding did not hold up if the analysis was restricted to major power wars. Mansfield concluded that K-waves may have more influence on the incidence of minor power warfare than they apparently have on major power wars (spatiotemporal boundaries: world system from the late fifteenth to twentieth centuries).

Upswing-War-Downswing Relationship

The Bernstein Interpretation

Bernstein (1940) acknowledged that economic upswings produced favorable conditions for fighting wars (spatiotemporal boundaries: major powers in the twentieth century). Prospects for long-term economic growth depended on wartime and postwar monetary policies. Major wars cause major price distortions. If decision makers adjust their exchange rates accordingly, the probability of a smooth postwar economic transition is maximized. The failure to adjust exchange rates will lead to more severe postwar depressions due to the effect of high interest rates on investment and business activity in general. Yet Bernstein was quick to note that depressions were not entirely products of warfare. In the absence of war, economic downturns would still occur. Wars simply made them worse.

The Imbert Interpretation

Imbert's (1959) economic upswing (spatiotemporal boundaries: major western states from the late thirteenth century onward) is fueled by innovation in dynamic industries. The surge in economic activity communicates a boom mentality and places strain on markets. The demand for raw materials is apt to increase which leads to colonial expansion and rising competition among industrial producers for control over the sources of the raw material. In general, interstate tensions become more acute. *Markets?*

In response to the rise in tension, decision makers allocate more state expenditures to the military sector. Tax burdens increase and the state finds itself competing with private capital for loans. As the initial industrial innovations encounter various types of rigidities and lose their capacity for leading growth, the economy's dependence on military spending increases and arms spending takes the place of public projects. The expansion of the military helps deal with rising unemployment.

When war breaks out among the main economic competitors, at a point demarcated in figure 2.1, the immediate economic effects depend in part on the circumstances. Production is likely to increase rapidly unless the state is invaded. But the boom is short-lived because the dependence on military spending cannot be maintained indefinitely. Four types of war effects will make postwar stagnation quite likely:

1. War participants suffer financial dislocation.
2. The abrupt increases in wartime demand and wartime destruction tend to be destabilizing.
3. States are likely to assume some greater level of control over production and pricing decisions during wartime, thereby increasing the rigidities encountered by producers.
4. War affects mortality and birth rates through war deaths and the increased probability of epidemics and disease. The ratio of the nonworking to working population increases and, in the process, creates a greater welfare burden.

During the ensuing stagnation phase, a generation traumatized by their war experiences places a premium on preserving the peace. Order, reaction, and conservatism are favored. In turn, insurrection and revolution become more likely. The stagnation will continue until the economy manages to stabilize itself and wean its activities away from the distortions created by war-

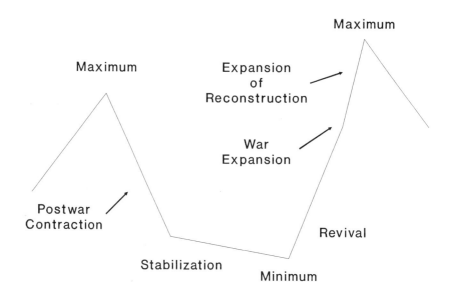

Source: based on Goldstein (1988: 37).
Figure 2.1. Imbert's Interpretation

induced state controls. When this occurs, the foundation for the next innovation impulse is established.[2]

The Goldstein Interpretation

Goldstein (1985, 1987, 1988, 1991a) has probably contributed more than anyone else to reviving the question of how wars and prosperity are linked. His 1988 analysis went some way in summarizing many of the arguments concerning economic long waves and war. His 1991 analysis is one of the more sophisticated empirical studies to emerge after nearly a century of controversy (spatiotemporal boundaries: world system from the mid-eighteenth to the mid-twentieth centuries).[3] The basic perspective that emerges from his analyses, outlined in figure 2.2, sees economic upswings increasing the probability of severe wars. Severe wars usher in a phase of stagnation from which the world economy eventually recovers leading to another resurgence of robust economic growth. Goldstein's analysis suggests that this process has gone on since at least 1495.

Economic upswings create economic surpluses and full war chests. The

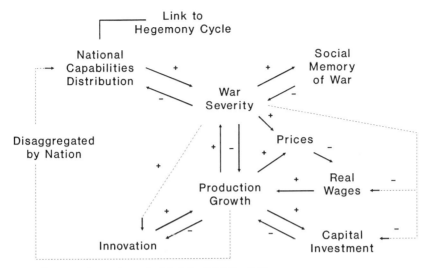

Source: based on Goldstein (1991b: 311).

Figure 2.2. Goldstein's War-Economy Theory

ability to wage war makes severe wars more likely. Severe wars, in turn, consume the surpluses and war chests and put an end to the growth upswing. Decades are required to rebuild. While there may be some gains registered in terms of resource mobilization for combat purposes, these gains are offset by the losses brought about by wartime distortions and destruction.

Goldstein is careful to distinguish between production and prices. Prices, in his view, are functions of war. Other things being equal, the severity of the war greatly effects the rate of war-induced inflation—in other words, the greater the severity, then the higher the rate of inflation. When prices rise, real wages decline. Yet he also notes that production (production waves are said to precede war/price waves by some ten to fifteen years) is already stagnating toward the end of the upswing. This phenomenon is explained in terms of demand increases outstripping supply. As a result, inflation occurs.

The lack of clarity on this issue may be traceable to the lack of specification among innovation, investment, and production. Cycles in innovation and investment are viewed as reinforcing the production long wave. Increases in innovation facilitate economic growth but growth discourages further innovation. Investment increases on the upswing but, eventually, over investment results. Investors retrench and growth slows down as a consequence. What is not exactly specified is whether innovation, investment, war, or some combination of the three processes is responsible for ending the upswing.

Goldstein also raises the question of how these economic/war cycles impact the distribution of capabilities among the major powers. War severity increases capability concentration. Relative capabilities then begin a process of diffusion as they move toward equality among the major powers. Another bout of severe war ensues and the cycle repeats itself. In addition to war, differential rates of innovation and production influence relative capability standings. Presumably, all three factors share some responsibility for generating the fluctuations in capability concentration.

Curiously, though, Goldstein does not regard this question of the distribution of national capabilities as being very closely connected to hegemonic cycles (even though hegemony can be a synonym for high levels of capability concentration). There seem to be two related reasons for this assertion of a weak linkage. First, Goldstein recognizes three hegemons (the Netherlands, Britain, and the United States) and three to four times as many long waves. Thus, he argues that there is no fixed number of long waves that correspond to a cycle of hegemony. Second, each long wave is associated with a war peak but only some war peaks are also hegemonic war peaks. Nonhegemonic war peaks are described as mid-course adjustments in the political arrangements of the world system, whereas hegemonic war peaks lead to a rewriting of the arrangements. So, hegemonic cycles and economic long waves overlap but only in an irregular fashion.

The Boswell and Sweat Interpretation

Boswell and Sweat (1991; Boswell, Misra, and Brueggemann 1991) were interested primarily in further testing some of Goldstein's (1988) arguments. In the process, Boswell and Sweat also generated a distinctive argument they called a resource theory of the size of wars that is predicated in part on some assumptions that differ from those adopted by Goldstein (spatiotemporal boundaries: world system from the seventeenth to twentieth centuries). Boswell and Sweat see no reason to anticipate any more competition when markets are expanding than when they are contracting. They also expect that hostilities among the major economic powers will be displaced by colonial expansion in periods of economic contraction. Contraction also means that fewer resources are available for waging major power wars. Major wars, therefore, should only break out if there is no longer room for colonial expansion as might be the case if all possible territory had already been allocated to someone's sphere of influence.

Nonetheless, the resource theory is predicated on the assumptions that (1) major wars require an extensive supply of military and human resources; (2)

decision makers are rational and initiate wars only when they perceive the benefits to outweigh the costs and their own capabilities to exceed that of the enemy; and (3) long economic upswings generate the scale of resources necessary for engaging in major power conflict.

Several factors make some decision makers more likely to exaggerate the net benefits and their own relative capability position. For example, decision-maker perceptions may be influenced by two types of bias: egocentrism and ethnocentrism. The first type of bias, which presumes greater information on internal developments as opposed to those taking place abroad, can lead to an inflated sense of one's own resources growing faster than others within the context of upswings. The second type of bias, ethnocentrism, may encourage decision makers to overvalue their own capabilities while discounting the opposition's resources as inherently inferior. Both biases may encourage leaders to view their upswing expansion as relatively unique. Other states may be expanding as well, but not at the same pace or with the same results.

The decision makers who are most likely to initiate a war are those who believe their resources are superior to those of the opposition and who believe their upswing gains have been unmatched by all other economies. Should war break out, a large and sustained conflict is possible because the resources are available for such a conflict. Indeed, the upswing is not viewed as absolutely necessary to war breaking out. If at least one state's decision makers have sufficient insulation from mass discontent, are able to build up military resources despite economic stagnation, and are able to successfully promote ethnocentrism, the initiation of major power war is at least conceivable. World War II, an anomaly for most upswing-war arguments, is offered as an example.

The resource theory of the size of war has relatively little to say about the impact of war on economic conditions. The authors were content to note that major wars initially spur production but eventually lead to economic stagnation. How much of the blame for the ensuing downswing is attributable to the major wars is not entirely clear.

Boswell and Sweat also questioned whether one should expect the long wave-war relationship to be consistent across several centuries. They doubted that long waves before the Industrial Revolution existed or, if they did exist, whether they exerted predictable effects on the probability of warfare. They also predicted that there would be less evidence of hegemonic restraints on warfare before 1790 as well.

For the most part, Boswell and Sweat's empirical findings were supportive even though not all of their specific predictions were realized. A positive relationship between long-wave expansions and war was found, but it was not confined to the post–1790 era. After 1790 imperial expansion did seem to displace major war as argued in the resource theory. Evidence for hegemonic restraint of warfare was also more statistically significant after 1790 than before.

Upswing-War/Downswing-Downswing Relationship

The Early Leadership/Long-cycle Interpretation

Modelski (1981, 1982) proposed what he labeled an alternating innovations model to explain long-wave fluctuations (spatiotemporal boundaries: global polity and economy in the late eighteenth to twentieth centuries). The model assumes that the global polity and economy are both propelled by a stream of innovations that can assume different forms as demonstrated in table 2.2. The model further assumes that the polity and the economy must be related structurally since they both draw on the same population and resource base. Conceivably then, the polity and economy can either grow simultaneously or in an alternating pattern. Of the two possibilities, the latter seems more likely. "The more goes for economic growth, the less is left for other social purposes. The more politics consumes attention and resources, the less can be invested in wealth creation" (Modelski 1981, 75).

Another reason for the appeal of the alternating pattern is that each set of activities creates problems that need to be addressed by the other. When politics receives too much attention, the resulting destruction of resources creates a need for renewed wealth construction. Economic growth, on the other hand, creates its own set of problems that require political solutions. An alternating pattern thus offers some level of self-regulation.

There is also an important linkage between polity and economy emphases and resource scarcities. As the demand for guns (excessive politics) increases, resources become more scarce and prices rise. As the demand for guns declines, resources become relatively abundant and prices decline as well. Economic innovations are more likely to emerge as leading sectors of growth in these periods of relative resource abundance than in periods of high prices and resource scarcity.

Modelski superimposed a second pattern on the basic alternating framework. In every other period when the demand for political innovation is rising, there is "an extra strong upbeat." The need for a major political overhaul leads to global war, the main pulse of the world system, and a new world power, the primary organizer of political innovations. These world powers rise and fall in terms of their capacity to perform a leadership role in ordering and maintaining global level transactions and interactions. Their status as lead economies—the world economy's centers of commerce, finance, and indus-

Table 2.2

Alternating Waves of Innovation, 1763–1980

Political Innovations	Long-Cycle Phases (Price Trends)	Leading Industrial Sectors*
American Revolution	Deconcentration 1763–1782 (stable)	Cotton Textiles (Britain, 1780s)
Britain as World Power French Revolution Vienna Congress Concert of Europe Latin American Independence	Global War 1792–1815 (up)	
	World Power 1815–1848 (down)	Railroads (Britain, 1830s)
Revolutions of 1848 Italian and German Unification Russia Checked (Crimean War)	Delegitimation 1848–1873 (up)	
	Deconcentration 1873–1913 (down)	Steel (Britain, France, Germany, U.S., 1870s) Sulphuric acid (Britain, German, U.S., 1870s) Electricity (U.S., 1880s) Motor vehicles (Britain, France, Germany, U.S., 1900s)
U.S. as World Power Russian and Chinese Revolutions Nuclear Weapons United Nations Indian Independence	Global War 1914–1946 (up)	Plastics (U.S., 1940–1945)
	World Power 1946–1973 (stable)	Synthetics (U.S., 1950–1955) Electronics, Aerospace, Travel, Education, Health (U.S., 1960s)
SALT OPEC	Delegitimation 1973– (up)	

Source based closely on Modelski 1982, 111.
*The maximum rates of expansion for the leading sectors are given in addition to the country or countries first in the expansion of that sector. The identifications are based on information in Rostow 1978.

trial innovation—is the resource foundation that funds the exercise of global leadership. The identity of the leading sectors that fuel the lead economy status has changed over time. Nevertheless, the main division is between the mercantile era in which economic innovations were centered on oceanic commerce and the more recent industrial era that is featured in table 2.2.

Wars are thus one of the expressions of the rising demand for political innovation in the up-periods (upturns from a price perspective; downturns from a production perspective), but it is the wars (in particular, the period of global war) in every other upturn that are most critical to the functioning of the global polity and economy. Consequently, the pattern is one of price downswings and production upswings that precede war that are followed by phases of price downswings and production upswings. Note, however, that in this interpretation, unlike any of the others, war is equated with a phase of price upswing and production downswing.

War-Downswing Relationship

The observation that war has negative economic consequences is hardly controversial. In fact this observation is quite common in the nonlong-wave literature on the consequences of war. Long-wave analysts are not likely to be content with the generalization that wars produce downswings. However, we find it interesting to note that Ricardo's early observation (1817) that long wars tended to produce a peace characterized by ''considerable distress in trade'' and considerable change in capital utilization (cited in Bernstein 1940, 530) never quite became institutionalized in economic theory. Perhaps if more economic theory had been formulated immediately after the Napoleonic Wars rather than much later in the nineteenth century more attention might have been given to the economic effects of major wars.

War-Downswing-Upswing Relationship

The Rose Interpretation

Rose (1941), a University of Illinois economist, contributed one of the shortest treatments of the war-prosperity relationship. While his analysis is less than two journal pages long, its line of attack is fairly distinctive and worth reviewing (spatiotemporal boundaries: industrialized states in the twentieth century).

Rose argued that long waves were not only centered on major wars, but were also primarily driven by them. A major war is destructive and stifles consumer demand through appeals to patriotism and high prices. An interval of postwar prosperity is to be expected as pent-up consumer demand and reconstruction make up for the losses and opportunity costs of the previous war. But when these extraordinary demands decrease, an extraordinarily deep depression is likely to follow.

Paralleling the decline in demand is the decline in prices and interest rates which had been grossly distorted by war. The movement toward some type of equilibrium position seems to facilitate an outburst of Schumpeterian innovation. That is, after the effects of the last war have been purged, the economic situation again becomes favorable for a new phase of prosperity based on carrier innovations.

Post Cold-War?

Rose did not really address the question of why major wars occur. He did note, however, that the role of modern war was similar to the role of innovation in the economic system. Inefficient, noncompetitive states are forced out of existence by war and, in the process, the nature of the world economy is altered. Since war has an important economic outcome, Rose implies that wars must also have important economic roots. At the same time, modern war, which Rose seemed to equate with the expanded scale of twentieth-century warfare, was dependent on innovation in armaments, such as the airplane. While Rose thought that the era of Schumpeterian innovations had ended (for unstated reasons), he did not predict that a pattern of prosperity and depression, keyed on major wars, was likely to disappear in the near future. For Rose, modern war was the innovation and, therefore, "the dominant cause of long waves in economic activity."

The Silberling Interpretation

Silberling (1943, 63), a former business school professor at Stanford University, credited major wars with creating long-term economic fluctuations (spatiotemporal boundaries: United States from the nineteenth to twentieth centuries): "great wars generate not only temporary economic or financial dislocation but disturbance of such magnitude that the broad course of industrial progress may be appreciably modified for several decades."

If war leads to economic downturn, what processes, other than the cyclical boost to urban wages, lead to renewed growth? For Silberling, the most dependable sources of long-term economic recuperation were major innovations in power utilization and transportation. Steam engines, railroads, electrical energy, and the internal combustion motor led his list of examples. "New discoveries and inventions and the application of new ideas to the acts of production'' were the root sources of economic progress and the restoration of prosperity (Silberling 1943, 69).

Silberling also endorsed the idea that the long-term economic fluctuations inspired by war participation are correlated with alternatives in prevailing political philosophies. Left or liberal ideas flourish in periods of stagnation. More conservative policies predominated in periods of economic boom.

War-Upswing-Downswing Relationship

Analyses that fall within this cluster usually relate war to prices. Rostow (1980), for example, argues (spatiotemporal boundaries: world economy in the late eighteenth to twentieth centuries) that specific wars (first K-wave: the Napoleonic Wars; second K-wave: Crimean, Indian Mutiny, the U.S. Civil War, and the three Prussian wars of the period; third K-wave: Spanish-American, Boer, Russo-Japanese, Balkan Wars, and World War I; fourth K-wave: World War II and the Korean War) reinforced the inflationary tendency of long-wave upswings. Rostow also argued that none of these wars initiated the upswings, and contrary to Kondratieff's argument, most of the wars were not made more probable by the upswing. More quantitative analyses (Thompson and Zuk 1982: world powers in the eighteenth to twentieth centuries; Craig and Watt 1985: world system in the nineteenth to twentieth centuries) have found support that some wars, if not all the wars mentioned by Rostow, did lead to greater price inflation that eventually recedes (the price downswing) as the impact of war and other factors is eroded.

Downswing-War Relationship

Examples for this category are not plentiful. Frank (1978) once suggested that different types of war were likely to be associated with upswings and downswings. Wars on the downswing are more likely to represent defensive attempts to eliminate economic competitors while upswing wars are more likely to be expansionary wars. Frank was writing specifically about eighteenth-century trade wars but, presumably, his hypothesis need not be restricted to that century.

Another example of a downswing-war argument is advanced by Russett (1983) who contends that the lion's share of the systematic evidence on the war-economic conditions relationship points toward the period following a sustained stagnation or downswing as the most war-prone. While it is not clear what body of evidence he refers to, Russett also suggests that wars that do break out during upswings may have had their roots in the earlier downswing period. It may simply have taken time for the economic conditions to have their political impact and for war preparations to be advanced (spatiotemporal boundaries: specific time not given).

In a related vein, Chase-Dunn (1989, 164) has noted that if Goldstein is right that wars tend to peak between peaks in production and prices, then wars are most likely to occur at the beginning of the downswing in investment and production (spatiotemporal boundaries: world systems in the late fifteenth to twentieth centuries). States still have ample war resources. The competition for markets should be increasing thanks to overproduction that, in turn, should increase the pressure to use state power to protect market shares and investment opportunities. The probability of interstate conflict and war should increase accordingly.

Downswing-War-Upswing Relationship

The Bergesen Interpretation

For Bergesen (1985), war serves an important function in the economic upswing/downswing cycle (spatiotemporal boundaries: world system, nineteenth to twentieth centuries). Overproduction in the long upswing leads to a long downturn. Violence is necessary to remove the limitations on renewed growth and the next upswing. War is then critical to the periodic reorganization and continued functioning of the world economy.

A principal root of the problem and the reason that a downturn follows an upswing is that the nature of aggregate world demand is fixed during the forced economic reorganization of a downturn. The absence of coordination among producers in an interstate world makes it inevitable that the world supply eventually will outrun the structural limitations of world demand. With the onset of the downswing, the competition between various types of actors intensifies. Capital and labor fight over wages, benefits, and working hours. Firms engage in price wars, takeovers, and mergers. The most powerful states conflict over access to markets and the control of the periphery.

Economic reorganization requires coercive hegemonic dominance:

> if you cannot have a new period of economic expansion without a reunification of the world market and pacification of core rivalries, and if that politically comes about through the dominance of a single state, then war becomes the means through which the bickering and protectionism of the downturn is turned into the seeming peace and free trade regime of the succeeding upturn. (Bergesen 1985, 329)

War thus has several functions. War ends the distribution of power equality of the downturn by proclaiming a new hegemonic victor. The new hegemon establishes a new division of labor, suppresses conflict, opens up new markets in the periphery and old markets in the core, and generates a new type of dominant business enterprise that makes older types obsolete. All of this adds up to a dramatic reorganization of the world economy—a setting highly conducive to renewed capital accumulation. The alternative is a permanent breakdown of the system that either reconstitutes itself or ceases to function altogether. Needless to say, the latter option has not yet occurred.

Downswing-War-Downswing Relationship

The Mensch Interpretation

Mensch (1979) is best known for his argument that depressions are necessary for the development of innovations that stimulate the next upswing. But he also has a reasonably distinctive interpretation of how war fits into the long-wave sequence (spatiotemporal boundaries: industrialized states in the late eighteenth to twentieth centuries). His theory appears to be the only downswing-war-downswing argument in the literature.

When a phase of prosperity gives way to stagnation, governments turn to armament programs as a substitute for flagging consumer demand. To be able to increase the level of a state's defense commitments without a great deal of domestic resistance, however, it is necessary to raise expectations about the level of external threat and the prospects of war. Tensions increase and the probability of war escalates.

An economic crisis follows the large-scale wars identified in table 2.3. The end of war removes the justification for economic pump-priming via military spending. The prewar stagnation reappears and the economic situation is made even worse by demobilized soldiers seeking civilian employment. Mensch notes that only World War II failed to follow this pattern. Whether the 1939 to 1945 combat period was a temporary aberration or the end of an era is not made clear.

An Evolving Costs Relationship

The Williams, McGinnis, and Thomas Interpretation

Williams, McGinnis, and Thomas (1992) begin their analysis with the observation that Goldstein's (1988) interpretation of the war and growth relationship lacks a specification of the mechanisms that encourage decision

Table 2.3

Mensch's Stagnation Wars

Inflection Points in Growth Trend (Increased Risk of War)	When Major Wars Begin	Wars
1801	1799	1799–1802 wars of the Second Coalition against France; Napoleonic wars
1858	1854	1854–1856, Crimean War; Sardinian War, 1859; U. S. Civil War, 1860–1865; European War, 1864–1866
1912	1914	World War I, 1914–1918
?	?	Vietnam War

Source: based on Mensch 1979, 80. No dates are given for the Vietnam War in the original source. Mensch (1979, 79) comments that "the contention that the United States became involved in Vietnam for primarily economic reasons has been discussed too thoroughly to require elaboration."

makers to choose war in an upswing period (spatiotemporal boundaries: world system in the mid-eighteenth to mid-twentieth centuries). If war is sometimes the preferred strategy, under what conditions will it not be the preferred strategy? To construct a model of the incentive structures, Williams et al. turn to a consideration of changes in the political-economic environment and how these changes influence cost-benefit calculations.

The basic relationship between upswings and war is straightforward. Periods of economic expansion contribute to the capacity to engage in war. As a consequence, the difficulties likely to be encountered in financing a war effort will seem less daunting. Other things being equal, a decrease in the anticipated costs of war will increase the net benefits of going to war.

But other things have a way of not remaining equal. Prior to the advent of industrial capitalism, land provided the principal basis for state wealth. To gain more national wealth, one needed to acquire additional territory through conquest. With time and the evolution away from the dominance of agrarian economies, alternative ways of acquiring national wealth became increasingly available. Concurrently, the net economic benefits of war strategies were declining for at least four reasons: (1) conquered populations were becoming increasingly resistant to working for alien rulers; (2) the development of industrial techniques was escalating the physical and economic costs of engaging in war; (3) growing intra-capitalist interdependence was also raising the opportunity costs of wartime trading disruptions; and (4) as domestic and international capitalist market institutions continued to develop, decision makers' levels of information about the relative costs and benefits of their strategic options improved just as the transaction costs associated with the expanding range of nonwar options declined. The combination of these factors worked to lower the perceived net benefits of war strategies.

The increasing irrationality of warfare does not preclude the outbreak of war. Rather, it implies that the wars that do occur will more likely be fought for noneconomic reasons. For that reason, these less frequent wars should also be more destructive because the intensity with which they are fought is likely to increase. More destructive wars will translate into greater war impacts on economic growth. Thus, the linkages between war and economic growth should be expected to change in two ways: the link from war to growth should strengthen due to the greater damages inflicted in pursuit of irrational goals, while the growth to war linkage should weaken because the perceived costs of war have been increasing and the perceived benefits have declined.

One other variable worth considering in estimating these calculations is the presence or absence of a hegemon. Basically, a hegemon would be expected to discourage the outbreak of war. If they are both willing and able, hegemons are believed to support the functioning of market institutions. The value of nonwar options will thereby be enhanced. More directly, the value of the war option should be depreciated by the presence of a strong supporter of the status quo. Potential war makers would have to calculate the likelihood of hegemonic intervention to preserve the prevailing distribution of resources during or immediately after the conflict.

The empirical findings of Williams (1993), however, do not support the significance of the hegemonic variable. Over the whole 1750 to 1935 period that he examines, the effect of war on economic growth, as measured by world industrial production, was greater than the effect of growth on war. One reason for this outcome was that a production-to-war relationship was only evident prior to 1858 while the war to production relationship, as expected, became more evident in the second half of the period examined. The theoretical problem, however, is that the production to war relationship faded away at the very height of British nineteenth-century hegemony. The subsequent decline of the British hegemony should have increased the incentives for war which would imply the continuation of a production to war relationship and not its fading away. The implication is that the presumed influence of hegemony may be a spurious factor in estimating incentive structures.

Hegemonic Phase Dependency

Perhaps the most awkward material to integrate with the literature on war and prosperity linkages is the world-economy arguments about the linkages among Kondratieffs, hegemony, and conflict. The material is awkward because it is both more ambiguous and more complicated than many of the other arguments.

The World-economy School's Interpretation

Some of the basic ideas regarding this interpretation (Research Working Group 1979; Hopkins, Wallerstein, and Associates 1982) are that long waves are controlled by relative profitability considerations in the core and periphery, they come in pairs with two sets of upswing (A) and downswing (B), and they correspond to hegemonic ascent and decline and the level of conflict among major powers (spatiotemporal boundaries: world system in the fifteenth to twentieth centuries).

One assumes that demand in the low-wage zone (the periphery) is a function of demand in the high-wage zone (the core) which, in turn, is a function of world demand and the world distribution of income. At the onset of the ascending hegemony (A1), demand in the core exceeds core supply and periphery demand exceeds periphery supply. Production in both core and periphery increases. But at some point, periphery supply becomes greater than periphery demand and core demand approximates core supply. Investment slows and stagnation sets in—first in the periphery and then in the core. The root problem is traced to the inelasticity of world demand and the relative absence of production coordination.

In the hegemonic victory (B1), productive capacity is demobilized and unemployment increases. The difficult economic climate intensifies class struggle which leads to some redistribution of world income and an increase in demand that creates the setting for the hegemonic maturity (A2). The economic expansion associated with the A2 phase proceeds until, essentially, core demand diminishes in comparison to core supply. Stagnation and hegemonic decline (B2) are the outcome. The return to A1 is then predicated on the conjunction of several factors that either increase demand or facilitate expansion: the centralization of capital, class struggles leading to a redistribution of world income, and the creation of new groups of low-wage workers in the periphery.

Imposed on this analysis is the historical schedule of long-wave phases and hegemonic movements portrayed in table 2.4. A1 is a period of ascending

Table 2.4

Hegemonic Phases and Economic Long Waves in the World-Economy Perspective

Hegemon	Economic Expansion	Economic Contraction	Hegemonic Phase
Netherlands	1575–1590		Ascending Hegemony (A1)
		1590–1620	Hegemonic Victory (B1)
	1620–1650		Hegemonic Maturity (A2)
		1650–1700	Hegemonic Decline (B2)
Britain	1798–1815		Ascending Hegemony (A1)
		1815–1850	Hegemonic Victory (B1)
	1850–1873		Hegemonic Maturity (A2)
		1873–1897	Hegemonic Decline (B2)
United States	1897–1913/1920		Ascending Hegemony (A1)
		1913/1920–1945	Hegemonic Victory (B1)
	1945–1967		Hegemonic Maturity (A2)
		1967–	Declining Hegemony (B2)

Source: based on information in Research Working Group 1979.

hegemony. The various rivals for succession are locked in acute conflict in this period. In B1, the next hegemon transits past the old hegemon. However, the true period of peak hegemony is A2 in which the hegemon establishes a new era of systemic openness and reduced conflict. B2 is a period of hegemonic decline where acute conflict between the old hegemon and possible successors is to be expected. This period is also marked by attempts to preempt control by core rivals over portions of the periphery.

One problem in this interpretation is that the relationship between the core-periphery dynamic supposedly governing the long-wave and the hegemonic/rivalry cycle needs further elaboration. As it is, the two sets of processes are simply introduced side-by-side without much discussion of how they overlap. The immediate problem for this review, however, is how to interpret their argument in terms of upswings/downswings and war. The hegemonic/rivalry cycle suggests that A1 and B2 are the phases of the most acute conflict. That prediction might be interpreted as implying that war leads to both upswing and downswings at various points in the paired long-wave sequence.

However, the world-economy school also singles out three major wars that are critical to encrusting the dominant position of the hegemon (Wallerstein 1984): Thirty Years War, French Revolutionary/Napoleonic Wars, and World War I and II. The Thirty Years War (1618–1648) began at the end of a

B1 phase and continued through most of the following A2 phase. The 1792–1815 period encompasses part of the end of a B2 phase and all of the next A1 phase. World War I and II took place during a B1 phase. Thus, the first two major wars gave way to downswings and the third war preceded an upswing. Alternatively, the first two wars were preceded by downswings while the third was preceded by an upswing. The pattern is:

1. Thirty Years War   downswing-war-downswing
2. French Revolution/Napoleonic Wars   downswing-war-downswing
3. World Wars I/II   upswing-war-upswing

Yet no explanation is offered on why the pattern might have shifted in the twentieth century. For that matter, there is little discussion of the role of war in creating economic conditions or vice versa. It is quite possible that these arguments were not meant to be interpreted so literally. Still, it is difficult to know just what to make of these conflicting inferences.

The Vayrynen Interpretation

A significant variation on this approach is offered by Vayrynen (1983) who disagrees with the conflict intensity rank order of the hegemonic phases (spatiotemporal boundaries: world system in the nineteenth to twentieth centuries). He predicted that the most conflictual phases in descending order should be: ascending hegemony (A1), hegemonic victory (B1), hegemonic decline (B2), and hegemonic maturity (A2). This schedule is based on several assumptions. The economic predominance of the hegemon should work to suppress conflict. That is why A2 has the lowest expectation. A1 is expected to encompass the most conflict because major power rivalries over power and markets should be the most intense in this phase. The precise order of B1 and B2 seems a bit arbitrary. Hegemonic decline should be more conflictual than hegemonic maturity because some early challengers to the weakening hegemon will have emerged. Yet a hegemon remains in place and therefore the conflict level should not be as great as in the hegemonic victory phase that brings the conflicts fought in the ascending hegemony period to some semblance of a conclusion. Much as in the world-economy approach, this logic is based primarily on the hegemonic cycle and hardly at all on the long-wave phases.

Vayrynen explicitly states that he, more or less, expects major wars to occur during the upswing and possibly contribute to the peak of the upswing through a brief postwar boom. He does suggest, however, that this pattern may vary by war participant. A postwar boom is more likely, for instance, if the war is fought on the opposition's home ground. At the same time, Vayrynen also argues that major wars alter the course of economic cycles and contribute to a postwar downswing. Basically, these statements would seem to suggest a variation on the upswing-war-downswing pattern.

Yet, there are the theoretical problems of the influences of the hegemonic cycle and the restraining effects of alliance management systems. Of the three, long waves are hypothesized to have the weakest influence with the hegemonic phase and nature of the alliance system exerting more significant impacts (and in that order of causal priority). This is an interesting feature of Vayrynen's argument since it is rare to find an explicit rationale for the relative influence of several separate but overlapping processes.

Vayrynen seems to put the hegemonic transition process first because the economic long waves tend to reinforce the transition of power that, in turn, tends to produce new management systems of diplomatic restraint. Ascending states (challengers) are hurt less by downturns than declining states (former hegemons) due to the reliance of rising states on industrial innovation accompanied by political protection. The hegemon's economic base has become more internationalized and more exposed to competition. Moreover, during downturns states must make their investments in new technology and infrastructure. If challengers are hurt less, than they should be in positions to invest more than the declining hegemon.

Challengers have strong incentives to improve their economic position. If they truly wish to catch up to the former leader, they will have to do so at the expense of the once dominant state. It is not inevitable that this will happen. The former leader may still rejuvenate its hegemony. Or, it is possible that some new power could assume hegemony peacefully? Historically, however, major power war has been the outcome. The set of predictions found in the top half of table 2.5 summarize how Vayrynen linked the various influences to the incidence of major power warfare.

The second half of table 2.5 discloses what Vayrynen found when he tested his predictions. Focusing on nine wars between major powers, with minimal thresholds of ten state months of magnitude (the number of participating states times the duration of the participation) or ten thousand battle deaths, as many as seven were initiated during an upswing phase. Of these seven, five were initiated during the most prosperous and fastest economic growth segment of the upswing. The two downswing wars began in a segment in which the economy had started to expand and accelerate its rate of growth just before the commencement of the upswing. Vayrynen concluded that his

Table 2.5

Major Power War Proneness

	Accelerated Growth	Decelerated Growth
	War Predictions	
Ascending Hegemony	much (1892–1929)	
Hegemonic Victory		little (1825–1845)
		some (1929–1948)
Hegemonic Maturity	some (1845–1872)	
	little (1948–1973)	
Hegemonic Decline		little (1872–1892)
		little (1973–)

- -

	War Observations	
Ascending Hegemony	Russia-Japan	
	(1904–1905)	
	World War I	
	(1914–1919)	
	Russian Civil War	
	(1917–1921)	
Magnitude	685.8 state-months	
Severity	9,180,000 battle deaths	
Hegemonic Victory		Soviet Union-Japan
		(1939)
		World War II
		(1939–1945)
Magnitude		900.5 state-months
Severity		15,028,000 battle deaths
Hegemonic Maturity	Crimean War	
	(1853–1856)	
	Prussia-Austria	
	(1866)	
	Prussia-France	
	(1870–1871)	
	Korean War	
	(1951–1953)	
Magnitude	672.1 state-months	
Severity	2,469,800 battle deaths	
Hegemonic Decline		no major power warfare

Source: Vayrynen 1983, 409–11.

outcome supports the notion that a sudden and rapid expansion of the economy is particularly conducive to the outbreak of war.

Note that the hegemonic phase conflict intensity rank order does not work out as predicted thanks in part to the placement of World War II. The observed order is victory, ascension, maturity, and decline rather than ascension, victory, decline, and maturity. Either way, the implications for the designation of the placement of long-term economic swings before and after war are roughly similar. Conflict intensity predicated on hegemonic transitions does not discriminate between upswings and downswings all that well. Nobody has argued that it should, but it does make the integration of these hegemonic phase-dependent hypotheses with the other war-growth arguments awkward.

Intermittent Reinforcement

The Trotsky Interpretation

Trotsky (1923; see Goldstein 1988) argued that capitalist systems were subject to phases of accelerated/retarded growth that were due to exogenous influences (spatiotemporal parameters: capitalist states in the late eighteenth to twentieth centuries). Wars could play this role along with a number of other types of events taking place in the system's superstructure.

The Hansen Interpretation

Hansen (1964) apparently became a skeptic on the existence of long waves. In a 1932 study, he had argued that wars do not follow long periods of depression because upswings generated conducive conditions (war chests, armies, navies) for fighting wars (spatiotemporal boundaries: industrialized states in the late eighteenth to twentieth centuries). The inflation and price instability associated with long bouts of war, on the other hand, was responsible for the beginning of the long downswing. A generation later and despite his agnosticism, Hansen changed his mind. The impact of war on long price trends was only sometimes significant. Hansen thought that the Napoleonic Wars might have been as important as the Industrial Revolution's innovations toward creating the first upswing. Each reinforced the other to such an extent that it was difficult to disentangle their relative impacts. Warfare played only a small role in the second wave's upswing and downswing phases that were due largely to railroadization. Similarly, the spread of electricity and motorized machines was primarily responsible for the third wave's upswing. World War I reinforced the upward price movement toward the end of the wave, but the adjustments to that war may have been as important to the downswing as the problems associated with adapting to innovational developments.

Differential Outcomes

Occasionally, authors of studies on long waves and war have suggested that not all states are equally susceptible to either the economic waves or the war impacts. Bernstein (1940) distinguished between participants and neutrals. Vayrynen (1983) differentiated ascending challengers from declining hegemons. The usual pattern, nevertheless, is to make generalizations as if all economies were equally affected. In this context, there is some literature that contrasts the war impacts of winners and losers. The authors who discuss this topic do not do so from the perspective of economic long waves. However, their logic is focused on postwar growth patterns and, therefore, should be of some interest.

There seem to be three basic hypotheses:

1. War increases the gap between winners and losers, with losers falling further behind (Keynes 1919).
2. War harms everyone, but winners lose the least amount. Therefore, the gap between winners and losers remains roughly constant (Angell 1933).
3. War losers may lose more in the short run than winners, but in the long run the war losers benefit more by losing the war than the winners gain by winning the war (Organski and Kugler 1980; Olson 1982; Brenner 1985).

What do these arguments have to do with waves of economic growth? Quite possibly, the answer is nothing at all. Ultimately, it will depend on how important war is to the fluctuations in growth. If war is tangential, who wins and who loses should make little difference to the course of the long-term economic rhythms. If war is not tangential, then winners and losers are unlikely to experience postwar conditions in precisely the same way. But as the three hypotheses illustrate, who really wins and loses in the macroeconomic environment of growth spurts and waves continues to be contested by analysts.

No Relationship

The argument that long economic waves do not exist has always had a number of supporters. This is hardly surprising because this argument has remained the majority opinion on the subject throughout the twentieth century. There are a number of empirical analyses that support this point of view. Conybeare (1990) is an example of such an analysis that also looked at the relationship between war, measured in terms of battle deaths and price cycles (spatiotemporal boundaries: world systems in the late fifteenth to twentieth centuries). Cycles with strict or regular periodicities were not found in either series. In addition, no statistically significant Granger causal relationship was found to work in either direction—from war to prices or prices to war.

Lest we end this literature review with the impression that only long-wave debunkers or analysts engaging in statistical examinations are likely to fall into this category, it should be noted that a strong opponent of the idea that long waves and wars were systematically related was none other than Joseph Schumpeter (1939, 2:697). In particular, he saw no reason to believe that upswings made war more probable because upswings did not give rise to a more intensive search for new markets (spatiotemporal boundaries: industrialized states in the nineteenth to twentieth centuries).

CONCLUSION

The mere existence of fourteen different interpretations suggests at least one conclusion: it is unlikely that these theories are all accurate models of the processes at work. Of course, it may be that none of them are very accurate. The appropriate question remains one of how are we to decide which interpretation is the most credible? To simply pick and choose among the alternatives idiosyncratically is not likely to improve the situation represented by a confused and confusing literature. Two things are needed to impose some analytical order on the question of war/long-term economic growth linkages. The first item is a slate of criteria by which we could evaluate which interpretations are most deserving of further attention. For instance, arguments that do not specify with any degree of precision how war is linked to economic growth are going to be less helpful theoretically than those that do offer explicit linkages. Once the criteria are developed and applied critically to the literature, the preconditions for the second item—explicit tests of the presumed linkages—will have been established. In the next two chapters, we focus on the development and application of the criteria essential to a critical evaluation of the competing arguments.

Chapter Three

A Critique
of the Literature

SEVEN QUESTIONS ABOUT THE WAR AND
LONG-TERM ECONOMIC GROWTH LINKAGE

As suggested by the review of the literature in the preceding chapter, there is a wide array of ideas about the relationship between war and long-term growth. While it may be possible to isolate only fourteen types of emphasis, the reader is apt to receive the impression that every author's argument is relatively unique. Regrettably, there is some truth underlying this impression. The literature on this topic has not been cumulative and has not shown a tendency to engage in comprehensive examinations of the phenomena at stake.[1] Many of the arguments gloss over important questions. Only a few of the authors have even bothered addressing the war/long-term growth linkage question more than once. In addition, the literature has, until very recently, not been much concerned with evidence.

These observations are not coincidental. A number of observers have noticed some general patterns that seem to link war to prosperity and depression. While there are certainly some degrees of overlap in the subsequent interpretations, each reconstruction of the pattern tends to have a number of idiosyncratic elements. Precisely whose behavior is being modeled is not always clear although there is some propensity to depend upon the experience of the United States in the twentieth century as implicitly prototypical. An irony of the literature is that, despite the focus on long-term relationships, the analyses are often not conducted on a long-term basis. Moreover, many of the interpretations are presented as if questions about the relationship between war and long-term economic growth had not been raised before. A further problem that may not seem obvious in the above review of the literature is that most, but not all, of the arguments have difficulty dealing with the apparent anomaly of World War II. Despite the record-setting destructiveness of this war and its well-documented impacts on economic growth, World War II simply does not seem to fit a number of the proposed patterns.[2] Is this an exception that does not detract from the ability to generalize? Or, does this war's apparent exception suggest that significant evolutionary tendencies are at work?

In any event, there are at least fourteen different views on how the linkages are thought to relate. These fourteen explanatory emphases vary on the extent to which their arguments are detailed, sophisticated, and validated. Even so, the extent and persistence of disagreements, as well as the significance of the processes involved (war and economic growth), suggest that there is an interesting puzzle here that deserves resolving.

The puzzle cannot be resolved by merely coding the arguments and weighting the various explanatory elements by the number of times that they appear in the literature. The repetition of a generalization does not make it any more accurate or plausible. Nor is it advisable to mix and match disparate elements of multiple interpretations of reality. What is needed instead is a relatively fresh approach that is: (1) explicitly theoretical (as opposed to intermittently descriptive); (2) fully cognizant of previous approaches to the subject matter and thus sensitive to the types of issues that need to be addressed; and (3) highly committed to providing systematic empirical evidence for the claims advanced.

Of course, explicit theory and systematic evidence are normally preferred to their alternatives. But precisely to which issues should we be most attentive in an attempt to resolve the war/long-term economic growth puzzle? There are at least seven major questions that should be addressed:

1. How do long-term economic fluctuations influence the probability of war?
2. How does war influence long-term economic fluctuations?
3. Are all actors equally susceptible and important to the war-growth linkage?
4. How far back in time does the war/long-term growth linkage hold?
5. Is there reason to anticipate evolutionary changes in the nature of the war/long-term growth linkage?
6. Is there systematic evidence to support a war/long-term growth linkage?
7. Are there major anomalies to the hypothesized pattern?

How Do Long-term Economic Processes Influence the Probability of War?

The first basic question—how do long-term economic processes influence the probability of war—should include such ancillary questions as: (1) when is the probability of war most likely to be influenced (upturn or downturn and trough, peak, or somewhere in between); and (2) which types of war are most likely to be affected (all wars, only major wars, or some subset of all wars or major wars).

The literature offers five basic choices on how long-term economic fluctuations make war more or less likely:

1. Periods in which financial resources are relatively ample improve the possibility of war.
2. Periods in which the demand for raw materials, access to markets, and control of the periphery are raising the probability of interstate conflict and tension.
3. Periods in which elites and masses are more likely to feel overconfident, optimistic, efficacious, excited, and/or interested in external affairs increase the probability of interstate conflict.
4. Periods of accelerated economic growth create problems that require political solutions—of which war is an extreme example.
5. Periods in which decision makers and economies become dependent on military spending as a countercyclical stimulus increase the level of threat perception and interstate tension.

The first four of these nonmutually exclusive conditions tend to be associated with upswings while the fifth one is more likely in a downturn setting. While authors have designated a number of positions on the upswing and downswing as the most dangerous, the logic of the arguments is that the probability of warfare increases linearly as economies move toward the crest or trough. In most interpretations, only major wars are thought to have sufficient economic impact to end an upswing or downswing. Therefore, it is major wars that are of most interest to this question.

How Does War Influence Long-term Economic Processes?

The second basic question reverses the first one. How does war influence long-term economic fluctuations? While a number of choices of linkages are available, the fundamental choice is between assigning a major or a minor role to the impact of war. War impacts, of a major magnitude, significantly distort the course of economic processes. Some time is required for the war impact to be absorbed and for economic processes to return to some state roughly equivalent to prewar conditions.

Authors who see war impacts of a minor magnitude assume that the economic fluctuations run their course more or less despite the ravages of war. An upturn or downturn may make war more probable, but the subsequent change in the direction of economic growth is due less to the intervention of war and more to the inherent cyclical course of the economic processes.

Naturally, an in-between position is conceivable. Wars could have a major impact on inherently cyclical economic processes. Presumably, war would then be most likely to accentuate the cyclicality of the economic processes. If war systematically worked against the long-term economic cycle, we would be far less likely to recognize the inherent cyclicality. Moreover, anticyclical war impacts would most closely resemble the significant distortion choice and, therefore, would not really represent a genuine intermediate position.

The ways in which the literature suggests that war might influence long-term economic processes are no more mutually exclusive than the possible influences of economic fluctuations on war. There are basically seven possibilities:

1. War distorts price levels leading to an inflation-deflation sequence.
2. War interrupts a trend toward the expansion or stagnation of production.
3. War encourages state intervention in the economy, thereby increasing the number of rigidities that the economy must overcome.
4. War alters the national demographic profile (births, deaths, marriages) with a number of implications for future economic growth.
5. War facilitates economic innovation either directly or indirectly.
6. War is necessary to establish new growth-promoting systemic leadership.
7. War is necessary to remove barriers to, or restrictions on, renewed economic growth.

The first three possibilities are likely to lead to downswings. The last three should lead to upswings. The impact of demographic change could work in either direction, depending on the extent of the impact. For example, a minimal loss of life which still leads to a baby boom should have a positive effect on economic growth (other things being equal). A major loss of life, on the other hand, might lead to a compensating baby boom, but it might take a number of years to attain the level of prewar output given the loss in the number of producers.

Are All Actors Equally Sensitive and Important to the War-Growth Relationship?

As for which actors are most vulnerable to the war/long-term economic growth linkage, the long-wave literature tends to be divided or vague. A number of authors have not examined more than one country. As a consequence, the question of what spatial scope their generalizations may possess hardly arises. Other analysts give the impression that all countries of some type, such as major powers, are equally subject to war-related economic disturbances and, therefore, it is the states who participate in the greatest wars that are most

Table 3.1

Spatiotemporal Boundaries Cited in Chapter 2

Author	Spatial Parameter	Temporal Parameter
Kondratieff	industrialized states	late 18th–20th centuries
Macfie-Blainey	industrialized states	19th–20th centuries
Shuman-Rosenau	United States	late 18th–20th centuries
Doran	major powers	19th–20th centuries
Mansfield	world system	late 15th–20th centuries
Bernstein	major powers	20th century
Davis	United States	19th–20th centuries
Dickinson	United States	19th/20th centuries
Imbert	major western states	late 13th–20th centuries
Goldstein	world system	various
Boswell-Sweat	world system	17th–20th centuries
Modelski	global polity/economy	late 18th–20th centuries
Rose	industrialized states	20th century
Silberling	United States	19th/20th centuries
Frank	core economic powers	18th century
Rostow	world economy	late 18th–20th centuries
Thompson-Zuk	world powers	18th–20th centuries
Craig-Watt	world system	19th–20th centuries
Chase-Dunn	world system	late 15th–20th centuries
Bergesen	world system	19th–20th centuries
Mensch	industrialized states	late 18th–20th centuries
Williams et al.	world system	mid-18th–mid-20th centuries
Hopkins-Wallerstein	world system	15th–20th centuries
Vayrynen	world system	19th–20th centuries
Trotsky	capitalist states	18th–20th centuries
Hansen	industrialized states	late 18th–20th centuries
Liska	European system	16th–20th centuries
Conybeare	world system	late 15th–20th centuries
Schumpeter	industrialized states	19th–20th centuries

likely to manifest the various economic effects hypothesized to follow war participation. Still another cluster of authors choose to link long waves in economic growth to long waves in political-economic leadership. Hegemons and system leaders are then in some way principal agents of the war-growth relationship. Table 3.1 illustrates these options by summarizing the spatiotemporal parameters encountered in chapter 2.

Since there is a very strong tendency to associate the advent of long-term economic growth fluctuations with the late-eighteenth-century development of industrialization, industrialized states are thought to be more at risk than agrarian states. As the principal participants in major wars, major powers are presumably more at risk than minor powers. Combining these derivations suggests that we should most expect to find the linkages between long-term economic growth and war manifested in the histories of industrialized major powers. Taking this logic one step further, the leading major power in at least the past two centuries (i.e., Britain in the nineteenth century and the United States in the twentieth century) has been the industrial leader as well. Thus, it is in the political-economic histories of the successive system leaders that we should expect to find the strongest evidence for the hypothesized relationships between long-term growth and war. Such an assumption often seems implicit to many analyses but the question remains whether it is simply a matter of convenience or something more. Do the experiences of successive system leaders merely provide the best opportunities for examining the war-growth linkage (big wars, good serial data) or are they the ultimate sources of the linkage?

How Far Back in Time Does the War/Long-term Growth Linkage Exist?

The majority opinion on this question (see table 3.1) dates the advent of long waves to the late-eighteenth-century British Industrial Revolution. But this approach is largely predicated on two assumptions. First, it is assumed that agrarian economies were less vulnerable to long-term economic fluctuations and that most economies were fundamentally agrarian before the nineteenth century. Second, it has been assumed by most, but again not all, empirically oriented analysts that even if long waves predated the 1780s, sufficient data simply did not exist to study them.

The second assumption has been proven false by the analyses of Goldstein (1988, 1991a); Conybeare (1990); Boswell and Sweat (1991); W. R. Thompson (1992a); Williams, McGinnis, and Thomas (1992); Sayrs (1993); and Williams (1993). Sufficient production and price data do exist to test hypotheses about war and long-term economic growth before the 1780s. To be sure, the empirical outcomes of these tests are decidedly mixed. Nevertheless, there can no longer be any doubt about the possibility of testing hypotheses over a genuine long-term span.

The first assumption is also problematic. The agrarian-industrial dichotomy has value, but it can be misleading. Industry and industrialization certainly predated the revolutionary changes in late-eighteenth-century textile and iron production. At the very least, one should attempt to test the assumed threshold effect. The dichotomy also ignores the significance of intercontinental commerce, especially of emerging market economies such as China in the modern era. All pre-nineteenth-century economies did not engage equally in trade, but those that were heavily involved in interregional transactions were vulnerable to the distortions of warfare. To the extent that trade was characterized by long-term fluctuations of expansion and contraction, we might expect to find similar linkages between commercial growth and war (as are often hypothesized for industrial growth and war).

Is There Reason to Anticipate Evolutionary Change in the Nature of the War/Long-term Economic Growth Linkage?

Although the work of Williams (Williams et al. 1992; Williams 1993) was singled out in table 2.1 as the principal examples of evolutionary arguments in this context, evolutionary arguments and assumptions are actually more common. The Williams et al. interpretation argues that as war costs increase, the linkage from industrial expansion to war should weaken—just as the reciprocal linkage should become stronger as the intensity of war increases. However, the most common evolutionary assumption in the long-wave literature points in the opposite direction. As noted above, greater industrialization is expected to lead to a stronger relationship between war and long-term economic growth.

Both of these assumptions portray economic activities as aggregated industrialization. What evolves are the relationships between economic activity and war. However, there is another type of evolution. Analysts who stress innovation as critical to spurts of growth see evolution in the types and locations of economic activities that are most likely to be associated with long-term upswings and downswings. The sectors that lead economic growth will change from era to era as in the sequence in which iron production gave way to railroadization that, in turn, gave way to steel and motor vehicles.

At the same time, an economy that pioneers in one era will not necessarily continue to do so in future eras. Historically, past pioneers are unlikely to lead indefinitely for a variety of reasons. One has to do with the tendency for competitive resource requirements to escalate with less-endowed leaders that give way to rivals with greater resource bases.

Another tendency is that the resource endowments of different countries are favored or discriminated against according to which sectors lead economic growth. One leading sector era may bias growth toward countries with large coal deposits while another gives the edge to economies with large domestic markets for mass consumption.

Thus, there are three different types of evolutionary tendencies to consider. One involves relationships; another type refers to kinds of economic activities; and the third type involves shifts in the spatial focus of growth activities. Once again, these three types of evolution need not be considered separately.

Is There Systematic Evidence to Support the Existence of a War/Long-term Economic Growth Linkage?

Too many of the models listed in table 2.1 were presented without accompanying evidence. It is hard to imagine fourteen different answers to the war/long-term growth question emerging if more attention had been paid to testing the arguments that were advanced. Yet it must be acknowledged that the linkages are elusive and not necessarily easy to test. No one has attempted to test all the variations and it would be difficult to make a case for such a comprehensive examination.

Most of the systematic evidence that is available is of quite recent origin and vulnerable to criticisms concerning the types of statistical techniques employed and/or the way in which economic activities or war have been measured. For example, almost all empirical efforts have measured war in terms of battle deaths (usually army). Battle death data are available for a long period of time and are of reasonably high quality. The question remains whether battle deaths accurately capture the appropriate wars. If all wars are thought to play some role in the war-growth linkage, battle deaths may be quite reasonable as a measure of comparative intensity. The only problem then is that army sizes and the lethality of weapon systems have evolved over the past five hundred years to such an extent that it is difficult to empirically compare sixteenth-century casualties with those of the twentieth century. If, on the other hand, only some wars are theorized to play a role in the war-growth linkage, battle deaths are only likely to introduce noise to the analysis unless only the most bloody wars happen to be the appropriate wars.

Another substantial measurement problem is that prices have been easier to measure than production. As a consequence, most empirical analyses have focused on the war-price relationship. But most of the arguments arrayed in table 2.1 are focused on war-production relationships. Findings based on war-price modeling, therefore, are less than conclusive. The rare studies employing some form of production variable tend to use the same series—a series of fairly obscure origins (Haustein and Neuwirth 1982) said to measure the pace of world industrialization over the past two centuries. Thus, it is difficult to regard these studies as conclusive.

Finally, there is the continuing debate on what types of statistical techniques are most appropriate to the detection of war/long-term growth relationships (Beck 1991; Goldstein 1991b). The strict constructionist school argues that if there is a long cycle of war and economic growth, the periodicity should be reasonably uniform. Techniques assuming exact periodicity are therefore appropriate. However, analysts who are most familiar with the history of long waves favor a less exact periodicity. Rather than insisting on fifty years for each and every upswing/downswing-war sequence, it is acceptable if one cycle is only forty years in duration while the next two may last sixty years and fifty-four years, respectively. If this perspective is appropriate, statistical techniques assuming strict periodicity are inappropriate tools.

One need not accept all of these claims—that decisions to emphasize battle deaths, prices, an unvalidated measure of world production, and strict periodicity are less than ideal—to acknowledge that the jury must still be considered out on whether and how war and long-term economic growth are related. The important thing to emphasize is that we have reached a point in the debates on long-wave processes where the sensitivity to evidence on long-wave generalizations has become fairly acute. That development should prove to be beneficial in sorting out the claims advanced for each of the fourteen models in table 2.1. While it may have taken some six to seven decades to generate fourteen different models, it should not take an equal length of time to ascertain which models are supported by the historical evidence.

Are There Major Anomalies to the Hypothesized Pattern?

If the predominant pattern in the literature is the upswing-war-downswing scenario, one of the major weaknesses of this model is the World War II anomaly. World War II was preceded by an impressive downswing and followed by an equally dramatic upswing. But then if World War II is a true anomaly, analysts who favor downswing-war patterns have a major problem because their best case is an exception to the rule.

Several of the models listed in table 2.1, along with a large number of other international relations theories, were based explicitly on the World War I experience. What would be more desirable is an argument that could handle World Wars I and II simultaneously without resorting to an ad hoc explanation (or simply writing off one of the wars as an exception to the general pattern). The two world wars of the twentieth century are simply too important to dismiss as exceptions, especially if the war/long-term growth linkage is limited to the past two centuries. If one of these wars appears to be an exception to the rule, it may be that either the rule is being misinterpreted or that the rule underwent some type of change during the twentieth century. Alternatively, depending on the envisioned temporal scope of the generalizations being advanced, there may be no systematic rule but only an intermittent process at work.

While the possibility of intermittent processes cannot be dismissed out of hand, there is a good possibility that something more systematic is at work in the causal sequencing of war and long-term economic growth. Yet the possibility is only as good as the theory or theories that exist to explain what forces drive the system. If no theory exists that can satisfy the seven criteria developed in this chapter, the processes may or may not be systematically related. It may be unlikely that we will be able to recognize how these processes are related.

Our position is that none of the existing literature fully satisfies the evaluatory criteria, but that some arguments come closer than others. The one that comes closest, in our estimation, is the long cycle of global politics that can be adjusted (or further elaborated) with only slight modifications to propose a sophisticated and testable answer to the war/long-term economic growth puzzle. In the next chapter, we discuss more explicitly just how the seven criteria fare within the long-cycle context.

Chapter Four

Long Cycles, War, and Long-term Economic Growth

In this chapter, we provide more background on what our version of a long-cycle interpretation represents and elaborate how it addresses the war/long-term economic growth linkage via the seven questions discussed in chapter 3.

THE LEADERSHIP/LONG-CYCLE INTERPRETATION

The long cycle of global politics theory brings a time dimension to the study of world politics: it highlights certain notable recurrences—in particular, those linked to leadership, alliances, and global war. It also raises questions about evolutionary trends.

One of the most distinctive aspects of the long-cycle theory is its emphasis on a global political system. Most historical interpretations of world politics are strongly anchored in the regional-territorial affairs of Western Europe; long-cycle theory is focused instead on an intercontinental-transoceanic layer that involves long-range transactions and issues of policy (order, security, stability) that are specific to those transactions. Although it is customary to accept the globalization of world politics by the late nineteenth century, long-cycle theory argues that a global layer began to emerge as early as the end of the fifteenth century. The theory itself pivots on the central observation that the management of this global layer and its problems fluctuates according to the relative efficacy of a system leader, which is referred to as the world power. After emerging from a global war succession struggle, the world power is in the best position to provide some level of global governance, but as its lead in economic innovation and naval power deteriorates, so too does the quality and quantity of governance. Ultimately, another succession struggle becomes probable.

The emphasis on the global political system influences the unusually strong theoretical bias toward translating global reach capabilities in terms of sea power. As discussed at greater length in Modelski and Thompson (1988), sea power is critical for a number of reasons. During global wars, the winning world power's navy, and those of its allies, exercises command of the sea. The challenger's fleets are rendered less effective than they might have been. The mobility of the challenger's attacks is restricted. It is the challengers that have to worry most about amphibious invasions and seaborne supplies reaching the enemies' troops in the field. It is also the challengers who are most likely to feel the pinch of a worldwide economic blockade supported by a superior naval force. To win a global war, therefore, one must have (among other attributes) superior naval strength.

After the global war has been won, sea power continues to be important as it becomes a principal military instrument in enforcing the new, postwar order; in policing sea lanes; and in deterring potential attacks on the world power and its allies and clients. Even after the development of air power in the twentieth century, naval forces, especially those vessels that merge air and sea power, continue to represent a highly significant component in a nation's ability to project power on an intercontinental scale. In or out of war, sea power is a necessary attribute for an active participation in global politics.

Yet sea power, or more generally the development of capabilities for global reach, constitutes only one of four necessary conditions for leadership. Development of the system's lead economy is certainly as important as sea power. Growth and prosperity are fundamental to the ability to pay for the global reach capabilities and the implementation of world order. Economic growth, in turn, is predicated on the pioneering innovation of leading commercial and industrial sectors that periodically reshape the nature of the world economy. They also bestow the benefits of monopoly profits on the pioneer until diffusion and imitation transform industries that were once considered radically innovative into fairly routine and widespread components of the world economy.

The most specific linkage to the concern over the relationship between war and long-term economic growth is found in the long-cycle contention that the rise and decline of leading sectors of economic growth in the global economy are closely linked to the rise and decline of global system leaders. Moreover, one era of global leadership encompasses two long economic waves based on innovative sectors in world commerce and industry. The linkages between and within the political and economic processes are multiple and concentrated geographically and chronologically. The innovations of the first wave shape the developments of the second wave. The first wave also generates the financial and economic resources needed to put together a winning coalition and a strategy in the global war that takes place between the two economic waves. Victory in global warfare paves the way for the second growth wave just as participation in the war effort may have significant effects on the creation of new markets, products, and technologies.

Via these processes, the ascending global system leader becomes the principal source of long-term economic growth. Eventually, however, the innovations are diffused to competitors, the monopoly benefits decay, and the economic foundation for political leadership is eroded. The possibilities for renewed political leadership must then be coordinated with a resurgence of economic innovation.

Table 4.1 imposes some additional structure and rhythm on these generalizations. Each period of ascendancy by the global system leader is divided into four phases: agenda setting, coalition-building, macrodecision, and execution. The first two phases, agenda setting and coalition-building, are preparatory periods characterized by the initial emergence of a new global system leader. The third segment, macrodecision, is the period of global war in which the ascending system leader actually rises to its lead political position. The fourth segment, execution, is the period during which systemic leadership is most in evidence. The fourth period is followed by two segments of leadership delegitimation and capability deconcentration that occur before the question of whose policies, rules, and vision of order will prevail in global politics once again becomes the central issue of world politics (in the macrodecision/global war phase).

Spurts of innovation and growth peak toward the end of the coalition-building phase and in the following execution phase. The precise nature of the innovations has changed over time as the world economy evolved over the past five hundred years. In the fifteenth through eighteenth centuries, the global lead industries were predominately commercial in nature: African gold and Indian spices in the Portuguese era; the Baltic and Asian trades in the Dutch era; and Amerasian products (tobacco, sugar, tea, Indian textiles) in the first British era. The emphasis shifted to industrial production in the late eighteenth century: cotton textiles, iron, and railroads in the second British era; steel, chemicals, electricity, motor vehicles, aerospace, and semiconductors in the U.S. era.

While the development of global reach capabilities and the lead economy is essential, it does not exhaust the prerequisites for leadership. A third necessary condition, societal openness, appears to be critical to fostering eco-

Table 4.1

Periodic Table of the Long Cycle of Global Politics

Agenda-setting (global problems)	Coalition-building (core alliance)	Macrodecision (global war)	Execution (world power and challenger)
	Phases		
	(West European)		
1430 discoveries	1460 Burgundian connection	1494 Wars of Italy and the Indian Ocean	1516 Portugal Spain
1540 integration	1560 Calvinist international	1580 Dutch-Spanish Wars	1609 Netherlands France
1640 political framework	1660 Anglo-Dutch alliance	1688 Wars of the Grand Alliance	1714 Britain I France
1740 industrial revolution	1763	1792 Wars of the French Revolution and Napoleon	1815 Britain II Germany
	(post–West European)		
1850 knowledge revolution	1873 Anglo-American special relationship	1914 World War I and II	1945 United States
1973 community	2000 democratic transition	2030	

Note: When looked at from the perspective of decline, the four phases of interest are world power (execution), delegitimization (agenda-setting), deconcentration (coalition-building), and global war (macrodecision).

nomic innovation. It also contributes to the stabilization of national politics by encouraging policy debates about strategies and rights. Relatively open societies also seem to have an easier time organizing the international coalitions that are critical to winning global wars and the peace that follows.

Responsiveness to global problems is the fourth necessary condition. The cooperation of coalition partners and the perceived legitimacy of proposed solutions to global problems will hinge on the degree to which aspiring leaders can convince others that their preferred policies serve interests that go beyond the national interests of the world power. Cooperation was most evident during global wars in which world powers skillfully practiced coalition leadership. This in turn served as the basis of their postwar influence. World powers must also recognize that their national interests are linked to wider policy concerns. Without this recognition, world powers may possess the capability to act but lack the willingness to lead or the ability to command a following.

These emphases on the global political system, global reach, lead economies, and global problem responsiveness influence how the world power's role is interpreted. In contrast to images of hegemonic preponderance and imperial control, world powers start out preponderant only in terms of naval forces and the dynamism of their economic system—which is the world system's leading economy for a time. The concentration of these capabilities is empowering, but only within very real limitations. World powers are unable to exercise the same type and degree of command and control often attributed to imperial centers.

There are some overt temporal limitations on the influence of successive world powers as well. Within a generation after the last global war, the relative decline of the world power becomes apparent. Old contenders are emboldened, and new contenders begin to emerge. Global problem management becomes increasingly difficult. There is a long cycle of leadership in the global political system because there is a tendency for post-global-war orders to be temporary; yet the impulse to create order in the global layer recurs with some regularity.

These temporal aspects are fairly structured in the sense that the behavior of the global political system is time patterned. Over the span of just about a century, the system passes through four characteristic phases. The four phases form one entire cycle, and over the history of the modern world system, several such cycles of global politics have been completed.

The four-phase model of the long cycle, which is so basic to this analysis, assigns a central role to the five global wars of the modern world system (the 1494–1516 wars of Italy and the Indian Ocean, the 1580–1609 Spanish-Dutch Wars, the 1688–1713 wars of the Grand Alliance, the 1792–1815 wars of the French Revolution and Napoleon, and the 1914–1945 world wars of the twentieth century). The macrodecision (global war) phase—encompassing the largest, best-known wars of the modern period—is the major beat of each long cycle. No one would dispute the status of such major conflagrations as World Wars I and II or the revolutionary conflicts opening the nineteenth century.[1]

Nor is the list of world powers generated by these wars particularly surprising. The majority are household names—except, perhaps, for Portugal. The list of challengers is also not surprising. Spain and France were central to earlier global wars, and Germany to the last one.

Yet the long-cycle perspective reveals features that are not only cyclical but also strongly evolutionary. It is quite remarkable that global wars have repeated themselves in the modern world in a decidedly regular pattern. Furthermore, each has been greater and more complex than the preceding one, and the underlying system also has grown: not linearly, but stepwise in punctuated form with the global wars acting as the principal form of punctuation.[2]

For an evolving system of that kind, an evolutionary learning model supplies an explanation. This model argues that expanding social systems need to pass through a regular sequence of phases governed by the functional requirements of that system and by the logic of the evolutionary process. From the perspectives of macrosociology and evolutionary theory, the macrodecision phase can be seen as one during which the system undergoes a collective decision that selects from the available candidates for leadership, and from the available programs for the future of the global system. Past global wars have selected such leadership and have embodied programmatic choices—hence, their importance.

LONG CYCLES AND THE SEVEN CRITICAL QUESTIONS

Armed with this brief summary, we have enough information to return to the seven questions derived from the earlier literature review.

In looking at the first question—how do long-term economic fluctuations influence the probability of war—the long-term economic fluctuations are identified as paired spurts of innovation. Prices are regarded as a derivative phenomenon. And it is only the first spurt of each pair that is thought to increase the probability of war. Of course, the probability of global war is not simply a function of the presence or absence of economic growth in the world economy. Other factors include the strength of global leadership and the relative strength of rising and falling regional leaders (Rasler and Thompson 1994). Over the past five centuries, global wars have been clashes between declining global leaders and rising regional leaders in Europe. Therefore, the pace of the respective global and regional declines and ascents can make a great deal of difference to the likelihood of war.

Nevertheless, the first growth spurt does facilitate the ascension of a new global system leader (usually allied with its declining predecessor) which organizes the resistance to the expanding regional hegemon. It is not likely that resistance would be entirely absent without the first growth spurt. Britain's resistance to German expansion twice in the twentieth century is a case in point—it can be speculated that the probability of successful resistance would be much lower without the first growth spurt. Wars might then still be fought but they might not have lasted as long as they did and they would probably have resolved the issues differently.

The first growth spurt also tends to intensify the competition for succession to the leading position in the global system. While the ascending global system leader is the primary beneficiary of the first growth spurt, it may take a global war for such an outcome to emerge fully. For example, before World War I, both Germany and the United States led the world in producing innovative technologies. One of these two states won the ensuing war; the other state was one of the principal losers. It is possible to argue that the United States would have pulled ahead with or without the war. Even so, the outcome of the war dramatically signaled the winner of the technological race, albeit temporarily.

It may also be that in the earlier commercial era the leading regional power could have benefited from the economic growth associated with the initial spurt. If it did, and more research needs to be done on this topic, the expansion of the regional leader may be linked to general fluctuations in economic expansion and contraction. Certainly, it seems likely that regional hegemonic aspirations are encouraged by the long period between the second spurt of the former paired growth set and the first spurt of the next pair. This is a period in which the decline of the incumbent global leader is most evident.

Finally, there is another way in which the first growth spurt may intensify the competition between the main rivals. It can be argued that the French Revolution and the French Revolutionary Wars were likely to occur because of French perceptions of economic gains made by their long-time rivals, the British (Wallerstein 1989). The fear of losing the ability to compete and the associated domestic costs in employment and standards of living can contribute to global war propensity.

Note that nothing has been said about war chests in general or tensions derived from competition over control of raw materials—two of the literature's most popular explanations for global use. However, neither explanation contradicts the more specific answers advanced with the leadership/long-cycle perspective. The emphasis on successful resistance to regional expansion depending on the first spurt and the possibility of regional leaders benefiting from the first spurt has clear ''war chest'' overtones.

Whether the first spurt of commercial/industrial innovation invariably generates increased competition for raw materials seems more debatable. Zero sum perspectives on resource and market control have always seemed more likely in downturns rather than in upswings. But in the pre-nineteenth-century commercial age, innovative spurts often focused on new ways of obtaining access to raw materials. In that sense, commercial innovations and increased competition tended to be synonymous—at least initially. In the industrial age, the prospects for increased competition over raw materials would seem to depend on the nature of the leading industries. France and Britain were not fighting over access to raw cotton in the 1790s nor were Britain and Germany struggling over control of petroleum sources in the twentieth century. Growth spurts increase international tensions, but not necessarily because of their ramifications for access to raw materials.

We now turn to the second question—how does war influence long-term economic fluctuations? The literature available frequently emphasizes the downswing implications of war. In marked contrast, the leadership/long-cycle argument posits instead that global war makes a second innovation spurt more likely after the war is concluded—the war effect is both direct and indirect. Global war facilitates innovation in all war participants, but the facilitation should be most obvious in the primary war winner—especially one that does not bear the brunt of the war's costs in personnel and infrastructure. The war also eliminates some of the winner's competition. In some cases, the elimination is only temporary, but then so is the winner's economic lead that is at least reinforced by the reduction in rivals. Moreover, a war fought to determine whose rules will govern interregional transactions is apt to prove beneficial to the winner's economic fortunes.

As regards the third question—are all actors equally susceptible and important to the war-growth linkage—note that any war participant may suffer economic impacts. However, the long waves in growth are keyed to global system leaders who become the lead economies of the world system. Lead economies initially come close to monopolizing the launching of innovations. Spurts of innovation are thus highly centralized spatially. Growth waves are then created primarily by activities that take place within the lead economies of each era; these waves are then emulated by other economies that are capable of participating in the global lead industries.

Global system leaders are not hegemons and do not dominate all economic and political activity. They specialize in long-distance commerce and advanced industrial production. They dominate for finite periods of time only in terms of global lead industries and the provision of political and military leadership at the global (intercontinental) level. Only four states (Portugal, the Netherlands, Britain, and the United States) have so far attained this particular pinnacle.

In evaluating the fourth question—how far back in time does the war/long-term growth linkage exist—the interaction of global war, growth, and leadership can be readily traced to Portuguese explorations of the West African coast in the fifteenth century. But these processes seem to have even earlier roots. We argue that long waves can be traced directly to a Sung economic revolution in the tenth and eleventh centuries that influenced the Mediterranean nautical and commercial revolutions of the twelfth and thirteenth century. These revolutions were centered around several Italian city-states, but ultimately were focused on Venice until the fifteenth century. These early long-wave manifestations can be considered prototypical for what was to come after the fifteenth century. They were also more delimited spatially. However, the result of these manifestations is an interconnected chain of nineteen innovation spurts beginning in Sung China in the tenth century and continuing through the present era.

For the fifth question—is there reason to anticipate evolutionary changes in the nature of the war/long-term growth linkage—it would be difficult to imagine a ten-century-long process that was not characterized by considerable evolution. Nevertheless, the type of evolution that is claimed has to do with the nature and locus of economic activities (the identities of the leading sectors and lead economies). Although war did not play quite the same role in the pre-fifteenth-century prototypical behavior, after the late fifteenth century the relationships among the pairs of innovation spurts and the intervening global war assume a remarkable temporal uniformity. It is conceivable that this pattern could change if the perceived costs of war were universally regarded as too high for the ostensible benefits that might be gained. The intervening global war might disappear as an overly crude problem-solving technique, but there is no reason to anticipate the disappearance of systemic crises over the future of global leadership. Alternatively put, and barring a fundamental change in the nature of economic innovation, there is no compelling theoretical reason to anticipate a substantial deviation from the first innovation spurt—macrodecision phrase—to the second innovation spurt pattern.

For the sixth question—is there systematic evidence to support a war/long-term growth linkage—the systematic evidence for the leadership/long-cycle interpretation takes two forms. In chapter 7 of this analysis, we will provide specific predictions of when paired innovation peaks should have been expected based on the four-phase chronology of the long cycle generated

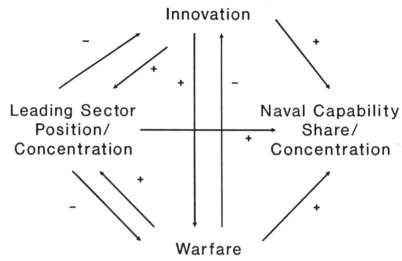

Figure 4.1. Innovation, Naval Capability, and War

earlier. The examination will encompass all phases between 1430 and 1973, and data are available to construct a schedule of global lead industries for this period. At the risk of getting ahead of the presentation, each peak prediction was supported by the data; no nonpredicted innovation peaks were uncovered. Moreover, in every case, the global system leader's share of global reach capabilities (as measured by naval power) exceeded the anticipated fifty-percent leadership threshold in between the paired innovation peaks. Evidence for the claim that the global system leaders have virtually monopolized the introduction of economic innovations is also supplied. Chapters 9 and 10 focus on the five centuries preceding the Portuguese breakthrough to the Indian Ocean and the beginning of the modern era. While the empirical evidence is understandably slim for the Chinese centuries, some useful data are available for Italian economic activities in the thirteenth and fourteenth centuries which prove to be equally supportive of our hypotheses.

A second form of systematic support for the leadership/long-cycle interpretation is advanced in Rasler and Thompson (1994). Four variables are subjected to Granger causality analysis for the British (1780–1913) and U.S. (1870–1980) cases. The four variables, outlined in figure 4.1, are leading sector growth rates, shares of leading sector production, shares of naval capability, and war (measured in terms of national resource mobilization—military expenditures as a proportion of gross national product). The basic Granger question is which variable antecedes the others—a necessary but not sufficient criteria for causality. The pattern shown in figure 4.1 is not simple, but it can be interpreted as supportive.

The most critical antecedence arrows are the ones between leading sector growth rates, leading sector production share, and war. Positive leading sector growth rates lead to economic leadership. War improves leading sector growth rates, naval leadership, and economic leadership. The only arrow that may seem puzzling is the negative arrow from leading sector growth rates to war. If global war breaks out between successive peaks in innovation, one would think the relationship would be positively signed. However, the link from the first innovation spurt to war would be negatively signed if the spurt had peaked immediately before the outbreak of war. That is precisely what happened between 1430 and 1973. Thus, instead of locating the outbreak of war somewhere on the upswing, the leadership/long-cycle perspective pinpoints the very beginning of the innovation downswing—that is, immediately after the peak. Does this contradict the asserted upswing-war/downswing-upswing pattern? The answer is no because leading sector innovation peaks can be expected to peak before economic growth does. Although we do not know the exact nature of the lag structure, it seems safe to presume that a point falling immediately after the innovation peak would still be a period of general positive economic growth.

In evaluating the last question—are there major anomalies to the hypothesized pattern—unlike most of the arguments summarized in table 2.1, the leadership/long-cycle interpretation has no problem dealing with World Wars I and II simultaneously as long as one views World War II as a continuation of World War I. The phrase of macrodecision/global war is then 1914 to 1945. The first growth spurt of the U.S. era peaked in the 1900s; the second growth spurt of the pair peaked in the 1960s. The pattern of a phase of global war bookended by growth spurts is therefore maintained. Since the long cycle of global politics has been consistent in treating the 1914 to 1945 period as a single phase of global war since the origin of the general perspective in the middle to late 1970s, the merging of the two twentieth-century wars cannot be viewed as a recent expedient to save the long wave-global war pattern. Overall, the leadership/long-cycle interpretation yields no other major anomalies, either.

Does this evaluation imply that the "twin peaks" interpretation of the leadership/long-cycle perspective has fully resolved the global war/long-term economic growth puzzle? The answer must be no, or, at least, not yet. Empirical corroboration is essential and, so far, it is only promised in subsequent chapters. Other aspects of the argument deserve further elaboration as well.

For instance, why do leading sectors give way to new leading sectors? Alternatively, should we expect the pattern of upswing-war-upswing to continue indefinitely? If not, why not and what should we expect instead? These are some of the questions that require more attention before we will be able to claim a comprehensive explanation of the fundamental relationship between war and long-term economic growth.

We will deal with these questions in subsequent chapters—but not all at once. The immediate priority is assessing whether the empirical evidence is supportive or discouraging for the long-cycle interpretation. Such an assessment is not quite as easy as it may sound. Testable hypotheses must be advanced; a number of concepts need to be translated into more specific variables and indicators; and appropriate data must be culled from the annals of economic history. Only then may the hypotheses be confronted with the empirical evidence. These are the tasks of the next section and chapters 5, 6, and 7.

Part Three

Testing the Leading Sector-Global War Relationship

Chapter Five

Do K-Waves
and Long Cycles Coevolve?

Are K-waves and long cycles two autonomous, unrelated processes, or are they in some sense related or coordinate (see also Modelski 1992)? Could they be said to be coevolving? This question, as we have shown in chapter 2, is hardly a new one, and has been attempted a number of times before.

To recapitulate what is still a reasonable opinion, let us look to Arnold Toynbee (1954, 234–35), the influential historian of world civilizations. In his major opus, *A Study of History,* Toynbee was struck by a number of regularities, including war-peace cycles and linking world politics and world economics. He observed that "alternating phases of peace and war" could be described as the "political counterparts of alternating waves of prosperity and depression." He was quite willing to seriously entertain the possibility of a law of nature that might relate these two sets of phenomena, but he did not investigate this matter at any greater detail. Instead, he voiced the concern that, among economists, the status of these later movements was uncertain and that this contrasted with his war-peace cycles (for which he provided a dating scheme starting in 1494) where the evidence for K-waves began only with the Industrial Revolution. Is it now possible to advance the investigation of this matter to a higher level?

IS THERE COORDINATION OR COEVOLUTION?

The answer to the question—is there coordination—is not really difficult: on general grounds, given what we know about the interdependence of economics and politics, we would not be surprised to learn that the two processes are coordinate. By using the term coordination we do not intend to imply the existence of a coordinator, but only the probability of self-organizing adjustment processes. In fact, we might for that reason prefer the term coevolution that is defined as diachronic changes in two or more interacting objects or systems—a term previously used in biological and ecological studies. This term captures the essence of what we are trying to depict: the relationship of mutual dependence between two or more processes of structural change.

We know that, today, government invariably absorbs a substantial portion of the gross national product in most countries—maybe one-third on average, perhaps as much as one-half during the two world wars of the twentieth century. In turn, the economy depends on peace, order, and security for carrying on its business; any disturbance of this political framework drastically affects the economy. These are all very good reasons for thinking that the political system of nation-states stands in a reciprocal relationship of mutual interdependence to the world economy, and absence of coordination would likely be a source of disturbance. Hence it is absence of coordination that would be surprising, and not its presence.

On similar, if not more specific grounds, we would also expect such critical global processes as the K-wave and the long cycle to be subject to mechanisms of coordination—both because they draw on a common pool of resources and because they respond to a common set of global problems. Unless these two processes dovetail, neither may operate successfully. To give just a few examples, new industrial sectors are a source of revenues and export earnings that help fund global operations. Innovative industries help stake out claims to political leadership. Political operations, in turn, build conditions of global security within which these innovative industries prosper and expand, and their logistical and other requirements, as in global wars, provide markets for their products.

Both the economic and the political processes are tied together as responses to perceived global problems. For instance, the Portuguese activities in which the political and economic considerations were closely intertwined responded to the widespread demand for discoveries. In the case of the United States, the heavy industrial expansion before 1914 laid the foundations for the military victories of 1918 and 1945. The order reestablished in 1945 put the world system on the way toward global integration that included a communications and information revolution and a better organized trading system. In fact we might advance the hypothesis that both processes have a common, broader, basis: the search for better forms of global organization.

Table 5.1

Long Cycle and K-Wave Process Sequences

	Phases			
Long Cycle	Agenda-setting	Coalition-building	Macro-decision	Execution
K-Wave	Start-up	High-growth odd-numbered	Start-up	High-growth even-numbered

Ever since Kondratieff introduced his theories, the length of the K-wave has been known to be between fifty and sixty years. Students of long cycles, furthermore, propose that world powers succeed each other, or experience re-selection, at intervals of some 100–120 years. This latter position was recently confirmed by measurements of sea power concentration that, as predicted, peaked at those intervals at the end of five past global wars (Modelski and Thompson 1988). Given agreement on those independent empirical data, it is reasonable to suppose that each long cycle resonates with two K-waves.

More specifically, when we view each long cycle as composed of four learning model phases, as in table 1.1, the first K-wave (hence odd-numbered) located in a rising economy might be expected to run in tandem with the phases of agenda-setting and coalition-building (of the rising power); the second K-wave (even-numbered) will be associated with the phases of macrodecision and execution. Since K-waves are S-shaped growth spurts, we might regard the first two phases of each K-growth spurt as start-up, and the two that follow as high-growth. Table 5.2 shows the postulated sequence for the two processes.

Empirical experience suggests that in the past expansionary high-growth periods have both preceded and followed the long-cycle phase of macrodecision (global war). Long spells of major war are inimical to the expansion of the global economy; they stimulate only the production of war-related material. They do, on the other hand, lay the foundation for the phases of postwar global expansion. Global war itself is a sequence of events that in the past has made use of capacity employing innovations brought into full production in the high-growth period preceding that war (as World Wars I and II fed on iron and steel, and on energy and chemical industries brought on line in the decades preceding 1914).

Considering this, we hypothesize the following relationships:

1. Odd-numbered K-waves peak in the (long-cycle) phase preceding macro-decision/global war.
2. Even-numbered K-waves peak in the (long-cycle) phase following upon macro-decision/global war.
3. The attainment of global leadership follows the peak in the odd-numbered K-wave and precedes the peak in the even-numbered K-wave.
4. World powers, in their learning cycles, account for the majority of basic economic innovations.

If sustained, the first two propositions would make it possible to assert that success in the odd-numbered K-wave serves as a necessary condition for attaining global leadership, and that the start-up phase of the even-numbered K-wave occurs during macrodecision/global war. Its high growth thrives upon the consolidation of the global economic order in the execution/world power phase of the long cycle. In this way, not all wars become central to understanding this interaction—with the exception of global war. National basing of innovative industries is not a historical accident but a product of that interaction.

While there are very real limits on the extent to which we can establish necessary conditions, it is possible to advance a third hypothesis on the timing of the attainment of global leadership. If the odd-numbered K-wave is a prerequisite to leadership, then it must precede it. Yet leadership is assumed to be most evident in the execution/world power phase. Leadership is also assumed to facilitate the development of the even-numbered K-wave. Presumably, then, leadership should be attained before the even-numbered K-wave peak.

The prediction embodied in number three is expressed in table 5.2. The list of global lead industries reflects the contemporary consensus of K-wave studies from Britain II onward; the earlier ones are informed by a close reading of economic history (see W. R. Thompson 1992a).[1] The predicted dates for start-up, and high-growth periods of each K-wave are derived from the long-cycle dating scheme found in table 3.1. In other words, our prediction as to the timing of the peaks is theoretically based upon a postulate of coordination, or possibly coevolution. Evidence confirming these predictions would tend to substantiate our hypothesis of the existence of coordination.

WORLD POWERS AND INNOVATION

In short, our hypotheses predict that states exercising (or successfully learning to exercise) global leadership are also the principal (and initial) sources of K-waves. In other words, global (political) leadership is closely synchronized with global economic leadership. In view of the fact that

Table 5.2

The Hypothesized Relationship Between the Learning Long Cycle
and Global Lead Industries

Learning Long Cycle	Global Lead Industries	Predicted "Start-up"	Predicted "High-growth"
LC5 Portuguese			
K9	Guinea Gold	1430–1460	1460–1494
K10	Indian Pepper	1494–1516	1516–1540
LC6 Dutch			
K11	Baltic and Atlantic Trades	1540–1560	1560–1580
K12	Eastern Trade	1580–1609	1609–1640
LC7 Britain I			
K13	Amerasian Trade (especially sugar)	1640–1660	1660–1688
K14	Amerasian Trade	1688–1713	1713–1740
LC8 Britain II			
K15	Cotton, Iron	1740–1763	1763–1792
K16	Railroads, Steam	1792–1815	1815–1850
LC9 United States			
K17	Steel, Chemicals, Electrics	1850–1873	1873–1914
K18	Motor Vehicles, Aviation, Electronics	1914–1945	1945–1973
LC10			
K19	Information Industries	1973–2000	2000–2030
K20		2030–2050	2050–2080

K-waves are animated by clusters of the basic innovations that restructured the global economy, we would also expect global leadership to be associated with such innovations. This leads to the fourth testable hypothesis mentioned above—world powers, in their learning cycles, account for the majority of basic economic innovations. This would predict that Britain, for example, would lead in basic innovations until 1850, but that the United States would account for the bulk of such innovations between 1850 and 1973.

We have asserted that the four hypotheses—which focus on the sequential timing of economic growth, global war, leadership, and economic innovation—are testable. In the next chapter, we explain how we propose to follow through on this claim and still encompass five hundred years of political and economic activity.

Chapter Six

Leading Sectors
in the Global Economy
Fifteenth to Twentieth Centuries, K-Waves 9–18

VARIABLES AND INDICATORS

Before examining the evidence, let us first discuss the relevant variables and indicators as follows:

1. lead economies and leading sector growth spurts,
2. K-waves,
3. the timing of growth spurts,
4. national success in exploiting growth spurts,
5. global leadership, and
6. the timing of leadership attainment.

LEADING SECTORS AND LEAD ECONOMIES

Leading sectors embody a basic innovation, or a cluster of innovations, which induces rapid growth. Such sectors lead to spillovers and produce multiplier effects—ultimately throughout the global economy. In these two respects, such sectors are said to be leading the economy. Their high growth rate and their impact are significant in propelling the growth of other sectors.

A central premise of the leading sector concept is that growth occurs unevenly and at different rates within (national and global) economies. Some types of activities or sectors expand steadily, but also very slowly. There will always be some sectors that are stagnating due to lags in technological change or, more simply, changes in demand. Significant rates of economic growth, however, are initially traceable to a few activities that are so transformed by

70

innovation that they experience abrupt and rapid expansion. These sectors lead their respective economies as vanguards of high growth. New ways of doing things are introduced. High profits are realized to the extent that leading sectors are monopolized by a few firms or a single economy; money for investment becomes less scarce; new industries and jobs are created; transportation costs may be reduced; and new markets are created. In sum, leading sectors act as the spark plugs of economic growth.

Growth occurs unevenly within the world economy as well. If leading sectors serve as basic stimulants of a national economy, lead economies are the spark plugs of the world economy. These lead economies are located at the apex of the world economy's technological gradient. For finite periods of time, they constitute the principal source of innovation and new technology that is used to develop new industries and other types of economic activities of global significance. The new products are then exported and diffused throughout the system. As the principal innovator of new products or processes, the lead economy determines the initial rate at which the fruits of innovation appear on the world scene. The economy's reward is that it profits most from the monopoly rents associated with pioneering economic activities. Yet the probability that imitation, diffusion, and increased competition will develop is high. The once-new products or technology will ultimately become more routine and will eventually be seen as old products or technology. The monopoly rents diminish accordingly. Thus, a lead economy status is not likely to be maintained indefinitely.

Not all fast growing activities will have secondary implications. At the same time, tracing intersectoral growth impacts is not an easy task. Ultimately, it requires the capability of fully modeling growth and economic interactions. Therefore, developing a schedule of which activities qualify at particular moments in economic history is not without controversy. Similarly, identifying lead economies is made more difficult by the relative scarcity of comparative data on economic activity before the nineteenth century. There are also important changes in the nature and composition of lead economies—for example, the shift from commercial to industrial emphases—to take into account.

Underlying our selection of leading sector indicators is the view that the principal structural change experienced by the global economy in the fifteenth to eighteenth centuries was the construction of the oceanic trading system. Pervasive commercial innovations in the Schumpeterian manner—the development of new sources of supply and new markets and the effectiveness of business organizations—centered around the pioneering of new trading routes, reducing of transaction costs, and opening of new markets. Radical innovations of the late eighteenth, nineteenth, and twentieth centuries centered on the formation of whole industries utilizing new and massively effective techniques of production and transportation that thrived on the basis of those new markets. The common denominator of both these types is innovation: creating new structures that have major implications for the pioneering economy, for the global economic system, and eventually for the entire world.

We tend to think of trade as an undifferentiated mass of exports and imports. Yet commerce, too, is subject to leading sectors of growth thanks to innovations in the development of access to the sources of prized commodities and changes in taste and income. The history of European expansion as the core of the world economy can be structured around sequential developments in gaining access to, and control of, certain Asian and American products. In each case, Europeans sought to develop monopolies of commodity control that were not unlike the more natural monopolies associated with a pioneering industry. In each case, the attempts to monopolize trade in these sectors eventually failed due in part to the sheer magnitude of the task and in part to the increased competition from commercial challengers.

In the absence of substantial evidence to confirm or deny the linkages involved, the assumption that Asian and American trade was important to European growth patterns remains controversial. Perhaps the strongest negative position is advanced by O'Brien (1982) who maintains that trade with the periphery was secondary to European growth. His argument rests on the small proportional size of core-periphery commerce, which he estimates in the vicinity of 2 percent of Europe's gross national product in the 1780s. O'Brien argues further that the proportional significance of trade must have been far less in the sixteenth and seventeenth centuries. Yet there is certainly a difference between Europe as a whole and specific lead European economies. O'Brien contends, however, that the claims for Asian-American trade in the context of the smaller, maritime economies—high profitability, the source of industrial investment capital, and various multiplier effects, including the construction of a global-maritime network—have been exaggerated.

Given the paucity of data, it is difficult to reject these criticisms out of hand. We do not have much precise information about multiplier effects. Nor is it clear just how critical investment monies were to the early industrialization efforts. Whether Asian-American trade profits were high or not depends in part on how they are evaluated. If they are averaged over a century, as O'Brien prefers, they will appear lower than if initial periods of near-monopoly and novelty are compared with later periods of strong competition and routine activities.

The issue cannot be evaluated strictly on the basis of the proportional volume or value of long-distance commerce. Jacob Price (summarized in Mc-

Cusker and Menard 1985, 44), for instance, suggests that British colonial trade encouraged innovation in production (e.g., cotton textiles) and institutions created to deal with long-distance transactions. In this fashion, the foreign trade sector is said to have functioned as an economic hothouse accelerating structural change. Much the same could easily be said of the earlier Dutch and Portuguese economies—even though the production implications were far less profound.

At some risk of sounding tautological, these maritime economies might still have become maritime economies on the basis of fishing and carrying intra-European trade alone. Yet, it is hard to factor out the consequences, intentional and otherwise, of the attempts to find new trade routes to Asia. The American territories were discovered by accident in this process. The opening of Russian trade with Western Europe was another unintended by-product. Or, as Tilly (1990, 93) comments, new phases of European imperialism were initiated by newcomer efforts to challenge or outflank regional trade hegemons. Not coincidentally, successful challenges tended to be highly beneficial to the newcomer's economic position and rate of growth. The most successful challengers became lead economies.

From a different angle, Mokyr (1990, 70) suggests that the age of discoveries was "the age of exposure effect, in which technological change primarily took the form of observing alien technologies and crops and transplanting them elsewhere." Whether the impact was to introduce new foods or drugs of choice, to change clothing styles, or to encourage import substitution, there can be little doubt that impacts were registered. We may not be able to measure these impacts precisely, but it does seem safe to argue that innovations in long-distance trade after 1500 represented a significant change in the scale and composition of European trade (Phillips 1990, 82). These same innovations were also responsible for creating new foci of economic growth. As Steensgaard (1990, 151–52) notes, intercontinental trade "showed vigorous and sustained growth during a period when growth in traditional sectors of the economy was sluggish and innovations in production and changes in consumer habits elsewhere were few." At the very least, the assumption that long-distance trade was an important (but not the only) source of dynamic growth for the Atlantic-based maritime economies of Europe (Portugal, the Netherlands, and Britain) in their respective systemic heydays does not appear to be all that unreasonable.

Economic historians tend to treat the eighteenth-century Industrial Revolution as a singular, unique event. David Landes (1969, 3) takes it for granted that:

The Industrial Revolution marked a major turning point in man's history. To that point, the advances of commerce and industry, however gratifying and impressive, were essentially superficial. . . . The world has seen other periods of industrial prosperity—in medieval Italy and Flanders for example—and had seen the line of economic advance recede in each case. . . . It was the Industrial Revolution that initiated a cumulative, self-sustaining advance in technology whose repercussions would be felt in all aspects of economic life.

The depiction of K-waves in table 5.1 advances a less singular explanation of the Industrial Revolution that began with the cotton and iron K-wave, and puts less stress on discontinuities produced by it. As an event, the wave was undoubtedly significant and constituted a major change in economic structures, and it also was the culmination of the West European phase of the global system. But our interpretation suggests that it was not unique in producing a cumulative, self-sustaining advance. It was just one in the sequence of K-waves, each a compound of technological, social, and other advances that have shaped the global economy in direct and cumulative linkage both to renaissance Italy and to other parts of the early modern world. The world system has been subject to cumulative and self-sustained evolution since its inception.

The list of indicators employed by us to capture the timing and shape of successive K-waves, summarized in table 6.1, extends, modifies, and simplifies the indicators used in earlier analyses (W. R. Thompson 1988, 1990, 1992a). The simplification occurs because we seek to bring our analysis to focus on the single best indicator (or as few as possible indicators for each K-wave episode). As a consequence, some indicators relied upon in earlier studies do not appear in this analysis.[1]

LEADING SECTORS: FROM GUINEA GOLD TO AEROSPACE

The Framework of Global Trade: Portugal, K-Waves 9–10

Conventional treatments of the Portuguese arrival in the Indian Ocean often overlook or understate one of the most important reasons for the Portuguese being the first West Europeans to directly intervene in the Asian spice trade and circumvent the Venetian-Mameluke middle persons. This early breakthrough in the formation of the oceanic trading system is variously attributed to such motivations as religious fervor, Prince Henry's vision, or Portugal's favorable position on the oceans.

Yet something more was involved as well. The Portuguese Crown began its maritime mission with attempts to break into the Saharan gold trade in a

Table 6.1

K-Wave Leading Sectors and Indicators

Leading Sectors	Indicators
West African gold	Volume of Portuguese gold imports from Guinea
Asian pepper	Volume of Portuguese Asian pepper imports
Baltic shipping	Frequency of Dutch Baltic shipping
Asian shipping	Value of Dutch East Indies Company Asian imports
Sugar	British American sugar imports
Tobacco	British American tobacco imports
Indian textiles	English East Indies Company Indian textiles imports
Tea	British tea imports
Cotton textiles	British raw cotton consumption
Iron	British pig iron output
Railroads	British railroad track open
Steel	U.S. crude steel output
Chemicals	U.S. sulphuric acid output
Electrics	U.S. electric power production
Automobiles	U.S. motor vehicle production
Electronics	U.S. semiconductor industry sales
Aerospace	U.S. civilian jet airliner seat production

century when all of Europe suffered from a shortage of precious metals. Attempts to seize Moroccan ports from 1415 onward, in part, were efforts toward that direction. But Morocco proved difficult to conquer and the gold-seeking Portuguese found themselves working their way down the African coastline (figure 6.1), looking at first for easier points of entry. Ultimately, in a major innovation that was a victory of caravels over caravans and camels, the Portuguese succeeded in outflanking the Moslem-controlled land network. By establishing a presence on the coast of West Africa, especially at Al Mina where they built a substantial fortress, the Portuguese gained direct access to the sources of gold in the interior. They concluded by circumnavigating the Horn of Africa, after finding much of the gold they and other Europeans needed to pay for Asian spices, other goods, and the fleet ships.

According to Scammell (1989, 228), West African gold doubled the royal income of Joao II (1481–1495). Far more profitable and ambitious, however, were the commercial opportunities opened by the voyage of Vasco da Gama (1497–1499). Entrance into the Indian Ocean meant the creation of a truly oceanic trading network (figure 6.2) that would link the rich and complex maritime Asian trade with the Atlantic. The Portuguese were initially quite successful in

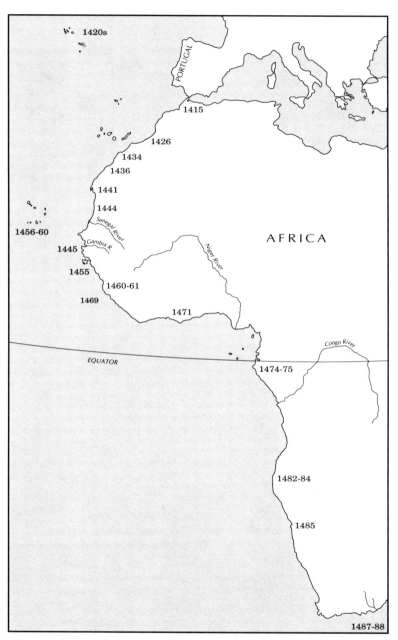

Figure 6.1. Portugal's Movement Down the African Coastline

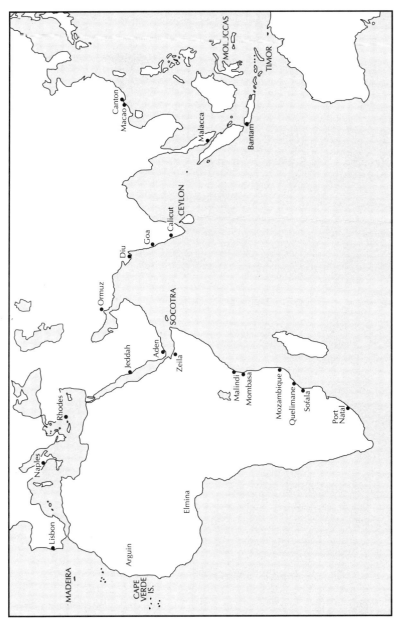

Figure 6.2. Portugal's Asian Network

Table 6.2

Portuguese Sectoral Data and Growth Rates, 1450s–1590s

Decade	Guinea Gold Estimated Annual Averages (in cruzados)	Growth Rates	Pepper Imports Estimated Annual Averages (in quintais)	Growth Rates
1450s	5,700			
1460s	5,700	0.0		
1470s	16,605	1.913		
1480s	94,178	4.672		
1490s	161,368	0.713		
1500s	129,985	−0.194	11,717	
1510s	120,000	−0.077	23,893	1.039
1520s			13,750	−0.425
1530s			17,054	0.240
1540s			30,120	0.766
1550s			17,100	−0.432
1560s			17,100	0.0
1570s			20,000	0.170
1580s			15,771	−0.211
1590s			9,300	−0.410

Data Sources: for gold and pepper, see Godinho 1963–1965; for pepper, see Mathew 1983 and Wake 1979.

monopolizing Eurasian maritime commerce. That monopoly was most fully realized in respect to spices—pepper in particular. For instance, between 1496 and 1498 the Venetians acquired 460 to 630 tons of pepper per year at Alexandria. Between 1501 and 1506 the average had declined to 135 tons (Subrahmanyam 1993, 66). Portugal's initially strong control did prove rather short-lived, yet their success as the dominant maritime power in Asian waters made them unusually prosperous for a time. It also initiated the movement of the hub of European intercontinental trade away from the Mediterranean to the Atlantic.

Table 6.2 summarizes decadal information on the two most direct indicators of Portugal's innovative economic activities of the fifteenth and sixteenth centuries: West African gold and Asian pepper imports. The influx of gold was not unlike a brief and restricted boom. We say restricted because the Portuguese basically failed to fully reroute gold destined for the North African caravan routes. But until the first decade of the sixteenth century, West African gold remained an important portion of Portuguese trade. Around 1500 the gold boom abruptly died. The gold declined to around 15 percent, instead of the fifty-percent share of Crown revenues that it had once constituted, as the focus shifted to spices. Even in terms of West African trade, the importance of gold faded as its trade share declined from about 58 percent between 1499 and 1501 to around 13 percent in 1508–1511 (Ebble 1986, 449). Instead, the slave trade became more important in that part of the world.

A virtual boom in spices followed this short-lived influx of gold. Duncan (1986) describes several phases in the *Carreira da India* (the India Run) by which Asian spices were carried back to Portugal. A pioneering phase from 1497 to about 1520, characterized by considerable navigational trial and error and relatively small ships, initiated the spice commerce. A second phase, from 1521 to 1590, was the most profitable even though the number of ships involved were reduced in quantity (while their size grew). Problems proliferated in the third phase from 1591 to 1630.

Then the violent challenge from the Dutch and English forced the Portuguese to increase their shipping to India (during the years 1591–1630), but with negative results: many shipwrecks, poor returns to Lisbon, recurrent fiscal losses, and military defeats undermined confidence and discouraged further efforts. After 1630 the Portuguese did little more than try to keep open some kind of annual communication by sea between Lisbon and Goa. Finally, with Portugal's Asian enterprise deprived of its most lucrative trading entrepots, even the coming of peace in 1668 [with Spain] produced no revitalization of the *Carreira*. By the end of the seventeenth century the once proud *Carreira da India* functioned as little more than a small appendage of Brazil's extensive Atlantic commerce. (Duncan 1986, 18)

Of particular importance for our purposes, Portugal's participation in the pepper trade was described as shrinking into insignificance during the fourth phase of the *Carreira da India* (1631–1670).[2]

The Framework of Global Trade: The Netherlands, K-Waves 11–12

The factor that figures most prominently in accounts of the emergence of the Netherlands, and of Amsterdam in particular by 1600, as the entrepot of intra- and intercontinental trade is the Baltic *moedernegotie* (mothertrade). The carriage of bulky, low-priced commodities (such as grain, salt, herring, and timber) to and from the Baltic region led to early Dutch specialization in inexpensive but numerous freight-carrying ships (such as the *fluyt*) and the development of an efficient shipbuilding industry.

The southern counterpart of the Baltic trade was Atlantic Spain—based in Seville and fueled by American silver. When rich deposits were found in northern Mexico and in Peru in 1545–1546, silver mining on modern lines was organized largely by Germans who introduced the mercury amalgamation process to Zacatecas, Mexico, in 1556 and Potosi (now in Bolivia) in 1573. By then, Potosi, with 120,000 people, was already the largest town in either new or old Spain (Davis 1973, 51–53).

The output of silver reached unprecedented levels, and imports at Seville tripled between 1540 and 1580, and peaked in 1595. Silver had, of course, been mined for many centuries in Europe, but the output of American mines lifted world output to an entirely new order of magnitude. Central European production (some half-million ounces per year in the 1630s) was now dwarfed by Spanish American output (7 million ounces in the 1590s). This proved both stimulative and disruptive, and helped set off a price revolution in Europe. The movement of silver also constituted the backbone of the Atlantic trade. The Netherlands became "the distribution center from which American silver was passed to Germany, Northern Europe, and the British Isles," and Antwerp became a city that was "as much (if not more) the true capital of the Atlantic as Seville or Lisbon" (Braudel 1972, 480, 481). After 1570 that role shifted to Genoa and to Amsterdam after "the Dutch took Seville . . . without firing a shot" (Braudel 1972, 636).

The Low Countries were the point at which Baltic trade met Atlantic silver. The Dutch and Spanish economies were at that time strongly interdependent—one-half of Spanish exports went to the Netherlands and one-third of Dutch exports went to Spain. But what is noteworthy is that neither the Netherlands nor Spain were in the relevant time-frame, roughly between 1520 and 1580, independent political entities. Both were parts of an imperial political organization headed by Charles V, a Hapsburg prince born at Ghent in Flanders. He was known as the Duke of Burgundy, the King of Castille and Aragon, and the Holy Roman Emperor (in Germany). As a consequence, and in spite of its "great, and growing importance," Spain "always took second place in any conflict of interest" when Charles' imperial designs came into play (Elliott 1970, 164). It was this Burgundian-based political system, whose afterglow may be said to have lasted until 1579 (with the defeat of the federal Eboli faction at the Spanish court), which served as the basis of what we have described as the first Dutch K-wave.

This helps clarify the global economic role of Spain which was sometimes regarded as the world power of the sixteenth century. Between 1516 and 1555 Spain did not exist as an actor in world politics. The bulk of the development that made Spain into a powerful challenger after 1580 occurred under the auspices of the Burgundian system. In the context of a global economy, this development centered on the Netherlands and Antwerp, in particular.

Once separated from the Dutch center, the momentum of that expansion slowed and soon came to a halt. Spain soon ceased to be a serious contender at the global level.

Israel (1989) traces the emergence of Dutch trading supremacy to the movement into, and control over (after the 1590s), the richer trades of Europe and the world. The bulk trade was not abandoned, but more profitable commodities were simply added to the commercial inventory. The most important one of the new circuits acquired after 1601 was the Dutch East Indies Company (VOC)—the first and most successful example of worldwide corporate business organization. Figure 6.3 identifies the main nodes in this circuit as they appeared around 1650. The value of the annual East Indies fleet was so high that its safe return was viewed as the central event in the commercial calendar of Amsterdam.

The Dutch were able to dispense with the services of intermediaries (as Portugal had used Antwerp) and recirculated the commodities they traded all around the world. The various trading circuits in which they were active—such as the Baltic, the Mediterranean, the Brazilian and Caribbean, the West African, and the Asian—were for the first time made strongly interactive and reinforcive. To emphasize a single commercial theater such as Asia, as we do in our indicator system, is therefore somewhat arbitrary. We do it partly in order to tap into the more global expansion of the Baltic base and partly because Asian trade was a critical component of the entire Dutch network.

Table 6.3 includes frequency and volume information on the Baltic and Asian trades. The frequency of shipping passing through the Baltic Sounds, and therefore subject to Danish tolls, is well known. The data in table 6.3 focus solely on eastbound shipping with an absolute frequency peak found in the 1610s. Several growth peaks are discernible. The Asian import data begins much later, but since it is expressed in value terms it is not subject to the problems of frequency interpretations. As in the case of the Baltic shipping data, prosperous or high growth decades are not concentrated at the beginning of the series. An initial period of extremely high growth is followed by clusters of positive and negative growth intervals. This seems to be a testimonial to the relatively long life of Dutch trade (see Israel 1989).

The Dutch chose to focus much of their Asian network around the production of spices in what is now Indonesia. An attempt to establish an American base in Brazil failed. Their Asian effort dwarfed the rival English company and displaced it to less desirable positions in the Indian subcontinent. But in the end, this turned out to be an advantage for the English when the demand for Asian goods shifted to Indian and Chinese teas and textiles.

Figure 6.3. The Dutch Network in the Mid Seventeenth Century

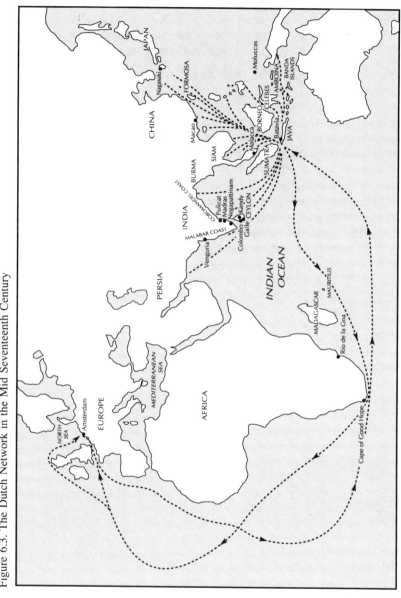

Table 6.3

Dutch Sectoral Data and Growth Rates, 1500s–1750s

Decade	Annual Average Baltic Shipping	Growth Rate	Annual Average VOC Asian Imports	Growth Rate
1500s	805			
1510s	733	−0.089		
1520s	631	−0.139		
1530s	764	0.211		
1540s	523	−0.315		
1550s	873	0.669		
1560s	2,333	1.672		
1570s	1,842	−0.210		
1580s	2,587	0.404		
1590s	3,275	0.266		
1600s	2,691	−0.178		
1610s	3,290	0.223		
1620s	2,405	−0.269	402.8	
1630s	2,028	−0.157	870.5	1.161
1640s	2,173	0.071	954.5	0.096
1650s	1,817	−0.164	1017.2	0.066
1660s	1,296	−0.287	980.8	−0.036
1670s	1,186	−0.085	1299.2	0.325
1680s	1,957	0.650	1669.8	0.285
1690s	1,149	−0.413	1592.9	−0.046
1700s	776	−0.325	2015.8	0.265
1710s	845	0.089	2370.0	0.176
1720s	1,514	0.792	3176.8	0.340
1730s	1,789	0.182	2506.6	−0.211
1740s	1,606	−0.102	2418.7	−0.035
1750s			3163.9	0.308

Note: Baltic shipping is expressed in number of ships; Dutch East Indies Company (VOC) imports are expressed as invoice values in thousands of pesos.
Data Sources: Boswell, Misra, and Brueggemann 1991 for Baltic shipping; Steensgaard 1990 for Dutch Asian imports.

Industrial Takeoff: Britain I, K-Waves 13–14

When the Dutch-Portuguese fighting in Brazil (1630–1640) forced the price of sugar upwards, English planters in Barbados stepped in and initiated the first sugar boom in the Caribbean. As sugar cultivation spread to other islands, another plantation-type crop, tobacco, was also being introduced. It was not that sugar suddenly became valuable in the mid-seventeenth century. Some would argue that Brazilian sugar was more important to Portugal than Asian spices. Not unlike Spanish gold and silver, the ultimate profit-takers from about the mid-sixteenth century were the Dutch who provided the initial capital and controlled much of the carrying trade, refinement, and marketing (B. L. Solow 1987, 66–67; Boxer 1957).

This meant that English trade, in the second half of the seventeenth century, underwent a transformation (Inikori 1987; Richardson 1987). The new commodities from Asia and the Americas displaced the traditional dependence on wool cloth as a principal export, and London began to rival Amsterdam as Europe's principal entrepot. The Navigation Acts from 1651 onward clarified this choice at the political level. According to Scammell (1989, 232), "for England at least the expansion in the nature and range of its entire commerce after 1650 was largely of oceanic inspiration, with the impetus coming from a surge in Asian and American imports and the simultaneous growth of a lively market in the Americas (North, South, and Caribbean) for domestic exports and reexports."

The plantation production techniques were also credited with substantially reducing the price of sugar and tobacco, thereby transforming one-time luxury goods into new habits of mass consumption (Mintz 1985, 63; Davis 1954). Several commentators attributed important spillover effects to these methods. Worsley (1984) argued that plantation techniques inspired the ways in which industrial factories were later organized.[3] Others suggested that experience with long-distance trade was a necessary condition for the Industrial Revolution because of the effects it had on the operating scale and sophistication of the British economy, on the working of critical institutions and availability of capital, and on the incentive structure for innovations—as exemplified by the development of substitutes for Indian textiles (Hobsbawm 1969, 51; McCusker and Menard 1985, 44).

It may be, as Solow and Engerman (1987) argued, that the colonial trade (Britain to Africa, to and from the West Indies, to and from New England, and to and from New England and the West Indies) was neither necessary nor sufficient to bring about the eighteenth-century Industrial Revolution, but they agree that it would be hard to argue that it did not affect its scale and timing.

Internal sources of economic growth were facilitated and encouraged by external stimuli to manufacturing, trade, and income expansion. The general timing of the colonial trade expansion was also fortuitous in the sense that the demand for spices had reached its limits and protectionist measures against the import of Asian textiles were soon to become more common within Europe (B. L. Solow 1987).

We are in a fortunate position to measure some of the most important commodities of this era's British trade. Table 6.4 lists information on the annual average size of sugar, tobacco, textiles, and tea imports into England from the middle of the seventeenth to the middle of the eighteenth century.

The amount of plantation crops, sugar, and tobacco clearly increases in the second half of the seventeenth century. During this time, their patterns of growth were unusually parallel. It was not until the 1740s to 1750s that they began to diverge. Accordingly, we have merged these two indicators by averaging their growth rates to create the single plantation crop growth rate shown in table 6.4.

The Asian indicators lacked this fundamental similarity in growth rates. Indian textiles became important about the same time as the American plantation crops. The importation of initially Indian, but increasingly Chinese, tea did not substantially accelerate until the early eighteenth century. Still, combining the two indicators into one Asian import growth rate, with textiles providing the sole focus initially, does not seem to constitute a major distortion of the economic activity of the time.

Industrial Takeoff: Britain II, K-Waves 15–16

Our choice of indicators for the Industrial Revolution—the two Britain II K-waves—should need little defense. As Cameron (1989, 196) succinctly summarizes the issue: "the industrial superiority that Great Britain had achieved by the first quarter of the nineteenth century rested on technological advances in two major industries, cotton textiles and iron manufactures, supported by an extensive use of coal as an industrial fuel, and by the growing use of the steam engine as a source of mechanical power."

Later, in the same survey of economic history, Cameron (1989, 223) suggests that railways were the most important new industry of the nineteenth century. While there may be some disagreement about the precise impact of various leading sectors between 1780 and 1945, there is a great amount of agreement on their identity (as there is in the K-wave literature). Landes (1969) supports this consensus by denoting the following sequence of industry as situated at the heart of these events: textiles, iron, steam engineering and

Table 6.4
British Sectoral Data and Growth Rates, 1650s–1760s

Decade	Annual Average Tobacco Imports	Growth Rate	Annual Average Sugar Imports	Growth Rate	American Plantation Crop Average Growth Rate
1650s			8,000		
1660s	6,798		8,555	0.069	0.069
1670s	9,028	0.328	13,278	0.552	0.440
1680s	11,630	0.288	18,000	0.356	0.322
1690s	13,189	0.134	20,236	0.124	0.129
1700s	12,565	−0.047	19,693	−0.027	−0.037
1710s	14,057	0.119	29,615	0.504	0.312
1720s	17,673	0.257	38,929	0.315	0.286
1730s	19,846	0.123	41,410	0.064	0.094
1740s	27,794	0.400	42,422	0.024	0.212
1750s	30,646	0.103	58,015	0.368	0.236
1760s	34,635	0.130		0.371	0.251

Decade	Annual Average Tea Imports	Growth Rate	Annual Average Textile Imports	Growth Rate	Asian Import Average Growth Rate
1660s			199		
1670s			578	1.905	1.905
1680s			707	0.223	0.223
1690s			296	−0.581	−0.581
1700s			277	−0.064	−0.064
1710s			552	0.993	0.993
1720s	401.4		783	0.418	0.418
1730s	527.2	0.313	765	−0.023	0.145
1740s	913.7	0.733	772	0.009	0.371
1750s	1,688.2	0.848	527	−0.317	0.266
1760s	2,803.5	0.644			

Note: All quantities are expressed in thousand kilograms with the exception of the English India Company's textile imports, which are expressed in thousand pieces. Data Sources: Schumpeter 1960; Price 1973; and Steensgaard 1990.

Table 6.5

British Sectoral Growth Rates, 1760s–1900s

Decade	Cotton Consumption	Pig Iron Production	Combined Average	Railroad Track Laid
1760s	−0.025	0.016	−0.003	
1770s	0.019	0.023	0.022	
1780s	0.196	0.067	0.131	
1790s	0.080	0.069	0.075	
1800s	0.131	0.030	0.075	
1810s	0.041	0.048	0.045	
1820s	0.078	0.072	0.075	
1830s	0.076	0.051	0.064	0.769
1840s	0.064	0.064	0.064	0.526
1850s	0.047	0.056	0.052	0.466
1860s	0.030	0.041	0.036	0.346
1870s	0.023	0.011	0.017	0.318
1880s	0.034	0.038		0.253
1890s	0.014	0.015		0.207
1900s	0.005	0.038		0.187

Data Source: calculated from Mitchell 1988.

railway transport, steel, heavy chemicals, internal combustion engines, and electricity. With some minor exceptions, the indicators we employ for the Britain II and first U.S. K-waves are taken directly from Rostow's detailed, empirical analysis of the world economy. We repeat his admonition (1978, 369) that "the sectoral data . . . stand as proxies for complexes which far transcend their narrow, literal scope."

Our indicators for the textile and iron industries, raw cotton consumption, and pig iron production are reported in table 6.5. As in earlier cases, we combine the two indicators to create a single growth series for the first wave of the eighteenth-century Industrial Revolution. For the second wave, in the early part of the nineteenth century, we rely on the pace of the amount of railroad track laid.

The Twentieth Century: The United States, K-Waves 17–18

For the latter part of the nineteenth century and the early twentieth century, we continue to follow the consensus emphasis on steel, chemicals, and electricity. Steel is measured directly by crude steel production in table 6.6. The chemical and electric industries are represented, respectively, by sulfuric

Table 6.6

U.S. Sectoral Growth Rates, 1870s–1980s

Decade	Crude Steel Production	Sulphuric Acid Production	Electricity Consumption	Combined Average
		Leading Sector Growth Rates		
1870s	0.367	0.132		0.250
1880s	0.153	0.112		0.133
1890s	0.140	0.052		0.096
1900s	0.137	0.068	0.175	0.127
1910s	0.059	0.065	0.110	0.078
1920s	0.090	0.049	0.086	0.075
1930s	0.070	−0.025	0.036	0.027
1940s	0.051		0.082	0.067
1950s	0.044		0.086	0.065
1960s	0.044		0.069	0.057
1970s	0.002		0.042	0.022
1980s	−0.056		0.012	−0.022

	Motor Vehicle Production	Aerospace Production	Semiconductor Production	Combined Average
1900s	0.452			.452
1910s	0.360	1.828		1.094
1920s	0.145	0.557		.351
1930s	0.037	0.069		.053
1940s	0.337	0.188		0.263
1950s	0.007	0.225	1.540	0.590
1960s	0.089	0.021	0.094	0.068
1970s	0.020	−0.010	0.088	0.033
1980s	0.010	0.058	0.103	0.057

Note: While we provide data through the 1980s following our full disclosure rule, the reader shoud keep in mind that we do not claim that these sectors were leading throughout the time period for which the data are available. The steel, acid, and electricity indicators refer to late nineteenth- and early twenty-century leading sectors while the vehicle, aerospace, and semiconductor indicators relate to sectors no longer leading after the 1970s.

Data Sources: U.S. Department of Commerce 1975 and U.S. Office of the President (multiple volumes) for steel, electric power consumption, and sulphuric acid production; Motor Vehicle Manufacturer's Association 1981 and Shapiro 1993 for motor vehicle production; *Aerospace Facts and Figures* (multiple volumes) for aerospace sales in constant dollars prior to the 1950s; Tyson 1992 for civilian jet airliner seat production after the 1940s; Semiconductor Industry Association Yearbook and Directory (multiple volumes) and Tyson and Yoffie 1993 for semiconductor production.

acid production and electricity consumption. All three growth series are averaged to form one combined series. For the first two-thirds of the twentieth century, an emphasis on motor vehicle production is unlikely to be challenged. This series is supplemented by information on semiconductors and aerospace production. However, in earlier analyses, aerospace production had been measured quite crudely in terms of civilian jet airframe production. This indicator has been replaced for the pre-1950 period by the more inclusive and reliable aerospace industry sales indicator.[4]

Growth Spurts and K-Waves

Even though the series relied upon are often continuous in form, each indicator of growth is converted to an average decadal growth rate. This procedure facilitates the comparison of the continuous series with those that are subject to missing data, as in the case of Guinea gold. But what is more important, it smooths what would otherwise be rather noisy year-to-year fluctuations in volume or frequency and allows one to see, more readily, the development of long-term patterns. In any event, the leading sector concept emphasizes patterns of growth as opposed to sheer volume of activity. While the decennial unit is arbitrary (but presumably neutral), dependence upon growth rates is problematic in cases where initially small units of volume tend to produce higher growth rates than subsequent higher units of volume. As a consequence, one has to be careful when to start measuring a series and how to interpret that start. The decadal aggregation technique reduces this problem somewhat, but it cannot eliminate it altogether.

Nevertheless, high growth spurts in leading sectors and the resulting K-waves can be readily identified. Each economic activity may be represented as a series of growth rates that can be rank-ordered to preserve comparability across different activities and centuries. If these growth rates rise and fall in each successive decade (or simply fluctuate erratically), it is unlikely that the K-wave appellation would be appropriate for such behavior. If, on the other hand, growth rates ascend abruptly and decay in a patterned S-shaped fashion with each maximal ascent separated from the preceding and following peaks by several decades, then we are presumably tapping into K-wave behavior in which each peak growth rate identifies the wave's initial spurt of high growth.

Both of these hypotheses predict when these peaks should occur within two to three decades. The peak of the first K-wave should occur in the coalition-building/deconcentration phase. The peak of the second K-wave should follow in the execution/world power phase. Yet should we expect all

A

B

C

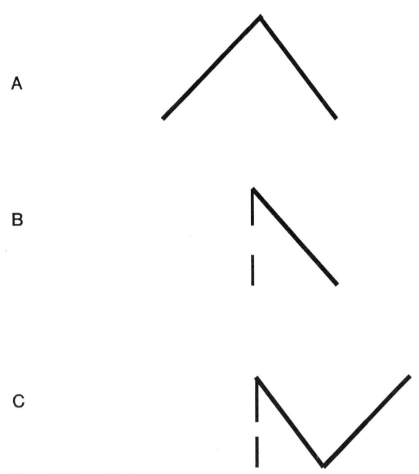

Figure 6.4. Types of Peaks

peaks to look exactly alike? Ideally the answer is yes but, in reality, three pos-sible peaking patterns are acceptable as outlined in figure 6.4.

Peak type *A*, an inverted *V*, is the most obvious form of a peaking growth spurt. However, early information on leading sector growth is not always available. In addition, limited production at the outset of a new activity tends to yield very high growth rates. Peak type *B*, therefore, represents a situation in which some unmeasured ascent to the highest growth rate is implied but not empirically demonstrable. A third possibility, the regular *V* of type *C*, is a double peak situation in which the initial growth spurt is high (frequently an artifact of the small numbers involved) but short-lived. Activity falls off in terms of growth rate but then builds up to a second peak before entering a period of slowing growth.

National Success and Global Leadership

The extent of national success that we have in mind is of the fairly extreme sort. One national economy literally dominates the leading sector during its phase of high growth and is the primary beneficiary of the immediate profits (even though the innovation is globally significant and the benefits spread wider over the long run). Neither dimension is easy to measure consistently over five centuries because relative production figures are possible only after the late eighteenth century—comparative data is quite scarce before that time.[5]

Table 6.7 contains information on the frequency of European shipping to Asia and the Baltic Sea. The Portuguese domination of sea traffic to Asia is clear in the late 1490s and early 1500s. While Portugal maintained this monopoly through the 1570s, pepper had begun to sporadically penetrate the Mediterranean area by overland routes as early as the 1510s. By mid-century, it is estimated that Venice was importing nearly as much pepper as Portugal. Wake (1979, 386) estimates the Portuguese-Venetian pepper import ratio at about 2.9: 2 in the early 1560s. Thus, the proportion of Portuguese outward-bound voyages in the middle decades of the sixteenth century is misleading as an indicator of who dominated pepper flows to Europe.[6] Figure 6.5 provides a more accurate picture of Portuguese economic ascent and decline by piecing together the information available on the Portuguese share of European pepper imports (Wake 1979).

The transition to Dutch dominance in Asian trade is captured in table 6.7 as well. The figures suggest that a peak relative trading position was reached by the middle of the seventeenth century. In contrast, the Dutch dominance in the Baltic trade was established much earlier and retained much longer. If we average the Baltic and Asian trade proportions, the trajectory of the Dutch lead resembles the curve shown in figure 6.6.

The nature of the British lead in the late seventeenth to early eighteenth century is more difficult to capture than the earlier Dutch position. Table 6.8 provides what comparative information we do have on Indian textile imports, American sugar production, and Cantonese tea imports. Comparative data on tobacco production was not uncovered although we do know that the British monopolized the American production of this leaf and that its main competition was tobacco grown in the Netherlands.

Table 6.7

The Relative Frequency of Shipping to Asia and the Baltic Sea

	Outward-bound European Shipping to Asia						
Decade	Portuguese	English	Dutch	(Percent)	French	Danish	Total
1490s	21						21
1500s	150						150
1510s	90						90
1520s	73						73
1530s	79						79
1540s	68						68
1550s	52						52
1560s	48						48
1570s	49						49
1580s	59	11					70
1590s	46	3	65	(57.0)			114
1600s	69	20	59	(39.3)	2		150
1610s	53	65	117	(46.4)	12	5	252
1620s	51	53	148	(56.5)	0	10	262
1630s	30	52	151	(61.4)	9	4	246
1640s	44	64	162	(58.9)	5	0	275
1650s	32	97	226	(62.6)	6	0	361
1660s	21	101	257	(60.8)	40	4	423
1670s	25	126	219	(55.4)	15	10	395
1680s	18	157	209	(48.9)	36	7	427
1690s	23	134	241	(53.3)	40	14	452

	Shipping to the Baltic Sea						
Year	Dutch	(Percent)	English	Swedish	Danish	German	Other
1500	711	(71)	0	0	5	92	190
1510	781	(68)	31	1	6	117	219
1520	674	(64)	45	1	7	108	222
1530	661	(60)	60	2	9	105	269
1540	890	(58)	65	2	4	223	283
1550	318	(48)	54	28	28	112	119
1560	1,391	(54)	18	36	39	584	663
1570	1,237	(36)	148	25	229	427	1,332
1580	2,058	(54)	113	17	268	619	757
1590	2,765	(56)	127	47	288	757	1,000
1600	2,312	(56)	162	11	316	583	904
1610	2,567	(64)	176	41	255	469	564
1620	3,843	(73)	116	25	187	527	542

(continued)

Table 6.7 *(continued)*

1630	1,467	(64)	95	59	173	209	332
1640	1,832	(55)	316	77	477	266	486
1650	3,127	(70)	94	145	210	362	471
1660	1,255	(62)	152	161	76	201	194
1670	1,821	(53)	205	540	138	311	411
1680	1,716	(52)	440	381	290	159	517
1690	1,165	(36)	157	595	474	204	626
1700	1,204	(39)	536	173	248	112	593
1710	724	(45)	238	18	116	90	227
1720	1,078	(46)	612	40	217	108	362
1730	2,064	(43)	852	832	357	173	660
1740	2,672	(47)	844	379	396	175	904
1750	1,835	(37)	837	436	670	201	1,041

Data Source: Asian shipping from Steensgaard 1970; Baltic shipping from Boswell, Misra, and Brueggemann 1991.

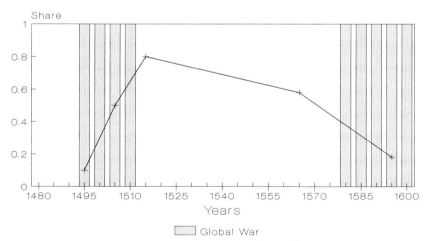

Figure 6.5. Portugal's Estimated Share of European Pepper Imports

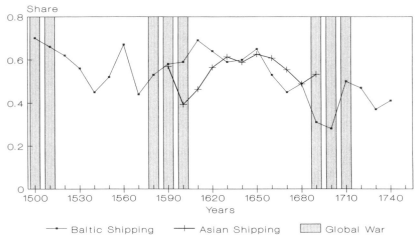

Figure 6.6. Netherlands' Share of Leading Sector Commerce

Table 6.8 demonstrates Britain's early lead (1660s) in Indian textiles over its main European competitor—a lead that is maintained for some time, with the exception of 1700–1709. The sugar data are more difficult to interpret due to the virtual absence of French data. Still, it is clear that the Portuguese position in Brazil was challenged briefly by the Dutch in the 1630s and 1640s, and more successfully by the English in Barbados as early as the 1650s. It is not clear what the level of Portuguese production was in the 1680s. If it resembled the production levels of the previous decade, the English then appear to have controlled 90 percent or more of the American sugar production in that decade. The British lead in American sugar production was then maintained through about 1766 (Watts 1987, 285). The tea data suggest a greater amount of competition than in textiles, sugar, or tobacco. Yet the British lead over its principal European competitor is still clear, except for the war years of the 1740s.

Combining the various observations that are available for this period still leaves much to be desired. One way to facilitate the creation of a series for British trade leadership is to introduce information on a related commercial sector—the import of slaves to American colonies.[7] The relationship to the innovative sectors of the time is quite direct in that the slaves were used primarily to provide labor for sugar and tobacco plantations. Table 6.9 pieces together a decadal flow description for the 1690s to 1780s era. Again, an early British lead is depicted giving way to increased competition later in the eighteenth century.

Table 6.8

Shares of American Sugar, Indian Textile Imports, and Cantonese Tea

			American Sugar Production			
Decade	French Colonies	Spanish Colonies	Portuguese Colonies	Dutch Colonies	English Colonies	(Percent)
1560s		649.2	2,070			
1570s						
1580s		243	4,025			
1590s		64.4				
1600s		65.6	6,900			
1610s		92.6	8,567.5			
1620s			5,321.9			
1630s			2,375.4	1,361.1		
1640s			1,203.7	1,897.9		
1650s		41.3	6,321.3		8,000	(55.7)
1660s		4.1	172.5		8,555	
1670s		35.9	766.7			
1680s	931.5	13.1			18,000	
1690s		0.7			20,236	
1700s				4,521.9	19,693	
1710s		30.9	178.3	6,686.7	29,615	
1720s		82.2	101.9	9,383.4	38,929	
1730s		168.0	75.7	8,243	41,410	
1740s		606.9	158	8,547.3	42,422	
1750s	47,400	1,904.9	104.1	7,462.2	58,015	(50.5)
1760s		2,730.1	199.4			
1770s		798.8				

Data Sources: Calculations based on data made available in Phillips 1990, Steensgaard 1990, and Watts 1987 in several different weight units. All of the entries above are expressed in 1,000 kilograms.

Estimated English and Dutch East Indies Companies
Average Textile Imports

Decade	English	(Percent)	Dutch	Total
1650s			89.8	
1660s	199	(69.4)	87.8	286.8
1670s	578	(80.8)	137.2	715.2
1680s	707	(67.0)	347.6	1,054.6
1690s	296	(51.6)	277.6	573.6
1700s	277	(44.2)	349.8	626.8

(continued)

Table 6.8 *(continued)*

1710s	552	(57.4)	409.6	961.6
1720s	783	(61.5)	489.8	1,272.8
1730s	765	(75.4)	250.0	1,015.0
1740s	772			
1750s	527			

Data Source: Steensgaard 1990, 126. The textile unit of measurement is 1,000 pieces of cloth.

Tea Exports from Canton

Years	EIC	Percent	VOC	Others	Total
1719–1725	417	54.1		354	771
1726–1733	498	43.7	181	460	1,139
1734–1740	629	30.6	392	1,034	2,055
1741–1748	899	24.1	916	1,918	3,733
1749–1755	1,390	26.1	1,275	2,661	5,326

Data Source: Steensgaard 1990.

If we utilize the relative proportions generated in tables 6.8 and 6.9, a number of holes remain, as demonstrated in table 6.10. Yet while the exact numbers may be inaccurate, particularly in the latter part of the seventeenth century, the general ascent and decline curve plotted in figure 6.7 seems plausible.

Much better data are associated with industrialization. After 1780 it is possible to focus on the system's major economies in the nineteenth and twentieth centuries (Britain, France, Germany, the United States, and Japan) and develop a series of proportional shares for each country. Since the data are available on an annual basis, tables 6.11 and 6.12 report the relative standings for each indicator every tenth year. By 1790 Britain had developed a commanding lead in cotton consumption and pig iron production—a lead that was maintained well into the nineteenth century. Britain also led in the next wave focused on railroadization, but its edge had begun to erode by the 1860s.[8]

Figure 6.8 offers two interpretations of the relative rise and decline of Britain's global economy. One simply averages all three sector scores from 1780 to 1900. The other switches from the averaged cotton-iron scores to the railroadization index in the 1830s. Ironically, the second approach signals a much faster rate of decline because the British retained their lead in the older sectors for some time, whereas railroadization was not an easy sector in which to remain dominant. Still, the general trajectory of the two interpretations is

Table 6.9

Slave Trade Estimates

Decade	Portugal	Dutch	Annual Average Imports Britain	Percent	France	Total
1690s	5,600	2,000	9,036	54.3		16,636
1700s	6,092	2,800	11,960	57.4		20,848
1710s	8,904	2,100	14,090	46.2	5,371	30,465
1720s	9,529	2,950	14,160	43.5	5,909	32,548
1730s	15,778	4,750	20,700	38.1	13,068	54,296
1740s	20,152	5,500	25,480	36.9	17,909	69,041
1750s	18,746	5,250	23,080	35.8	17,385	64,461
1760s	23,901	7,000	30,600	37.3	20,452	81,953
1770s	20,933	4,900	25,400	35.4	20,452	71,685
1780s	32,180	1,400	36,000	32.6	41,000	110,590
1790s		1,538	74,667			

Note: The Portuguese estimates are based on rather limited information. Figures are given for century aggregates (1601–1700: 560,000 slaves, 1701–1810: 1,909,730). The 1690s figure was arrived at by dividing the 1601–1700 figure by one hundred. The 1700–1780 estimates were obtained by assuming that the rate of growth in Portuguese slave imports paralleled the growth rate for the Dutch, British, and French. These ten-year growth rates were multiplied by a 1701–1790 estimate (1,562,159) and then divided by ten to reach an average annual figure. Data Source: Rawley 1981.

consistent. After the 1870s, if not before, the British lost their hegemonic position in the leading sectors.

Britain was also the initial leader in steel and chemicals as table 6.12 demonstrates. Within a few years, though, the United States had supplanted the British lead in both sectors. The United States has not seen a great deal of competition, at least among the major economies, in the consumption of electricity either. The mid- to late-twentieth-century experience has been a more mixed situation. The lead in the production of motor vehicles, for a time a virtual North American monopoly, eventually passed to the Japanese (see table 6.13). Semiconductor production has experienced a similar outcome, although in a much shorter period of time. While the American production shares in automobiles may improve (the share of semiconductors already had by the early 1990s), only civilian airliner production has so far remained an American preserve.

Figure 6.9 plots the two versions of the U.S. leads between 1870 and 1990. The first series averages all six sectors. The second series switches to

Table 6.10

Pieces of Information on British I Economic Leadership:
Proportional Shares of Leading Sector Commerce (percentage)

Decade	American Sugar	Indian Textiles	American Slaves	Chinese Tea	Average
1650s	55.7				55.7
1660s	98.0	69.4			83.7
1670s		80.8			80.8
1680s	95.0	67.0			81.0
1690s		51.6	54.1		52.9
1700s		44.2	57.4		50.8
1710s		57.4	46.3		51.9
1720s		61.5	43.5	48.9	51.3
1730s		75.4	38.1	37.2	50.2
1740s			36.9	24.1	30.5
1750s	50.5		35.8	26.1	37.5
1760s			37.4		37.4
1770s			35.5		35.5

Data Source: See tables 6.8 and 6.9.

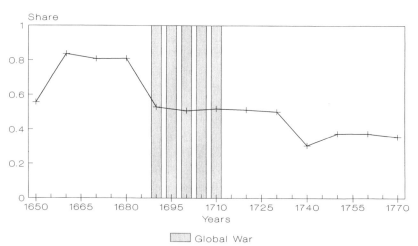

Figure 6.7. Britain I Share of Leading Sector Production

Table 6.11

Shares of Raw Cotton Consumption, Pig Iron Production, and Railroad Construction

Year	Britain	Percent	France	Percent	United States	Percent	Germany	Percent	Japan	Percent
				Raw Cotton Consumption						
1780	3	42.9	4	57.1						
1790	14	69.0	4	19.7	2.3	11.3				
1800	24	69.4	7	20.2	3.6	10.4				
1810	56	78.7	8	23.1	7.2	10.1				
1820	54	59.4	19	20.9	17.9	19.7				
1830	112	67.8	34	20.6	19.3	11.7				
1840	208	64.8	53	16.5	50.9	15.9	8.9	2.8		
1850	267	56.8	59	12.5	118.4	25.2	26.0	5.5		
1860	492	56.9	115	13.3	190.0	22.0	67.0	7.8		
1870	489	60.5	59	7.3	179.0	22.2	81.0	10.0		
1880	617	52.2	89	7.5	338.0	28.6	137.0	11.6		
1890	755	44.5	125	7.4	567.0	33.4	227.0	13.4	22	1.3
1900	788	35.8	159	7.2	830.0	37.7	279.0	12.7	143	6.5
				Pig Iron Production						
1780	45	42.9	26	24.8	17	16.2	17	16.2		
1790	61	40.4	36	23.8	27	17.9	27	17.9		
1800	171	57.6	54	18.2	36	12.1	36	12.1		
1810	225	57.3	77	19.6	50	12.7	41	10.4		
1820	374	62.0	130	21.6	18	3.0	134	22.2		
1830	688	56.7	266	21.9	149	12.3	110	9.1		
1840	1,419	64.0	348	15.7	258	11.6	190	8.6		
1850	2,285	67.0	406	11.9	507	14.9	210	6.2		
1860	3,888	64.2	898	14.8	739	12.2	529	8.7		
1870	6,059	60.6	1178	11.8	1,499	15.0	1,261	12.6		
1880	7,873	50.7	1725	11.1	3,452	22.2	2,468	15.9		
1890	8,031	35.9	1962	8.8	8,283	37.0	4,100	18.3		
1900	9,104	27.3	2714	8.1	14,010	41.9	7,550	22.6	31	0.1
				Railroad Construction						
1830		76.6		22.4		8.2				
1840		52.6		6.1		33.9		7.4		
1850		46.6		9.8		23.8		19.8		
1860		34.6		14.8		32.7		18.0		
1870		31.8		15.8		33.3		19.2		
1880		25.3		15.7		36.1		22.8		0.2
1890		20.7		16.2		40.9		20.8		1.5
1900		18.7		15.5		41.5		20.9		3.4

Note: The unit of measurement for cotton consumption and iron production is 1,000 metric tons. The railroad construction index is based on the sum of the relative proportions for railroad track laid and railroad track laid per square kilometer, divided by two.
Data Sources: Mitchell 1980 and 1982, with country size information from Banks 1971.

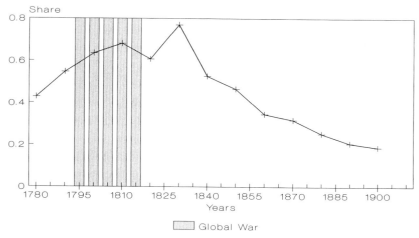

Figure 6.8. Britain II Share of Leading Sector Production

motor vehicles, jet airliner seats, and semiconductor production in the 1950s. As in the British case, it makes little difference which interpretation is utilized. The U.S. relative leading sector position peaked after each world war and is presently on a downward trajectory. Just where the U.S. relative position will be after the 1990s depends, in part, on whether (and when) a new group of leading sectors emerges. In this respect, it does not make sense to continue counting vehicles, airliner seats, and semiconductors into the 1990s. By our accounting system, these sectors ceased to be leading sectors in 1973. (See chapter 11 for more on this topic.)

Regrettably we are not in a position to currently measure the extent to which our choices for leading sectors were responsible for the consequent wealth of the respective lead economies, or the cumulative expansion of the world economy.[9] Still, there is little controversy (with, of course, the continuing exception of Portugal) that four countries were the leading actors in the global, intercontinental economy in their successive heydays after 1500.[10] We do not have to demonstrate their military or even economic hegemony within Europe for that is not what is meant by leadership in the global political economy.[11] Nor is the unusually wealthy status of the four states identified as lead economies—however temporary that status turned out to be—a matter of much debate.

Leadership suggests that an actor take the lead in some activity that others follow. At a minimum, lead economies do this by innovating economic activities. Figure 6.10 provides one way to summarily illustrate the extents to which

Table 6.12

Shares of Steel Production, Sulphuric Acid Production,
and Electricity Consumption

Year	Britain	Percent	France	Percent	United States	Percent	Germany	Percent	Japan	Percent
					Crude Steel					
1871	334	52.9	80	12.7	74	11.7	143	22.7		
1880	1,316	35.9	389	14.3	1,270	34.7	690	18.8		
1890	3,636	33.7	683	10.6	4,350	40.3	2,135	19.8		
1900	4,980	21.3	1,565	10.2	10,350	44.3	6,461	27.7		
1910	6,476	13.1	3,413	6.9	26,510	53.6	13,100	26.5		
1920	9,212	14.2	2,706	4.2	42,810	66.0	9,287	14.3	811	1.3
1930	7,444	10.2	9,444	12.9	41,350	56.6	12,536	17.2	2,289	3.1
1940	13,183	12.3	4,413	4.1	60,770	56.9	21,540	20.2	6,856	6.4
1950	16,554	12.7	8,652	6.7	87,850	67.6	12,121	9.3	4,839	3.7
1960	24,695	13.2	17,281	9.2	89,354	47.6	34,100	18.2	22,138	11.8
1970	28,316	9.2	23,773	7.7	118,363	38.3	45,040	14.6	93,332	30.2
1980	11,277	3.9	23,176	8.0	101,456	34.8	43,838	15.1	111,395	38.3
					Sulphuric Acid					
1870	590	68.3	145	16.8	78	9.0	51	5.9		
1880	900	60.2	200	13.4	264	17.7	130	8.7		
1890	870	38.8	271	12.1	683	30.4	420	18.7		
1900	1,010	28.9	625	17.9	1,108	31.7	703	20.1	50	1.4
1910	1,065	19.3	837	15.1	2,197	39.7	1,381	25.0	50	0.9
1920	942	14.0	1,250	18.6	3,422	50.8	792	11.8	324	4.8
1930	813	9.0	1,059	11.7	5,027	55.4	1,475	16.3	701	7.7
1940	1,215	10.5	729	6.3	5,245	45.2	2,140	18.4	2,278	19.6
					Electricity Consumption					
1910	2	6.7	1	3.3	21	70.0	5	16.7	1	3.3
1920	9	9.9	6	6.6	57	62.6	15	16.5	4	4.4
1930	18	9.2	17	8.7	116	59.2	29	14.8	16	8.2
1940	28	8.5	21	6.4	182	55.3	63	19.1	35	10.6
1950	63	10.8	33	5.7	396	67.8	46	7.9	46	7.9
1960	129	10.0	72	5.6	849	66.1	119	9.3	116	9.0
1970	230	8.8	141	5.4	1,642	62.8	243	9.3	359	13.7
1980	285	7.3	261	6.7	2,383	60.9	374	9.6	612	15.6

Note: The units of measurement are 1,000 metric tons for crude steel and sulphuric acid production, and gigawatts for electricity consumption.
Data Sources: Mitchell 1980 and 1982; U.S. Department of Commerce 1975; U.S. Office of the President (multiple volumes); and various U.N. Yearbooks.

Table 6.13

Shares of Motor Vehicle, Civilian Jet Airliner, and Semiconductor Production

Year	Britain	Percent	France	Percent	United States	Percent	Germany	Percent	Japan	Percent
				Motor Vehicle Production						
1900	2	13.6	3	27.3	4	38.1	2	20.9		
1910	14	5.6	38	15.7	187	74.2	13	5.2		
1920	55	2.3	40	1.7	2,228	95.2	18	0.9		
1930	237	6.0	23	5.9	3,362	85.6	96	2.4	1	0.0
1940	134	2.8	119	2.4	4,472	92.4	72	1.5	46	0.9
1950	784	8.3	357	3.8	8,003	85	301	3.2	32	0.3
1960	1,811	14.2	1,370	10.8	6,724	52.9	2,047	16.1	760	6.0
1970	2,099	8.7	2,750	11.4	10,206	42.2	3,825	15.8	5,305	21.9
1980	1,313	4.8	3,378	12.2	8,010	29.0	3,878	14.0	11,043	40.0
1990	1,566	4.7	3,769	11.2	9,778	29.1	4,977	14.8	13,487	40.2
				Semiconductor Production						
1960		4.0		4.0		78.0		4.0		10.0
1970		6.0		4.0		63.0		6.0		21.0
1980						51.4				35.5
1990						39.7				48.0

Note: European market share in 1980 and 1990, respectively, was 12.9 and 12.3 percent.

Year	Britain	Percent	France	Percent	United States	Percent	Germany	Percent	Airbus	Percent
				Civilian Jet Airliner Production						
1952	1,144									
1960	2,180	5.6	3,120	8.0	33,908	64.5				
1970	1,938	2.8	720	1.0	66,592	96.2				
1980	737	0.8			84,667	87.8			11,037	11.4
1990					107,930	84.3			20,169	15.7

Note: Motor vehicle production is stated per one thousand vehicles (Motor Vehicle Manufacturer's Association, multiple volumes; Shapiro 1993); semiconductor production market shares are based on the value of sales (Malerba 1985; Tyson and Yoffie 1993); civilian jet airliner production is stated in new seats per airliner, calculated from information supplied in Tyson 1992.

Portugal, the Netherlands, Britain, and the United States led in the generation of leading sectors in their respective centuries. Whether, and to what extent, such a position translates into political leadership is a separate question. Nonetheless, it seems likely that the lead player in the global economy, an arena structured around long-distance transactions, will develop the incentive and capability to manage or regulate problems pertaining to the stable functioning of commercial systems. To do so in a meaningful fashion requires global mili-

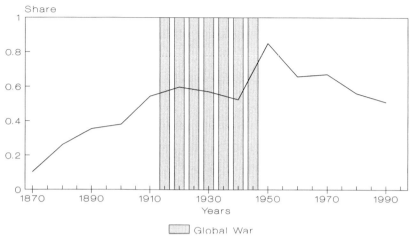

Figure 6.9. U.S. Share of Leading Sector Production

tary reach which, for the past several centuries, has meant an oceanic naval capability. For precisely this reason we have spent some time developing serial indices of naval capability (Modelski and Thompson 1988) that allow us to measure relative naval strength from 1494 onwards.

Hypothesis 3 implies that success in the first K-wave is a necessary condition of attaining global political leadership. Leadership in this connotation encompasses both economic and military-political processes. While economic leadership must be assumed, to a large extent, the attainment of military-political leadership in the global political economy can be tested with our data. We shall examine the timing of the naval ascents of the lead economies in terms of observations on relative naval power every fifth year. Elsewhere, we have argued for some time that a naval capability share equaling or exceeding 50 percent indicates a decisive foundation for exerting global reach and managing the resulting global problems. Thus we expect each of the four lead economies to attain a fifty-percent share of naval power after the peak of the first, but before the peak of the second K-wave.

Of course, evidence supporting this expectation will not constitute proof that the first wave is a necessary condition for global political leadership, but it would constitute a major step in that direction. If the fifty-percent threshold is attained before the first, or after the second, K-wave peak the nature of the presumed link between economic and military-political leadership might be less clear. Both K-waves might be necessary, or perhaps only the second one

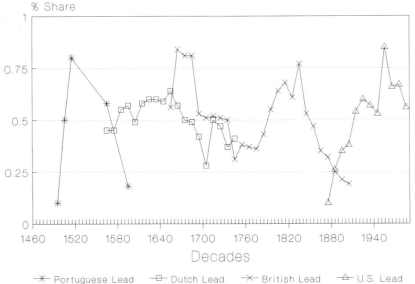

Figure 6.10. The Sequence of Lead Economies

was necessary. Alternatively, if the threshold was never attained, it would be difficult to advance an argument about any wave being a necessary condition for such a process of structural change in global politics.

To determine what thresholds were attained and when, as well as determining when the leading sector growth spurts peaked vis-à-vis the timing of global war, we turn to a discussion of the outcome of our tests in chapter 7. In that chapter, we will also analyze our fourth hypothesis about the timing and origin of economic innovation.

Chapter Seven

Testing for Coevolution

We have four hypotheses to test in this chapter:

1. Odd-numbered K-waves peak in the (long-cycle) phase preceding macro-decision/global war.
2. Even-numbered K-waves peak in the (long-cycle) phase following upon macrodecision/global war.
3. The attainment of global leadership (as indicated by exceeding a fifty-percent threshold of global naval capability) follows the odd-numbered K-wave peak but precedes the even-numbered peak.
4. World powers, in their learning cycles, account for the majority of basic economic innovations.

To simplify our presentation, we have broken the test results pertaining to the first three hypotheses into two parts. In the first test, we will concentrate on the timing of the growth spurts, as predicted by hypotheses 1 and 2. The basic questions are whether the first K-wave peaks immediately preceding the macrodecision/global war phase and whether the second K-wave peaks immediately after that same phase. Implicit in this question is the assumption that the successive leading sectors peak and then decay as demanded by this K-wave interpretation.[1] If the peaks are invisible or too numerous, the tests and the hypothesis will have little meaning. The second test introduces the naval power indicator as a proxy for global political leadership as required by hypothesis 3.

Figures 7.1 through 7.5 provide an illustrated summary of the results of the first test. Each lead economy and pair of K-waves are depicted on separate graphs. The temporal span of each plot is standardized. At the center of each plot is the demarcated macrodecision/global war phase period. The two phase

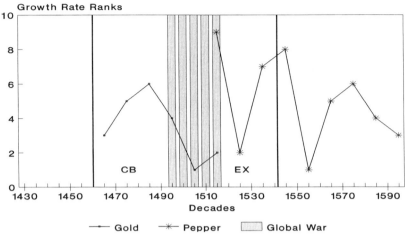

Figure 7.1. The Portuguese K-Waves, 1430s–1590s

periods immediately preceding and following this central interval are also included in each plot and designated with a *CB* (coalition-building phase) or *EX*
(execution phase) label.[2] Any data in our possession for the two phase periods
that are external to the three phases of primary interest are usually plotted unless their inclusion simply makes the graph too difficult to read. The idea is to
present the available information as neutrally as possible.

Our data support hypothesis 1 in all five cases. As predicted, the first K-
wave's growth peak occurs in each case in the phase of coalition-building/
deconcentration. In one case, though, the plot shows two peaks. The
exception, linked to the U.S. K17 wave, is not that exceptional since both of
the two peaks fall within the expected window. In this instance, the first of the
two peaks (1870s) is clearly a case of small volume numbers yielding high
growth rates. Focusing on the major peak of the coalition-building phase, it is
interesting to observe that the peak almost always arrived in the decade immediately before the decade in which global war began (1480s, 1670s, 1780s,
and 1900s). The only exception is the 1560s Dutch peak that is one decade off
from the generalization. The intensification of the revolt following the establishment of the nucleus of the Dutch Republic in 1572 probably accounts for
the poor showing of the 1570s.

The prediction derived from hypothesis 2 is as equally successful as the
first one. To summarize, it is fair to say that the second wave's peak follows
the period of global war. Precisely when it follows varies from case to case. In

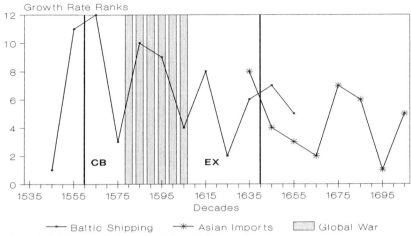

Figure 7.2. The Dutch K-Waves, 1540s–1700s

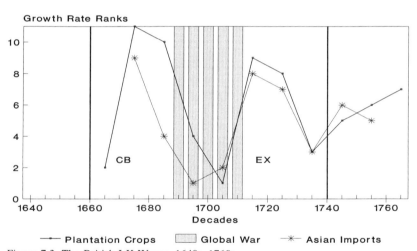

Figure 7.3. The British I K-Waves, 1640s–1760s

the Portuguese case, the second peak shown in figure 7.1 is dated in the 1510s. Since the flow of pepper back to Portugal began almost at the turn of the century, it is really the 1500s when this commerce would have experienced its greatest average annual growth. But a 1500s peak is too early for our prediction.

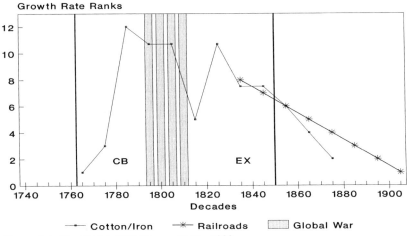

Figure 7.4. The British II K-Waves, 1740s–1900s

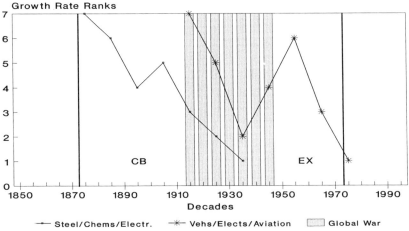

Figure 7.5. The U.S. K-Waves, 1850s–1980s

Duncan's (1986, 22) estimates of shipping arrivals in Lisbon, partially re-produced in table 7.1, help clarify this interpretation. Since only two ships ar-rived before 1501, any computation of the percentage increase from the 1490s to the 1500s in pepper volume needs to be viewed cautiously. After the ship-ping began to flow in the 1500s, tonnage peaked in the 1530s (still within the execution phase) at a level not exceeded until the 1580s. Pepper was not the

Table 7.1

Estimates of Portuguese Shipping From Asia, 1497–1700

Years	Ships	Tonnage
1497–1500	2	170
1501–1510	73	21,115
1511–1520	59	25,760
1521–1530	53	27,020
1531–1540	57	36,410
1541–1550	52	30,550
1551–1560	35	25,750
1561–1570	40	32,150
1571–1580	39	35,150
1581–1590	42	39,290
1591–1600	22	25,000
1601–1610	28	32,290
1611–1620	28	35,550
1621–1630	19	15,050
1631–1640	15	9,910
1641–1650	24	12,030
1651–1660	16	8,120
1661–1670	13	4,820
1671–1680	21	9,680
1681–1690	15	8,600
1691–1700	13	7,550

Data Source: Duncan 1986, 22. The tonnage is expressed in
terms of sixteenth-century Portuguese maritime tons (equal to
1,023 kilograms).

only commodity carried back to Lisbon by Portuguese shipping, but it was
certainly the principal cargo in the first half of the sixteenth century.

The second trade-based Dutch K-wave is depicted with a peak in the last
decade of the execution phase—no doubt the true peak occurred slightly earlier. Our Asian imports indicator series only begins in the 1620s (table 6.2),
but we know that Dutch shipping to Asia began in the 1590s and increased
dramatically in the 1610s (see table 6.7). Nevertheless, these considerations
would still place the second peak in the predicted phase.

The second Britain I and U.S. K-waves peaked immediately following the
cessation of global hostilities. In contrast, the second Britain II peak occurred
toward the end of the post-global war phase (execution/world power). Yet it is
interesting to observe the 1820s upturn in the first K-wave's production in the

Britain II case (figure 7.4). While we have argued that winning a global war is beneficial to the victor, it should also be noted that wars interrupt trade and production. Once a global war ends, there is likely to be some new growth in response to the restoration of normal economic conditions.

In general, then, the timing of the second K-wave peak seems to be sensitive to global warfare—underscoring how the lead economy's second wave is dependent on the postwar order. Obviously, other factors intervene as well for the leading sectors of the first and second K-waves are often linked.[3] Examples include African gold that paid for Indian spices; British innovations in iron and steam in the 1780s that were critical in developing the railroad industry of the mid-nineteenth century; and the interdependence of the American steel and auto industries. To what extent global war accelerates or retards the innovations at the heart of the second K-wave should also make some difference to the success and timing of that process.

Table 7.2 summarizes the outcome of the tests for the first two hypotheses more succinctly than is possible for five plots with a number of serial fluctuations. Again, both hypotheses 1 and 2 are quite strongly supported by the data that are available.

Turning to the second part of our test, matching K-waves to global political leadership, figures 7.6 through 7.10 depict the timing of ascendance to naval preponderance. A visual inspection of the figures may suggest a more mixed outcome than is actually the case. In each instance, the fifty-percent naval power threshold is breached well after the peak of the first K-wave. In four cases—the Portuguese, Dutch, Britain II, and U.S. periods—naval leadership was clearly attained before the second K-peak. In the case of Britain I, the 1715 attainment occurs at about the same time as the peak of the second K-wave (in the 1710s).

Table 7.3 again sets out the successful outcome of our test in each case, more starkly than possible with several longitudinal plots of multiple series. It also broadens the scope of the analysis by displaying certain other events that were occasions for global leadership, in addition to the hard data on the surpassing of the naval threshold (that assures power monopoly at the global level).

These soft data may be interpreted as showing the time when, originating in these countries, "declarations of intent, or major acts of assumption of leadership at the global level occurred" (Modelski 1987, 42; further documented in Modelski and Modelski 1988). Thus 1494 in table 7.3 refers to the global political regime established by the Treaty of Tordesillas between Portugal and Spain that granted Portugal the first exclusive access to the oceanic route. Britain's assertion of the principle of the balance of Europe in 1701, or the U.S. signing of the Atlantic Charter and entering World War II in 1941, were events of comparable

Table 7.2
Predicted Versus Observed Growth Peaks in Global Lead Industries

Learning Long Cycle	Global Lead Industry Indicators	Predicted "High-growth"	Observed Growth Peak*
LC5 Portuguese			
K9	Guinea Gold	1460–1492	1480s
K10	Indian Pepper	1516–1540	1510s
LC6 Dutch			
K11	Baltic Trade	1560–1580	1560s
K12	Asian Trade	1609–1640	1630s
LC7 Britain I			
K13	Tobacco, Sugar, Indian Textiles	1660–1680	1670s
K14	Tobacco, Sugar, Tea, Indian Textiles	1714–1740	1710s
LC8 Britain II			
K15	Cotton Consumption, Pig Iron Production	1763–1792	1780s
K16	Railroad Track Laid (absolute amount and per square kilometer)	1815–1850	1830s
LC9 United States			
K17	Steel, Sulphuric Acid, Electricity Production	1873–1914	1870s/1900s
K18	Motor Vehicle Production, Aerospace Sales, and Semiconductor Production	1945–1973	1950s

*All observed growth rate peaks fall within the predicted window.

significance. In each case they preceded the establishment of the naval threshold, but followed the peak of the first (odd-numbered) K-wave.

It is important to make clear at this juncture that we are not arguing that every K-wave fluctuation is mirrored in some way by a corresponding flux in the political standing as reflected in the naval score. The type of causal relationship we have in mind is more complicated.[4] As supported but not proven by our analysis, the first K-wave establishes a necessary resource and financial base for developing a global leadership position. These attainments both finance and justify global reach. Global war has been another necessary procedural precondition; it is the emergency stimulus of major crisis. This response is not limited to naval construction. Armies can be mobilized and coalition partners can receive subsidies

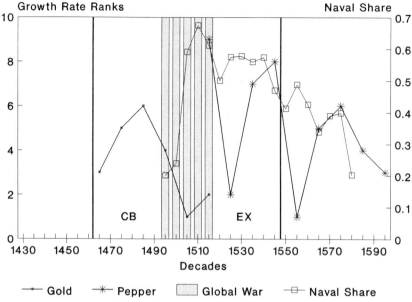

Figure 7.6. Portuguese K-Waves and Naval Capability, 1430s–1590s

and substantial aid. As we have seen, the first of each pair of K-waves has in the past generated the sinews of major warfare.[5]

The plots arrayed in figures 7.6 through 7.10 attest to the complex nature of the K-wave/naval global reach relationship. Thus, the second of the pair of K-waves does not appear to have much, if any, lasting positive impact on the global political position in any of the five cases. At the same time, it is likely to be more than a coincidence that economic leadership and naval preponderance decline in coordination with that K-wave's movement into a slow growth mode. In past centuries, a significant reversal of the slide away from global leadership has been arrested only by the emergence of new leading sectors (or simply a new K-wave). In the Portuguese and Dutch cases the next K-wave originated somewhere else. Britain I broke this incipient pattern by giving way to K15 and K16 in Britain II. The outcome of the current case (K19) remains to be determined.

But why do leading sectors give way to new leading sectors in the pattern that we suggest? We can explain the decline of each successive sector generally as a matter of it having played out its growth potential. When this occurs depends on the diffusion of the root innovation, the number of new competi-

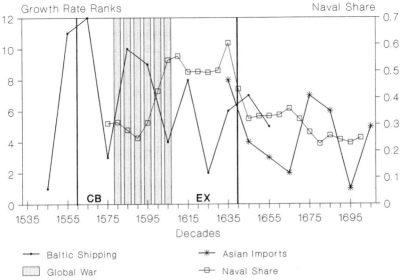

Figure 7.7. Dutch K-Waves and Naval Capability, 1540s–1700s

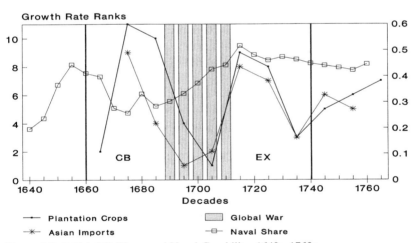

Figure 7.8. British I K-Waves and Naval Capability, 1640s–1760s

tors and their impact on supply, market saturation, prices, and the elasticity of demand for various products. Pepper, for instance, remained a leading trade commodity for the Italians, the Portuguese, and the Dutch before the European

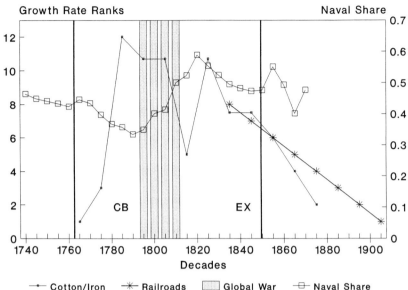

Figure 7.9. British II K-Waves and Naval Capability, 1740s–1900s

market became saturated in the late seventeenth century (Steensgaard 1990, 118–20). Wake (1979, 392–93) calculates that European pepper imports increased between 45 and 64 percent in the fifteenth century and accounted for 27 percent of the exports in the sixteenth century. In the seventeenth century, the Dutch and English imports of pepper more than doubled the supply available in the previous century, drove prices down by 30 to 40 percent, and finally ended Mediterranean participation in the trade. Yet in the process, pepper became a mere routine commodity—it had lost its leading sector quality.

Much the same process can be seen in table 6.8. American sugar production totaled less than 3 million kilograms in the 1560s. By the early 1600s, production had increased to 7 to 8.5 million kilograms. When the English colonies began to produce sugar in the middle of the century, total production doubled. By the early 1700s production had more than doubled again and by the 1750s production had quadrupled. New competitors greatly increased the supply, prices dropped, and demand increased—but not infinitely. Eventually, sugar too became a routine product.

Our examples of pepper and sugar represent old leading sectors, but the general process appears to apply to all leading sectors. An initial monopoly enjoyed by some pioneering groups of a singular nationality gives way to dif-

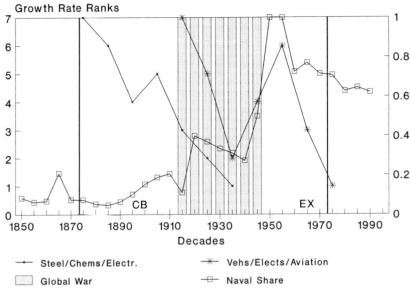

Figure 7.10. U.S. K-Waves and Naval Capability, 1850s–1980s

fusion and international competition. Supplies increase, prices fall, and depending on consumer tastes, the market becomes saturated. Pepper and sugar became routine commodities in this fashion, but so, too, did cotton textiles, steel, and automobiles. National and sectoral leads are closely linked and neither seems sustainable for long.

Transitions from one lead economy to the next reflect a variety of factors such as location, resource endowments, and the nature of indigenous technological problems. Portugal's limited resource pool could only go so far in monopolizing Asian trade. The Dutch did not have the coal deposits the English possessed and peat could not produce the heat necessary for late-eighteenth-century industrial production. Nor did the Dutch have a problem with draining mines—a technological nuisance that led to the development of steam engines. Similarly, the British lacked the home market for automobiles that only the United States possessed in the early twentieth century.

Yet it is also clear that the intensity of commitment to old leading sectors is crucial too. Some examples are the Dutch commitment to spices and the English settlement for Indian bases (due to Indonesian influences). The latter proved fortunate when the demand for Indian textiles increased dramatically. Not only were the Dutch at a disadvantage in this sector, but their insistence

Table 7.3
Attainment of Global Leadership and the Timing of K-Waves

World Power	First K-Wave Peak (observed)	Occasions for Global Leadership*	Naval Threshold Attained**	Second K-Wave Peak (observed)
Portugal	1480s	1494, 1499	1510	1500s/1530s
Netherlands	1560s	1601, 1608	1610	1620s
Britain I	1670s	1689, 1701	1715	1710s
Britain II	1780s	1793, 1815	1810	1830s
United States	1870s/1900s	1941, 1947	1945	1960s

*Modelski 1987, 42; Modelski and Modelski 1988.
**Fifty-percent share of capital warships of global power navies (Modelski and Thompson 1988).

on attempting to funnel Chinese trade through their Batavian entrepot (as opposed to going directly to the Chinese ports) gave the British another head start. Less than two centuries later, the British were slow to capitalize on an early lead in steel because they were overly committed to an early technology that was soon improved upon in Germany and the United States. Electrification was also slow to develop in Britain due to an earlier commitment to gas.

In the one case that we have so far where a lead economy retained its lead status through more than a pair of K-waves (Britain I and II), it is for the same reason that an odd-numbered K-wave tends to lead to an even-numbered K-wave. The first wave makes the second wave more probable. As discussed in chapter 6, Britain I made Britain II more probable—not so much in terms of direct technological transfer, but in modifying the economic environment and making it more conducive to new departures in industrial production. With the advantage of hindsight, we can see how the nature of the initial Portuguese and Dutch leads made the likelihood of a movement into the lead in the next pair of K-waves less probable. How such probabilities might be estimated for the ongoing U.S. case is a topic to which we will return in chapter 11.

THE WORLD POWER AND INNOVATION HYPOTHESIS

Since the original publication of Gerhard Mensch's *Stalemate in Technology* in 1975, the role of innovation in K-waves has received considerable attention. A number of lists of inventions and innovations have been compiled, and students of the subject have become well aware that the selection of cases

Table 7.4

Major Innovations and the World Powers

Cycle/K-Wave (years)	No. of Major Innovations*	Originating in (percent)
Britain II: K16 (1811–1849)	18	Britain: 44; United States: 22
United States: K17 (1850–1914)	67	United States: 45; Germany: 18
United States: K18 (1915–1971)	75	United States: 57; Germany: 17

*includes six cases described as originating in (unallocated) "various countries."
Data Source: based on information found in van Duijn 1983, 176–79.

for such lists entails a considerable amount of subjective judgment. Nevertheless, Mensch's theses have been reanalyzed and subjected to empirical testing (see, for instance, Freeman 1983). Most of the lists do not show the country of origin of the innovation, but van Duijn's work is an exception. As part of his discussion of K-waves he produces a list of 160 major inventions "introduced during the nineteenth and twentieth centuries" (van Duijn 1983, 176–79). This represents a consensus compiled from a number of sources and excludes cases mentioned by one source only. Van Duijn also shows the country where the innovation was first introduced, as well as the innovator—usually a business firm, but occasionally with the notation "various countries."

To test hypothesis 4, we group the innovations into three classes by the year they were first introduced: the Britain II cycle (until 1850) and the two K-waves of the U.S. (learning) cycle: 1850–1914 and 1915–1971.

As predicted, this shows that the world powers in our table account for the plurality, if not the majority, of basic innovations.[6] The challenger of the U.S. cycle, Germany, was the second ranking location of innovations. Moreover, the data in table 7.4 do not suggest any slackening of the U.S. rate of innovation in the most recently completed portion of the K18 wave. Between 1945 and 1971 69 percent of the thirty-five major innovations are reported to have originated in the United States—an even higher proportion than over the entire cycle. The Soviet Union appears only once on that list (communication satellite introduced in 1962, along with the United States) and Japan has no entry at all.[7]

The conventional approach to K-waves strongly implies and assumes that the eighteenth-century Industrial Revolution was necessary for the emergence of the K-wave phenomenon. We have shown that this was not the case. The rise and decline of leading sectors can be found in the seventeenth, sixteenth, and fifteenth centuries. But is that as far back as they extend? We think not. The next three chapters develop arguments and evidence for the continuous existence of K-waves since the tenth century. We contend that they began in Sung China, migrated westward to the Mediterranean, and then shaped economic life in renaissance Italy. The first eight K-waves were dominated by the Chinese and Italians. The next ten favored Portugal, the Netherlands, Britain, and, most recently, the United States. Who will benefit most in the nineteenth K-wave? The identity of the primary beneficiary, of course, remains to be seen, but some informed speculation seems warranted and will be discussed in chapter 11.

Part Four

THE COEVOLUTION
OF THE GLOBAL ECONOMY

Chapter Eight

An Enlarged Framework

Our work so far has tested K-waves actuating the global economy since the mid-fifteenth century. That considerably extends the scope of most of the studies that concern themselves primarily with events since the Industrial Revolution (in the convention initiated by Kondratieff). But the question arises: if the Kondratieff-type analysis can reasonably be extended back to 1430, does that date represent the true inception of the process, and what might be the grounds for thinking so? Or else, what are the reasons for supposing that such origins extend even further into the past? What general or theory-backed account might be adduced for such reasoning? A definitive treatment and explanation of our problem cannot be achieved unless the origins and true nature of these processes are better understood.

CAPITALISM IN THE WORLD ECONOMY

Nikolai Kondratieff (1984, 25–26, 35, 90) maintained that the long wave was part of the capitalist economic system that was constantly evolving, and that this evolutionary process possessed the property of directionality. He argued that ''a theoretical curve can represent real evolutionary trends in the development of an economy.'' But he (Kondratieff 1984, 32) was also acutely aware that the investigation of these processes was extraordinarily difficult because it presupposed a very long period of observation, and therefore called for going back in time as far as necessary. Two sets of conditions worked in the opposite direction, toward shortening the time span under investigation—''reasons of homogeneity and comparability of the phenomena under study,'' and ''lack of data.''

Kondratieff (1984, 32) took the view that ''we cannot go too far back'' because homogeneity required that "the basic principles of business organization" remained constant for the period under investigation, and for him that meant implicitly the period after the Industrial Revolution. However, if we take the principle of business organization to be capitalism as such, and not just industrial capitalism, then the relevant period might extend back further than Kondratieff thought necessary or possible.

In fact there is no universal agreement on what capitalism is, and when it may be said to have started. Successive waves of scholarship have steadily pushed the date back when it might be said to have originated. Joseph Schumpeter began the empirical investigation with his *Business Cycles* where he proposed the date of 1790, but admitted freely that "capitalism went as far back as the element of credit creation" which could have taken it "certainly as far back as the sixteenth century" and even earlier; he pleaded lack of data and the possibility that the capitalist sector was smaller at that time, as the reason for not dating capitalism before 1790 (J. Schumpeter 1939, 224–25). More recently scholars such as Immanuel Wallerstein saw capitalism rising in the "long" sixteenth century, while others such as Janet Abu-Lughod recognized it in Chinese, Arab, Indian, or Italian business practices of the twelfth and thirteenth centuries. Some authors such as Michael Rostovtsev claimed Hellenistic "city capitalism" to have flourished in the Roman Empire of the second and third centuries. For Fernand Braudel (1984, 620) capitalism has been potentially visible since the "dawn of history."

If we fix our sights on the market economy, instead of contending with so contested a concept as capitalism and the scheme of "stages of historical development" that it implies, then we might find that economies bringing together diverse business enterprises responding to the complex demands of their customers have been found in a variety of conditions throughout the past millennium. We view a market (or exchange) economy as one consisting of firms and households in exchange with one another, and as an economy that operates with internal self-organization and a degree of external autonomy (especially from politics). We know, too, that market economies are particularly favorable to innovation.

William McNeill (1982, 25) argues that in a world-historical perspective the inception of a market economy occurred in China circa 1000. If that were so, the required homogeneity of the economic system might extend all the way back to the two periods of Chinese history known as northern and southern Sung. Here we see, as we shall show at greater length in the next chapter, the inception of evolutionary potential for market economy on a global scale. That potential is not just in the growing complexity and specialization of the economy within a setting of high urbanization, but also in the successive waves of innovation that animated it via world-famous inventions involving paper, money and finance, weapons leading up to the development of fire-arms, and the use of compasses that opened the way for oceanic navigation. If we have globally significant inventions, then we also are entitled to expect that innovations implementing them would come in clusters and produce early K-waves which would gradually pervade the global economy.

We might then ask: why should the years around 1000 be any more com-pelling then, for example, 1430, or 1492, or even the onset of the Industrial Revolution? To answer that question we might approach this problem from another direction: that of world system evolution (see, for example, Modelski 1992).

EVOLUTION OF THE WORLD ECONOMY

In the big picture, let us view K-waves as processes that are nested within the larger framework of the evolution of the world economy. We might define the world economy as the set of specialized arrangements whereby the human species provides for the production and distribution of the material wealth of goods and services. Let us propose, further, that the beginnings of this world economy go back some five thousand years ago to the Near East when irri-gated agriculture began to yield surpluses that gave way to increasing and wide-ranging systems of exchange. We observe, finally, that these arrange-ments did change over time, and that over a very long time they have shown increasing specialization and greater frequency in exchange.

The processes by which the world economy has undergone such changes have been little studied but much speculated upon. The literature of economic history has neither a canonical periodization nor a "general theory of eco-nomic growth to which the economic historian can turn" (North 1968, 472).[1] There has been very little progress since the abandonment of the nineteenth-century attempts at establishing "stages of economic development," such as Carl Bucher's (1907, 89) three-fold scheme for Europe, of household, city, and national economy (Eucken 1951, 69–98).

Karl Marx's "law of the evolution of human history" proposed that eco-nomic development forms the foundation for political and social change through a series of major stages (each characterized by distinct forms of own-ership) beginning with primitive (tribal) communism, and proceeding through slave society, feudalism, and capitalism to socialism. His theory has had, at times, great political resonance, but less influence on the study of economic history.

The term capitalism retains much currency, but it is worth bearing in mind that, according to Fernand Braudel (1982, 237), it was not until the beginning of the twentieth century, after the publication of Werner Sombart's *Der Moderne Kapitalismus* in 1902, that it entered academic debate. Braudel used it extensively in his trilogy, but did not fit it into the framework of world economic history. We have already noted the imprecisions attached to that term— including the lack of consensus on the beginnings of that system—and observed the tendency to use that multidimensional concept that ranges over economy, politics, society, and culture as though it was something personifiable (i.e., capitalism is wreaking havoc upon society). We do not believe that a theory of economic change can be achieved which is limited in its application to capitalism.

Yet we do hold, along with John Hicks (1969, 7), that the economic history of the world can be treated as a single process. To that end we propose to devise the concept of the world-economy process and to view that as a sequence of major structural changes that might be reconstructed, as in table 8.1. This table shows the world economy, since its inception, passing though six major periods where the last one is still underway. The periodization is basically a conventional one, and adheres to the categories, established by nineteenth-century archaeologists, of Bronze, Iron, and Modern Ages. But within each of these major eras are two conditions: an initial period of concentration during which productive centers make headway in the establishment of new technologies and a follow-up phase of dispersion in which technologies and productive capacities diffuse, and trade and other forms of exchange become more prominent. In other words, our model proposes, within each major era, a regular alternation, or major swings, between supply and demand oriented modalities of the world economy—overall, in line with Hicks' argument, a movement from command economy, characterizing the first four such periods, to the market economy of the recent past.

That is how we distinguish between a Bronze period proper (the millennium during which civilization arose and bronze production methods first took hold in Mesopotamia and Egypt) and the Fertile Crescent period (that William McNeill calls the "Great Society"—where linkages between these centers of civilization, especially over the area of the Fertile Crescent and other civilized regions, developed in relation to them). In respect to the Iron Age we might speak, first, of the establishment of iron-based economies, as in the Iron period (-1200–100). This, in turn, is followed by a millennium whose most characteristic feature was the growth of the Silk Roads connecting the major regions of the world system.

Table 8.1

Evolution of the World Economy
(World-Economy Process)

World Econony Period	Description	Years
I	Bronze	−3500 – −2200
II	Fertile Crescent	−2200 – −1200
III	Iron	−1200 – 100
IV	Silk Roads	−100 – 930
V	Market Economy	930 – 1850
VI	World Market	1850 –

The world economy process describes structural changes in the world economy
over very long periods of one thousand years. It highlights sectors that are
undergoing transformation and describes qualitative change rather than fluctuations
in macroeconomic quantities such as prosperity/depression, or the rise and decline
in world output.
Periods of world economy process are numbered consecutively in Roman numerals.
Data Source: based on Modelski 1992, 20, table 2.

We might wonder if changes in metal-working techniques involved in the
making of bronze and iron artifacts were in fact so important as to lend definition to such long sequences of the world economic process. But it could be
argued that such tools, weapons, and ornament-making processes could have
been decisive factors in creating new forms of specialization and long-range
exchanges and trade (in copper and tin) in agrarian societies.

Our concept of the modern era starting in 930 broadly corroborates that of
William McNeill—of developments in East Asia (circa 1000) which set into motion a sequence of irreversible changes worldwide. These might be seen to consist
(1) in experiments in the buildup of active market societies of great productive
capacity in China and in Europe culminating in the Industrial Revolution (the
breakthrough to market economy); and (2) in the now unfolding period of diffusion of that potential on a worldwide basis via an increasingly capable world market. Such a scheme is in broad agreement with the thrust of Hicks' (1969) theory
of economic history as predicated upon the rise of the market.

Complementing McNeill's thesis, we might therefore argue that about the
year 1000 the world system reached a size (approaching one-half billion
people) and degree of complexity (especially in respect to urbanization and
long-distance trade via the Silk Roads) where new forms of world organization, and of the world economy, became feasible and the search for them became rewarding. At that point, the simple two-layer, pre-modern schema of

agrarian village and regional imperium began to be replaced by what might yet become a full-fledged, four-layer system allowing not just local and regional, but also national and global forms of organization. In respect to the economy, we witness the beginnings of global economic organization, both in the form of industrial sectors that proved to be significant in global proportions and of trading linkages of greater frequency, capacity, and reliability.

That process of the formation of a global layer of organization thus began in China and was then transmitted, via the Mongol world empire and well-established transcontinental trading networks, to the Mediterranean where the lead was first assumed (and the rewards reaped) by Genoa and Venice. The lead soon shifted to the Atlantic and northwest Europe. That process set in motion not just the evolution of a global economy, but also helped animate a global political system and sowed the seeds of global community.

EVOLUTION OF THE GLOBAL ECONOMY

Silk Roads

For over fifteen hundred years the Silk Roads, the main routes identified in figure 8.1, served as the basic framework of the world economy and the world system. We should note that the name, Silk Roads, was first coined by European geographers of the nineteenth century in relation to the northern overland part of this network that linked China, Central Asia, and Europe. Subsequently, the southern maritime linkages between the Near East, India, and China came to be known as the Spice Routes. Most recently, the name Silk Roads has also been applied to the entire system viewed as a single network of communications.

Table 8.2, which outlines the shifting fortunes of the Silk Roads, provides some additional information on this key structure. The table shows that, if this system is viewed as one whole, major shifts of emphasis can be observed to have occurred in this communication structure over its lifespan of more than a millennium. The initial breakthrough was affected by the advances made by the Han empire into Central Asia that paved the way for the importation of silk to Rome. The subsequent opening of Indian Ocean navigation paved the way for Greco-Roman ships to sail to India. The rise of Byzantium at about 500 seems to have shifted attention to the north once again, but when the Abbasids established themselves at Baghdad after 750, they gained control both over the Central Asian and the Persian Gulf routes. In other words, in its classical form the Silk Roads system of the world economy might have manifested some degree of regular alternation between a continental and a more maritime emphasis.

ERRATUM

The map on page 127 (figure 8.1) is reproduced incorrectly. It appears in correct form below:

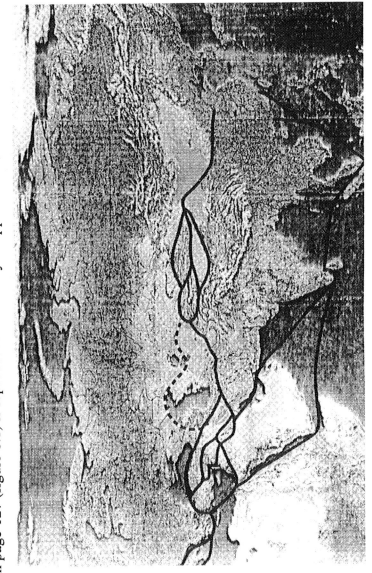

Figure 8.1. The Silk Roads

Table 8.2

Shifting Fortunes of the Silk Roads

Period	K-Waves	Major Linkages	Anchor Cities*
		World Economy Period IV: Silk Roads	
–100–250		Silk via Parthia	Rome–Lo-yang
200–500		Red Sea route to India	Alexandria–Muziris–Canton
500–650		Byzantium favors northern route	Constantinople–Ch'ang-an
750–1000		Abbasids for Persian Gulf route	Baghdad–Ch'ang-an
		World Economy Period V: Market Economy	
930–1125	K1–2	Northern Sung works northern route	Constantinople–K'ai-feng
930–1250	K3–4	Southern Sung enhances southern route	Cairo–Hangchou
1250–1350	K5–6	Mongols restore northern route	Genoa–Peking
1350–1500	K7–8	Mamluks, Venice build up Red Sea route	Venice–Cairo–Calicut– Malacca–Hangchow

"Silk Roads" is a generic name for the system of communications that, between the years 1 and 1500, linked the main regions of the Old World: China and East Asia, India and Southeast Asia, the Near East, and Europe. It refers both to the main northern overland (silk) road systems across Central Asia (south—and with a variant north—of the Tien Shan Mountains), and to the mostly maritime southern (spice) routes, also with two variants: via the Red Sea and the Persian Gulf.
*based on data supplied by Andrew Bosworth.

The Silk Roads continued to function right into modern times. In the Sung era, China strongly influenced both the northern and the southern branches of the system. For a while, the Mongols' peace restored trade over routes that Marco Polo traveled on in his best-selling reportage (published circa 1300), but the Black Death (1346–1353), the collapse of the Mongol world empire, and the depredations of Timur (d. 1405) put an end to the northern system. Cairo gained from the destruction of Baghdad and, with the help of Venice, profited greatly from its monopoly control over the Red Sea route to the East. The early modern pulsations of the world economy were transmitted over the established networks of the Silk Roads.

More to the point, the oceanic trading system that emerged after 1500 was

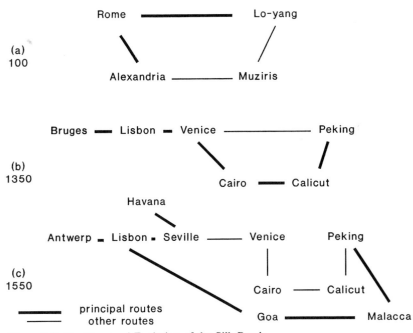

Figure 8.2. The Structural Evolution of the Silk Roads

a structural elaboration of the Silk Roads, and in particular of its southern variant. Portugal's route to India was a graft upon the maritime trunk of the, by then, traditional network of long-distance trade. This is illustrated in the depiction of the structural evolution of the Silk Roads in figure 8.2.

Part A in figure 8.2 shows the system (circa 100) in its early shape with emphasis on the northern route linking Han China with Roman Europe, but clearly exhibits its enduring feature of being the structure linking the four major regions of the classical world system: China, Europe, India, and the Near East. Part B in figure 8.2 displays its last form (circa 1400) centered on Venice, which was still basically quadrilateral, but already branching off into western Europe via the Venetian galleys routes through Lisbon to Bruges.

By 1550, as in part C of figure 8.2, the world trading system was transformed. The Venice-Cairo-Calicut connection was overlaid by the Lisbon-Goa-Malacca route which was soon extended to Macao and Japan. Bruges had been replaced by Antwerp, and Seville had become the base for the Atlantic route to the Caribbean. This route was soon extended via Acapulco and the Manila galleon across the Pacific. The modern global economic structure basically only extended the old system.

K-Waves Build the Global Economy

We have now shown that:

1. The world economy has been subject to structural change since its inception, with a major breakpoint appearing just before the year 1000; that breakpoint may be identified as the inception of the global economy process or the process of formation of the global economy; and
2. The global market economy of modern times was built on the foundation provided by the Silk Roads system of the classical world, and its maritime variant in particular. In other words, we have evidence of both continuity and change—continuity in that the oceanic trading system arose from long-standing structures of the world economy, but also change since the new structures elaborated upon turned out to be significantly more complex than the classic ones.

We now turn to the question: what shape did the global economy process assume over the past millennium. The short answer is: K-waves. K-waves do not just "nest" within the world economy, but they are driving forces behind global economic development.

We recall at this point that we think of K-waves as fifty- to sixty-year-long pulses of economic activity. They might animate sectors of industry or trade, or forms of business organization and their relations with other sections of society. Such bursts have their center of gravity in one national economy (that becomes the lead economy), but their influence radiates via mechanisms of trade, emulation, and competition throughout the world economy.

Our central contention is that K-waves build the global economy. That is, their significance lies not merely in enhancing the standing or wealth of one economy, and for a time adding to the power of one society, but it lies in making the economy of the world function more effectively and more productively. That is why we are justified in viewing K-waves as the mechanism through which the global economy grows and adapts to changing circumstances of the world system. To understand them better, we seek to monitor both their positive and their negative reverberations.

This point of view cannot be appreciated if each K-wave is viewed individually, and in its own terms. That is why early students of this subject failed to inquire into the connections between K-waves and neglected to view them as forming patterns. Such major bursts of activity cannot occur totally at random—each K-wave builds on the conditions created by earlier innovations, and in its turn, gives rise to problems that future innovations will have to resolve. In other words, K-waves are both path-dependent and future-oriented, and they are best understood if viewed in clusters.

We hypothesize that four K-waves add up to one period of global economic process, and that four such periods form one era of the world-economy
process. We think of the four K-waves in chapter 6 as animating the British
lead economy (K13–K16) and also as constituting the takeoff into the Industrial Revolution. We can furthermore think of that cluster as forming the last of
the four periods that brought about the "breakthrough to market economy"
era of the world economy.

We might therefore conjecture further that, in a rudimentary but gradually
more pervasive manner, K-waves began in China (circa 1000), traveled to
Italy via the Silk Roads, gathered speed in the fifteenth century, and achieved
mature form with the consolidation of the oceanic trading system by the Dutch
and the British. The industrial long waves investigated by Kondratieff were
the most recent manifestations of a process that started centuries earlier in another part of the world.

Table 8.3 represents this hypothesis in tabular form; it shows that the K-
waves previously documented in chapters 5 to 7 might best be thought of as
having been preceded by another set of eight growth spurts of the same structure. The nineteen waves postulated in table 8.3 (including the current one) are
not identical in that each "takes place under new concrete-historical conditions, at a new level of development of productive forces, and hence is by no
means a simple repetition" of its predecessor (Kondratieff 1984, 99). But they
may also be seen as so many stages in the evolution of the global market
economy—a process that still is underway, and far from complete.

Here we finally come to the other difficulty cited by Kondratieff and
Schumpeter—lack of data—as being the second reason why they were both
reluctant to reach deeper into the past. We have so far assembled information
going back to the mid-fifteenth century, but reliable and quantifiable knowledge for the postulated first eight K-waves is scarce. The search for it represents a challenge and a set of questions for our next two chapters. The naming
of the leading sectors for these eight cases is entirely tentative and subject to
confirmation. But (without going into greater detail on matters we shall look
into in depth in the next two chapters) we can say that we do know that the
Sung started the global economy process with a breakthrough to market
economy: a surge of the printing and paper industries, followed by consolidation of a huge national market. The political system then adjusted to changes
in the national economy with the end result of the transition being a tremendous expansion of maritime trade aided by the wide use of the compass. In the
next period of the global economy process, and as part of the commercial and
nautical revolutions, the Genoans first took the lead during the thirteenth century and then the Venetian system of trading galleys assumed shape after

Table 8.3

Evolution of the Global Economy: K-Waves

Global Economy Process	Phases Basebuilding	Networking	Breakthrough	Payoff
World Economy Period V: Breakthrough to Market Economy				
Sung Breathrough	930 K1 Printing and paper	990 K2 National market formation	1060 K3 Fiscal/administration framework	1120 K4 Maritime trade expansion
Nautical/ Commercial Revolutions	1190 K5 Champagne Fairs	1250 K6 Black Sea trade	1300 K7 Venetian galley fleets	1350 K8 Pepper
Oceanic Trading System	1430 K9 Guinea gold	1494 K10 Indian spices	1540 K11 Baltic, Atlantic trade	1580 K12 Asian trade
Industrial Takeoff	1640 K13 Amerasian trade (plantations)	1688 K14 Amerasian trade	1740 K15 Cotton, iron	1792 K16 Steam, railroad
Work Economy Period VI: World Market				
Information Economy	1850 K17 Steel, chemicals electrics	1914 K18 Autos, aerospace, electronics	1973 K19 Information industries	2030 K20

Note: Dates shown mark the beginning of each of the nineteen K-waves to date. Innovation and high growth in the sectors listed peak toward the end of each phase.

1300. It is also arguable that, judging by price levels, the Venetian pepper trade with Alexandria was routinized after about 1430—about the time that the Ming abandoned their expeditions to the Indian Ocean and the Portuguese launched seriously into their discoveries.

There is another aspect of table 8.3 that calls for discussion. As already remarked, the Kondratieff wave literature basically views each wave in its own terms as a response to a specific cluster of innovations, and forgoes the search for a pattern of waves. In a system of four or five such waves, patterns may be hardly discernible at all, even though Kondratieff (1984, 99) was quite explicit in expecting linkages among waves on theoretical grounds: "in accordance with the hypothesis I have set forth, each successive phase of a cycle is a consequence of conditions amassed during the preceding time interval; and . . . each new cycle follows another just as regularly as one phase of one and the same cycle follows another." In practice, such linkages have not been spelled out.

In table 8.3 individual K-waves, defined by the leading sector each pro-
motes, are also hypothesized to be part of a larger process—the evolution of
the global market system. We observe that K-waves span the entire range of
economic innovations that Joseph Schumpeter laid out in his analysis. Some
bring out new products, as in K18 (autos and airplanes); others highlight new
methods of production, as in K1 (printing and paper) or K15 (new techniques
of textile production). Some open new markets, as in K7 (Venetian galley
fleets), and others open up new sources of supply, as in K9 (Guinea gold) and
K10 (Indian spices). Yet others pioneer new forms of business organization, as
in K5 (Champagne Fairs), K12 (Asian trade via VOC, the Dutch East Indies
Company), or K17 and K18 (U.S. multinationals).

We note, too, that blocks of four K-waves each appear to exhibit distinct
themes: the Sung breakthrough to market society, the commercial-nautical
revolutions, the oceanic trading system, industrial takeoff, and the information
economy. Each of these has a special spatial aspect with a regional base in an
active zone (China, Italy, northwest Europe, and the United States), and each
also has a time-structured component in the building of the global economy:
experiments, clusters, critical mass, and takeoff. Finally, each of these zonal
and thematic periods of the global economy may also be said to have its own
phase-structure of base-building, networking, breakthrough, and payoff. We
have here a complex array of nested processes whose linkages and ramifications remain to be fully explored.

Two main eras of that process may, however, be clearly discerned: those
of market economy and world market—the first laying out the necessary conditions for such a system and the second, from 1850 onward, starting the
lengthy process of putting together the outlines of a structure of global economic exchange. Since 1850 a true world market has been shaping up as an
edifice of knowledge constructed in the information age, now in high gear,
which makes market signals available throughout. The construction of a true
world market, though, remains a project whose full completion remains an
agenda item for the more distant future. The search for patterns makes it easier
to think about the character of future K-waves.

Mechanism of Evolutionary Process

We have already established in part 3 that K-waves exist, and have now
shown that they are aspects of structural change in the world economy. That is,
we have both change and direction that spans long time periods. How do we
explain what appears at first to be a pattern of order?

Social change, in and of itself, is not really surprising. We might postulate that humans continuously search for ways of bettering their conditions, and will change their behavior as situations require it. Travelers between *A* and *B* will seek out the best route between these points—one that is shortest, safest, or the most economical—and they will change the routing arrangements according to the relevant circumstances guided by considerations of rational choice. In the economy, too, both producers and consumers are always on the lookout for improved performance.

What is not so easy to account for are patterns of change over long periods with pronounced directionality. These involve questions of a different order—not just how to get from *A* to *B*, but why not go to *C* or *D*, rather than to *B*, and in the process invent new ways that take us to *F*. When shifts in preferences come to the foreground, and the constraints on action are loosened, different modes of explanation usually prove more fruitful.

The paradigm best suited to explicating structural change in the global economy is an evolutionary one. Students of K-waves cannot be accused of having ignored this avenue of explanation. We have already noticed that Nikolai Kondratieff referred to the processes he uncovered as "evolutionary" and as having characteristics of directionality, but he did not pursue this line of reasoning to any great length. Joseph Schumpeter, who helped to popularize Kondratieff's findings in Europe and the United States, was a pioneer of an evolutionary approach to economics. More than any other economist, he helped to advance the view that innovation was central to the process of economic growth and to fluctuations that are a necessary consequence of growth. He opposed what he described as the Marshallian theory of evolution (J. Schumpeter 1954, 1165), and denied that the structure of the economy evolves in a steady or smooth fashion.

In the *Theory of Economic Development* (1934) Joseph Schumpeter sets out to construct a coherent account of economic change by showing how the economic system incessantly transforms itself. The mechanism of transformation consists of entrepreneurs (with access to credit) who exercise economic leadership by pursuing equilibrium-destroying innovations in continuous winner-and-loser producing competition. In *Business Cycles* (J. Schumpeter 1939) he introduced to English-speaking audiences the concept of long waves of fifty to sixty years as a bunching of innovations, and named them after Kondratieff.[2]

More recently, Richard Nelson and Sidney Winter (1982) have taken up the Schumpeterian themes in *An Evolutionary Theory of Economic Change.* Theirs is a critique of the neoclassical model based on equilibrium and rational choice, and a proposal for an alternative perspective based on the distinction between routine operations and innovative search and selection. In their view the main theoretical commitments of evolutionary theory have application in relation to transitions from one period to the next. While their focus is on the behavior of individual firms, it is also clear that their emphasis on transitions (and not equilibrium) is a great aid to understanding long-range processes.

Other students of innovation have also been drawn toward an evolutionary perspective. Gerhard Mensch saw these problems as necessary features of industrial evolution. For Christopher Freeman and Giovanni Dosi economic evolution is a succession of technological or sociotechnical paradigms with each K-wave embodying one such paradigm (the latest defined by the microelectronic revolution).[3]

K-wave studies find a good home in an evolutionary framework because innovation and transition are keys to understanding such processes of social structural change. The distinguishing characteristics of evolutionary processes include the following: (1) they embody mechanisms of search and selection; (2) they occur when the necessary and sufficient conditions are present; (3) they are constitutive of generational lineages; and (4) they coevolve with other evolutionary processes. Let us look briefly at the first three points, leaving the last for the next section.

Ever since Charles Darwin, search and selection have been the central mechanisms of the evolutionary process. Search is generated by variety or, in our context, innovation that advances solutions to global problems. In favorable conditions the economic system generates a stream of innovations that are then subject to a process of selection. In Darwinian theory this is the environment exerting selective pressure; in social contexts the process is a competitive one in a market sense. K-waves describe the rise of clusters of innovations that respond to the demands of a competitive marketplace and put in place new industrial or commercial sectors or new forms of economic organization. The rise of new firms and new sectors is the microlevel mechanism that drives growth in what becomes the lead economy. Economies that create the most favorable conditions for innovation and market selection are also likely to be those that originate K-waves.

The necessary and sufficient conditions for the initial rise of a K-wave in a potential lead economy are innovative entrepreneurs: (1) operating in market economies with access to resources and credit; (2) in the context of an open society; (3) in favorable political circumstances; and (4) in conditions of global competitiveness, including responsiveness to global problems.[4]

But the outcomes of evolutionary events do not exist in a vacuum, rather they are linked at the macrolevel in chains of processes that trace distinctive lineages. Darwinian macroevolution traces the origin of all life on earth

Table 8.4

Rational Choice and Evolutionary Paradigms

Characteristics	Rational Choice	Evolutionary
Ends/Means Schema	given ends, choice of means	preferences and constraints changeable
Criterion of Choice	ends-means rationality: plan, design	trial and error selection as collective phenomenon emerging from nonlinear interactions
Focus on	decision, equilibrium	institutions, transitions
Perspective	short-term	long-term

through lines of common descent. While social change is much faster, structures of behavior, too, are related in lineages and may be seen to build on antecedents and to accumulate. Table 8.3 presented K-waves as forming such a lineage across a period of one thousand years. By a process of cumulation a succession of K-waves have shaped the emergence and the functioning of the global economy.

Let us briefly contrast rational choice with an approach based upon an evolutionary paradigm, as seen in table 8.4 (see, among others, Elster 1989; Little 1991; Dosi 1992). We argue that evolutionary approaches furnish the better foundations for understanding long-term changes in the global economy and lay bare the mechanisms of the evolutionary process. That is one reason why the study of economics in the neoclassical mode is essentially an elaboration of ends-means rationality that has so far had scant success in attacking these problems.

WHY COEVOLUTION?

Coevolution is the last characteristic of evolutionary processes that does not proceed on a course in a vacuum, but may be presumed to relate in a determinate manner to other evolutionary processes; that is, the processes coevolve. World system evolution engages a spectrum of processes of which several components must be distinguished and their mutual relationship traced. We have already observed and confirmed in chapter 7 how globally significant K-waves mesh in a convincing way with long cycles that are the

Table 8.5

The Coevolution of Global Politics and Economics

Long Cycles (world powers)		K-Waves (global leading sectors)	
Preconditions		Market Economy	
LC1	Northern Sung	K1	Printing and paper
		K2	National market formation
LC2	Southern Sung	K3	Fiscal framework
		K4	Maritime trade expansion
LC3	Genoa	K5	Champagne Fairs
		K6	Black Sea trade
LC4	Venice	K7	Galley fleets
		K8	Pepper
Global Nucleus			
LC5	Portugal	K9	Guinea gold
		K10	Indian spices
LC6	Dutch Republic	K11	Baltic, Atlantic trade
		K12	Asian trade (VOC)
LC7	Britain I	K13	Amerasian (plantations)
		K14	Amerasian trade
LC8	Britain II	K15	Cotton, iron
		K16	Steam, rail
Global Organization		World Market	
LC9	United States	K17	Steel, chemicals, electrics
		K18	Auto, air, electronics
LC10		K19	Information industries

Note: Preconditions, global nucleus, and global organization are phases in the evolution of global politics; market economy and world market are periods in the evolution of the world economy.

moving wheels of global political evolution. Thus the existence of coevolution, at least for the period since 1430, is already established, and will be argued for early modernity in the next two chapters. In table 8.5 this fact of coevolution is summarized for the entire modern era to date.[5]

We now ask: what might explain this close meshing of the two processes? In other words, why does coevolution and diachronic changes occur in these two interacting systems? We shall argue this case on narrow grounds of the relationship of economics and politics at the global level, and we have already pointed out, in chapter 4, that coordination between two such structurally similar processes is not really surprising. But what might be the actual mechanisms of this coevolution?

We propose that coevolution occurs for two reasons: substantively, because of the necessity of coaction, and as regards form, because of synchronization—that is, the concurrence of events in respect to time.

Coaction

As previously argued, the K-wave and the long cycle are two structurally similar global evolutionary processes, and that structural similarity alone makes it more likely that the two processes are interrelated. But these processes are not just interrelated—each is the necessary condition of the performance of the other. In other words, coaction is called for and occurs in time because it is necessary over the entire length of that process. It occurs in space because, in all the cases we have looked at so far, both processes were based on one and the same area—in the four most recent cases, a nation-state.

What, then, might be the reasons for such coordination? In the first place, these are constraints of efficiency that have to do with ease of communications and costs of supplying inputs. Locational studies have shown that innovation is highest at sites at which communication is swift and easy between producers and their markets, and where a variety of input is available. Geographers (such as Hall 1985, 9–10) have pointed out that K-waves have not only been dominated by countries such as Britain and the United States, but also by regions within those countries. In Britain, for instance, the first industrial wave was dominated by Lancashire, Shropshire, and the Black Country, and the second by newer regions such as South Wales and the North East. In the United States, the west has now become a major center of the information industries with the Silicon Valley in California already becoming a textbook example of that process.

All this suggests that a nation-state, being the common site of these two processes, also serves as a coordinating factor because proximity helps to expedite both of them. Transaction costs are lowered, communication is cheaper, and factors of production common to these processes are more easily mobilized. This national "basing mode" affords both security and openness of conditions, and provides the arena within which all kinds of innovations thrive. We might add, though, that the specialization of one site, based on one innovative paradigm, also makes it more difficult to replace such a tradition with a new paradigm in the same place; that is why transitions to new waves and new long cycles tend to be associated with shifts of location.

Secondly, coordination occurs because both processes respond to a common agenda of global problems as transmitted by global politics. If we postulate that structural change responds to priority global problems—authoritatively formulated by global leadership—then such solutions might derive from both political and economic sources. More concretely we might think of such solutions being expected (or demanded) by world opinion via global media—as represented by markets, the press, and scholarly or scientific (epistemic) communities. Thus we might think of the problem of discoveries in the fifteenth and sixteenth centuries as being articulated by sets of opinion-makers in several parts of western Europe who viewed it as a search for new routes to India and responded to both through political and economic processes—thus innovating new sources of supply, as well as a new global political structure. Or we might think of contemporary global problems centered on integration of the global community as being responded to both through the building of a democratic community and the expansion of information industries without which a global community could not function.

We notice that in the experience of the past half millennium the coevolution of global processes occurred in a national basing-mode. We might attribute this both to the high costs of coordinating global activities in any other mode and to the fact that world opinion and world media, such as they were, could be found predominantly among the populations of the world powers. In the nineteenth century, and for William Gladstone, for example, the British public would have constituted the court of world opinion, especially as articulated by Parliament and the British press, and would play a privileged role in formulating global problems and translating them into actions.

But we notice, too, that costs of communication and transport at the global level have been falling steadily in the past century or so. The difficulties of coordination are declining in the information age and the base of world opinion has also expanded steadily. These developments suggest that the predominantly national basing-mode for coordination of global processes ought to be evolving in the direction of broadening.

Synchronization

In form, this coaction takes place via synchronization that shows up in the empirically confirmed fact that K-waves are one-half the length of a long cycle. In principle, synchronization should not be surprising because without it global processes would be chaotic. But for those raised on the idea that world politics is anarchic and global economics is no more than a jungle, some explanation might be in order.

Why then the synchronization of K-waves and long cycles or the effective coevolution of global economics and politics? In physics, the phenomenon of synchronization is known as the problem of "coupled oscillators"; the classic case is that of two close by pendulum clocks spontaneously adopting the same rhythm.[6] More recent research has extended this problem to biology, including that of biological clocks.[7] J. W. S. Pringle (Modelski 1990, 19) has pointed out that coupled oscillators possess a type of mechanism capable of "selection of variation over time" leading to an evolutionary increase in the complexity of rhythm, thereby leading to learning.

An oscillator is any system that exhibits periodic variation or fluctuation over time. We have reason to believe that the global economy, and the global political system, might properly be regarded as oscillators because they do execute periodic behavior. Our work (including chapters 9 and 10) now argues that the global economy has experienced regularly recurring K-waves over a period of a millennium, with an average period of fifty-eight years; these completed eighteen K-waves have ranged in length from forty to seventy-four years, with ten of them in the range of fifty to sixty years. The global political system may be estimated to have shown, over the same period, long cycles with a period of some 116 years.[8]

We notice that periodicity is average rather than strict but we have no reason to require that social periodicity be as precise as physical or mechanical systems. But biological systems also tend to have not only a characteristic period but also amplitude, for once disturbed they return to their accustomed path and are therefore known as limit-cycle oscillators. On our evidence we have reasons to think that both the global economy and the political system belong to that type.

Coupled oscillators exhibit more complex behavior, hence potentially learning. We have previously shown grounds for thinking that the global economy and global politics are a coupled system exhibiting coevolution. Just as in the case of two pendulum clocks where the coupling was a function of proximity, so also in our case: the coupling of K-waves and long cycles is a product of colocation—the fact of basing in one political-economic base and one opinion base, that, most recently, has been delimited by the boundaries of a nation-state. We have also shown that the rhythm of global war that was, until recently, the most spectacular event of the long cycle has also marked the coming and going of K-waves. That leads us to believe that this is a case of "pulse coupling" because interactions need not necessarily be continuous, but could be particularly marked when one or the other of the systems "fires" (as in producing a global war) or fails to fire (as in the case of a great depression).

For coupled oscillators, synchrony is the most likely manner of coordination. Physics and biology research has shown that oscillators started at different times will tend to become synchronous. Synchrony is not inevitable, but exhibits the general effect of phase locking. In communities of oscillators, synchrony depends on the strength of coupling and emerges cooperatively. We suspect that the same principles apply in the case of the two systems we have been studying.

THE EVOLUTIONARY PARADIGM

We have now cast our analysis in an evolutionary mold. In our opinion, it is one that is appropriate to the study of long-term economic processes and developments. Let us restate the advantages and special insights of that approach.

1. The paradigm explains structural change in the global economy as an evolutionary process of determinate shape in which K-waves are the pulses of growth in innovative sectors that help to build the global economic structure. It opens up a range of issues, both in respect to understanding past change and in looking to the future outside the ken of rational-equilibrium models. We need not postulate a rational plan or grand design to explain the emergence of a world market or global organization.
2. The idea of coevolution helps us conceptualize the relationship of the global economy to global politics. The broad concept of social evolution is made more tractable, yet analytically more useful.
3. Even while cultivating the big picture of global evolution, this approach enables us to view individual K-waves, the microfoundations via search and selection, of a global macrodevelopment in a new, sharper light and with greater analytical power. This makes it possible to say which economies, and what conditions, are likely to harbor new K-waves.

Before we attempt to deal with the uncertainties of the information age, we need to reach back and examine the asserted origins of the K-wave system in Sung China and its transmission to the West—the subjects of our next two chapters.

Chapter Nine

Sung China and the Evolving Global Economy
Tenth to Twelfth Centuries, K-Waves 1–4

The idea that the China of one thousand years ago (as shown in figure 9.1) was the most developed part of the world economy and the seat of a number of crucial socioeconomic transformations is now beyond doubt, and a thought familiar to scholars. But it is also widely noted that while these changes do not seem to have led to a takeoff into sustained growth in China, the innovations spawned by such changes did profoundly influence developments in other parts of the world.

That is why the transformations of the Sung era (960–1279) raise questions not only for students of China but also for those of world economics and world politics.[1] Were these bursts of growth merely a product of unique circumstances and the special characteristics of the Chinese experience, and must we depend, as Albert Feuerwerker (1992, 757) put it, on "specifically Chinese cultural features to construct a satisfactory paradigm?" Or are we entitled to regard such changes as regular manifestations of China's interaction with the world system?

We incline toward the second position and develop the argument that the Sung economic revolution might be seen as the world's first essay in the direction of a world market economy. That experiment consisted of four waves of innovation closely coordinated with two proto-global long cycles in the political realm. After about 1200 the locus of innovation shifted away from China, via the Mongol world empire, to renaissance Europe, but the innovations themselves became part of the experience of the evolving world system.

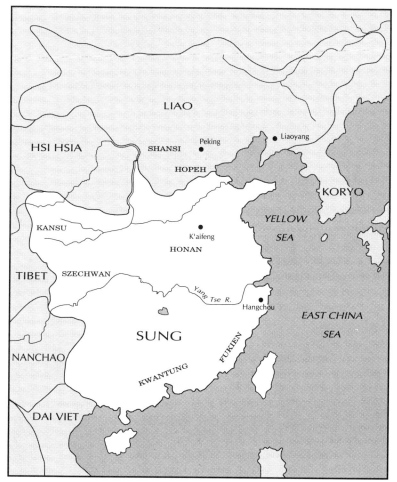

Figure 9.1. Sung China

RECOGNIZING THE SUNG ECONOMIC REVOLUTION

Students of world history have in recent decades come to recognize Chinese developments during the Sung dynasty as an economic transformation of a major sort. Prominently among them is William McNeill who has advanced the claim that, in world-historical perspective, developments in Sung society are the first instances of such a breakthrough to market economy. He wrote:

It is the hypothesis of this book that China's rapid evolution toward market-regulated behavior in the centuries on either side of the year 1000 tipped a critical balance in world history. I believe that China's example set humankind off on a thousand-year exploration of what could be accomplished by relying on prices and small group (the partnership or the company) perception of private advantage as a way of orchestrating behavior on a mass scale. (1982, 25)

Traditionally, scholars were more impressed by other, seemingly more brilliant eras of Chinese history (Liu and Golas 1969, vii). The Spring and Autumn period, or the powerful empires of Han or T'ang appeared particularly worthy of interest. The Sung, by comparison, seemed consumed by defense problems with its northern neighbors and was the first dynasty to succumb to foreign conquest.

The credit for first recognizing the importance of the Sung belongs to the so-called Naito hypothesis by a Japanese historian of that name (d. 1934) (Miyakawa 1955). Naito and his followers, known as members of the Kyoto school, argued that modernity in China began with the Sung—the period constituting a watershed in Chinese history (Shiba 1970, 1). E. O. Reischauer and J. K. Fairbank (1960, 211–19) endorsed this claim in a qualified fashion in their leading text and spoke of a "commercial revolution," while others were adding new empirical evidence and theoretical reasoning: Ping-ti Ho (1956) on the agricultural revolution, Robert Hartwell (1966) on iron and coal development, and Mark Elvin (1973) and E. L. Jones (1988, chap. 4) who provide synthetic overviews. In his last work, John Fairbank (1992, 88) titled the Sung era: "China's Greatest Age."

Mark Elvin (1973, 7) advanced the question: "what were the causes of the medieval revolution that made the Chinese economy after about 1100 the most advanced in the world?" Elvin identified a number of revolutions that made up this process: in farming and water transportation, money and credit, market structure and urbanization, and science and technology. But he did not provide an analytical statement of the causal mechanisms at work, but instead placed central emphasis on "changing patterns of the economics of technology" (Elvin 1973, 316). He stated that, between 1300 and 1500, "for reasons which are still largely inexplicable," the Chinese economy fell into decline and invention almost entirely ceased (Elvin 1973, 203–4).

In his *History of Chinese Civilization,* Jacques Gernet (1982, 298; French edition 1972) calls this the era of the Chinese renaissance—in conscious parallelism to the Italian period of that name which followed the Chinese, but belongs in that same general period. He does so on the grounds that we also wish to underscore—"the inventions which made their appearance about the year 1000, once grouped together, form such a coherent and extensive whole that we have to yield to the evidence: at this period the Chinese world experienced a real transformation.''

Another approach to recognizing the importance of the Sung proceeds from deductive reasoning about world system evolution (Modelski 1992). Such reasoning tries to make sense of the unfolding of the world system over the past five thousand years and sees that entire process, as does Frank (1990), as one subject to significant uniformities. But it also recognizes that the world system, being subject to evolutionary change, may be paced by major phases, as long as two thousand years in length, that broadly correspond to classic divisions of world history.

On such grounds, the world system may have entered its modern phase about the year 1000—about the time, as we have just pointed out, that contemporary scholarship extended the range of modernity, especially with regard to China. Analytically, we might call this the phase of collective organization—one that is still with us and is characterized by the rise of complex and diversified organizations (including nation-states, and business enterprises) and the formation of networks of organization at the global level. In turn, these organizations could not have taken shape without significant innovation in such respects as information gathering (printing), communication (oceanic), military (gunpowder weapons), and economic (media of exchange). A global economy, viewed as a pattern of interregional and oceanic trade and focused upon the institution of the world market, might be expected to have begun to take shape at about the same time.

The first item of business on the long agenda of world market formation might have been the laying out of the necessary foundations or preconditions of such a development (930–1850), and the second (since 1850) might have been the construction of a world market. This means that a global market economy could not have been created in a day, or by fiat, and that the two main steps along the long road toward such a condition would have been (1) a breakthrough away from command to a market form of organization at national levels; and (2) the gradual combining of the basics of a global structure—the world market constituting a web of interconnections within which a truly global economy might ultimately arise over the next few centuries.

A fine set of conditions for creating an initial base for a world market would be a large, vigorous, and innovative national economy that served a substantial population capable of exerting effective demand. Table 9.1 displays the place of Sung China in its world, and shows how significant that population was in global measure. In 1100, at the zenith of that era, China's

Table 9.1

Sung China in the World

Year	World* (in millions)	Population China proper (in millions)	China proper (percent of world)	Sung** (in millions)	Chin** (in millions)
800	220	50	23		
961				32	
1000	265	60	23		
1100	320	100	31		
1109				121	
1193				71	
1195					49
1200	360	115	32		
1300	360	85	24		
1975	3,900	720	19		

*Data from McEvedy and Jones (1978: 166, 170–4, 342) who define China proper as the area bounded by the Great Wall and the Tibetan plateau, but excluding Manchuria, Inner Mongolia, and Tibet.
**Data from Chao (1988:34–36), rounded; the Chin figure for 1195 includes Manchuria.

population accounted for close to one-third of the world's total—the highest proportion that country's population had attained so far in the world picture.

China of that time was also significantly urbanized: it accounted for the major share (at least seven out of twenty) of world cities.[2] This was an affluent market of global dimensions. On population figures (and, as we shall shortly see, also on grounds of productivity) China easily outranked any other country or any other region of the world. This made the designation "middle kingdom" singularly appropriate.

Other Regions of the World System

In our time frame, which is between about 900 and 1200, the Cola (or Chola) Empire in southern India (capital at Tanjore) probably was an entity that might have been comparable to Sung China in economic significance, but it did not really come close. The Colas ruled over both the Coromandel (eastern) and the Malabar (western) coasts of India and were strong in irrigation agriculture. They controlled islands in the Indian Ocean, including Ceylon and the Maldives; developed significant maritime interests; and had an important commercial stake in the flow of trade between the Middle East and the Far East. The Sung received occasional tribute from Cola—a total of four missions in 990–1126, including one modest one in 1077 carrying pearls, rosewater, and rhinoceros horn (Hartwell 1983, 189; 1989, 471). Their population probably was about twenty to thirty million, but was less urbanized and formed less of a coherent market than China. The time path of the Colas was not unlike that of the Sung: foundation 907–958; major impact 985–1044 (whose high point was a long-range naval expedition against Srivijaya, Sumatra, in 1025); another run in a Cola-Calukya mode 1070–1122; followed by decline. The Colas faded away about the same time as the Sung did, but obviously with a lesser record of achievement.

In the Middle East the rising power (circa 950) was that of the Fatimids—best known as a movement to reform and/or displace the Abbasid Caliphate in Baghdad. Based on the Ismaili branch of the Shia, the Fatimids spread, by missionary activities of propaganda and education, from an original base in the Yemen to North Africa where they seized Tunisia (909), and then Egypt (969) where they founded Cairo. With the help of a strong navy, they may have controlled, at their peak, some fifteen million people from the Maghreb to Syria and southern Arabia. They grew rich on trade (with a gold dinar), fostered the Red Sea route as an alternative to the Persian Gulf, and might have been in contact with the Sung via trade and tribute missions. But they were torn by disputes between radicals and reformers that ultimately brought tyranny and anarchy, a military regime after 1073, and collapse by 1171.

In the European-Mediterranean world around this time, Byzantium was staging a temporary comeback under the Macedonian dynasty. It was a rich Greek empire, centered on Constantinople with a population of some ten million people and a standing army of over one hundred thousand. Its gold coin, the bezant (unchanged in value between 476 and 1204), was a standard of regional trade. Its substantial, and the one truly effective, navy in this part of the world had just reestablished its command of the Western Mediterranean by retaking Crete (in 961, with a force of thirty-four thousand sailors and thirteen thousand soldiers). Byzantium had wealth, but it stood alone—embattled and set in its ways. Edward Gibbon (1910), in maybe too sweeping a judgment, said "in the revolutions of ten centuries, not a single discovery was made to exalt the dignity or promote the happiness of mankind," but he either forgot about, or disdained, the contribution made by Greek fire—a petroleum-based mixture fueling an early form of flamethrower first used in a sea battle against the Arab naval force besieging Constantinople in 672. The decisive signal of decline of Byzantium was the battle of Manzikert (1071) in which the Seljuk Turks crushed the Byzantine army, thereby opening the way for conquest of

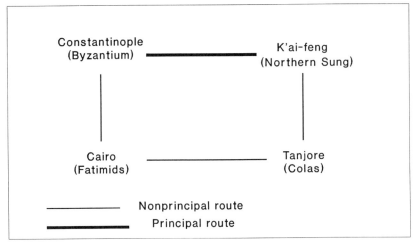

Figure 9.2. A Simplified Version of the Silk Roads System, circa 1000

Anatolia. This undermined the navy based on southern Anatolia, and increased the role of Venice that led the fourth crusade which seized the Byzantine capital in 1204.

Silk Roads

At the onset of the global system, these four imperial centers might be thought of as the principal contenders for world market evolution. Based on major cities, they each received a new impetus for growth in the tenth century, served as potential foci of innovations, and were each heavily involved in trade and naval affairs. Together they formed the four corners of the global economy jointly constituting what we have called, in chapter 8, the Silk Roads system—viewed as a set of linkages between the world's major regions. In place for at least the previous millennium, it had now reached clear definition. Its shape (circa 1000) might schematically be represented as the simple diagram in figure 9.2.

This diagram shows a network consisting of four major nodes—world cities each serving a major political system, but also linked, more or less directly, with at least two other such nodes. As the name itself suggests, the links have been, in the first place, economic in character—long-distance trade with the transport of silk westward being their most famous characteristic. The Silk Roads have also been the mechanisms for the slow transmission of social and cultural influences, as in the cases of the migration of peoples across Inner

Asia or the spread of Buddhism toward China and Japan. On the other hand, given the low speed of communications, it has not been a system of political alignment between the major centers of the world system, with the notable exception of the interlude of the Mongol world empire.

Hartwell's (1983, 1989) lists of tribute embassies received at the Sung court nevertheless show that eleventh-century China was not an isolated regional power but was also in contact with other major components of the world system. It received missions, as mentioned, from the Colas, but also from Arabia (Ta-shih), as well as from the Seljuk Turks who had just expelled the Byzantines from Anatolia and had supplanted the Abbasids at Baghdad. We might see these missions as consisting of relations of a predominantly symbolic and informational character, but also of some political and economic significance.

At the onset of globalization (circa 1000), it is our argument that China was the most active and vibrant part of that system. The Sung realm was the part of the world where demand and supply conditions strongly conducive to the emergence of a world market existed, and were capable of exercising a pull of attraction on the whole of the world economy. That is why the first breakthrough to world market formation occurred there or, as Reischauer and Fairbank (1960, 214) put it, "the first period of great oceanic commerce in the history of the world" occurred there.

PROTO-GLOBAL POLITICS IN SUNG CHINA

Another set of conditions (this time political) made it likely that yet another set of experiments (this time in global politics) occurred in China at the same time. Consider first the place of China in the East Asian regional system. As depicted in some detail in table 9.2, that place was, at least population-wise, a dominant one. If population predicted directly to political standing, the structure of that position should have been a unipolar East Asian political system.

Yet we also know that with respect to at least some of the states shown in table 9.2, the Sung administration conducted their political and diplomatic contacts on the basis of equality as shown in several studies in the illuminating collection edited by Morris Rossabi (1983). In spite of a continuing tendency to see relations with "barbarians" in terms of classical doctrine—formulated, for example, in the Confucian text *Spring and Autumn* (circa 480) and characterized by tribute missions received at the Sung court—the practice of relations with at least the more powerful of the barbarians (officially referred to as "Northerners") was conducted on an equal footing. Above all, the Sung had to contend with a series of aggressive political units in the north—those of the

Table 9.2

East Asian Regional System, circa 1100

Political Unit (number missions to Sung)	Population (in millions)	Major cities***
Sung	960–1125	ca. 120*	K'ai-feng Hangchow Soochow

Northeast			
# Japan		6	Kyoto
## Koryo (Korea)	935–1392	3	
Liao (Khitan)	930–1125	3.8**	Lin-huang
# Juchen	1069 (1115–1234)	>1	

Northwest and West			
Hsi Hsia (Tanguts)	990–1227	3	Ninghsia
## Khotan		>1	
## Kucha		>1	
# Ch'ing T'ang		>1	
## Tibet (autonomous lordships)		2	

Southwest and South			
# Hou-li	1094–1227	2	Ta-li
# Burma	849–1287	2	Pagan
## Vietnam	939–1407	1	
## Champa	192–1300	1	
# Cambodia	802–1444	1	Angkor
## Srivijaya	600–1400	1	Palembang

Population estimates based on McEvedy and Jones 1978.

*Kang Chao (1986, 35, 41) puts the Sung population in 1109 at 121 million (a high estimate, using a people to household ratio of 5.8); McEvedy and Jones (shown in table 9.1) give a figure of one hundred million for all of "China proper."

**Wittfogel and Feng 1949, 55–59; Lin-huang's population estimated at 182,000 (Peking at one hundred thousand per Wittfogel and Feng 1949, 62, 79).

***All capital cities except Hangchow and Soochow; all but Ninghsia and Palembang were among the twenty largest cities in the world in 1100.

Tribute missions received by Sung between 1060 and 1119 (Hartwell 1983, 1989, 470–75): ## indicates major activity (5–30 missions in period), # indicates minor activity (1–5 missions); others not listed from Cola, Arabia (Ta-shih) (##), Seljuk Turks, and others.

Khitans, Jurchens, and Mongols. These groups were on par with the Sung in respect to military power, and were also recipients of tribute (in silver and silk) from the Sung.[3] But they also had contacts with other important, but autonomous, political formations in their environment—Korea and Japan in the north; the Tanguts (Hsi Hsia, also receiving tribute from the Sung) in the west; and Champa, Vietnam, and Cambodia in the south.

In other words, the Sung operated in a multistate system of a bipolar, if not multipolar, character—one not really different from our contemporary experience. In that system, contacts were multiple, alliances and security were at a premium, and survival was precarious. There was little wonder, then, that in this competitive milieu innovation, military innovation in particular (such as gunpowder weapons), was thriving. Moreover, the Sung initially took shape in an even more multiplex system—the Five Dynasties (Wu-tai)—in which a rapid succession of regimes in the north contended with as many as ten independent kingdoms in the south of China.

Why then, despite a population disparity and striking achievements in social and economic realms, were the Sung in a position of political equality? Or were the Sung at a disadvantage as compared to their principal opponents such as the Liao empire, the Chin, or the Mongols? The answers to these questions have to do with the structure of military power in that system at that particular time, and may best be answered by a consideration of data on the strength of the Sung military forces and of the forces available to its opponents.

Sung army numbers shown in table 9.3 were indeed notable for their quantity. The maximum strength shown for the years 1041–1048 approached 1.3 million. Although much of its strength would be consumed in garrisoning of towns and frontier posts, such an army could field up to one-half million men in a single campaign. When the Chin emperor launched the (abortive) attack on the southern Sung in 1161, he fielded an expeditionary force of one-half million soldiers, including strong naval forces (Chan 1984, 67). The defending army commanded some 450,000 troops, as well as naval strength. A comparably decisive campaign in the Near East, ending in the battle that signaled the fall of the Byzantine Empire (Manzikert in 1071), probably involved fewer than 100,000 soldiers on both sides. William the Conqueror's landing in England in 1066 fielded a force of no more than twenty-five thousand, including twelve thousand cavalry. In other words, nowhere else at that time did armies exist, or operate, on a scale comparable to the Chinese. Armies of that size did not begin to make an appearance in Europe until the eighteenth century.

Nevertheless, one problem with the great size of the army was a concern over quality. According to Deng Guangming (Feuerwerker 1982, 83) ''the state opted for quantity rather than quality''; because although this was a pro-

Table 9.3

Military Forces of the Sung Era

Years	*Sung Total Number of Troops (in thousands)	Imperial Troops (cavalry & foot) (in thousands)	**Liao Mounted Troops (in thousands)	Mongol Army (in thousands)
926			6	
968–976	378	193		
969–983			36	
995–998	666	358		
1017–1021	912	432		
before 1031			61	
1041–1048	1,259	826		
1064–1068	1,162	663		
1078–1085		612		
1101–1125			76	
1142	215			
1160	318			
1163–1190	450			
1206	504***			
1218+				over 200
1225+				180

	Sung (in thousands)	Naval Forces++ Sung (squadrons)	Mongol ("wings")
1130	3	11	
1174	21	15	
1237	52	20	
1257			4
1275			41

Sources:
*Saeki in Kinugawa 1989, 282; total includes prefectural troops; Imperial troops were stationed in K'ai-feng and Honan.
**The *ordo* army (the emperor's elite guard), (Wittfogel and Feng 1949, 503); "ultimately a dozen *ordos* were set up in separate areas, totalling perhaps six hundred thousand horsemen, a mobile shock force held in reserve" (Fairbank 1992, 113).
***War ministry, Franke 1987, 16.
+Dupuy and Dupuy 1977, 336, 339; campaigns against Khwarezm (1218) and Hsi Hsia (1225), including the Mongol *ordo* army on the order of one hundred thousand.
++Lo 1955, 491.

fessional army, its training program was inadequate and "the great size of the army turned out to be a source of weakness." The key weakness was in respect to the cavalry forces needed for mobile warfare in the plains of north China. Our table does show separate figures for the emperor's army, mostly concentrated around the capital, together with mounted troops that were probably held in reserve, at the disposal of the political center. But the table also suggests that the Sung cavalry was at best only a match as compared to that of their enemies in the north. Shortages of horses also meant that the Sung armies in the northern plains would be restricted to the defense—town defenses in particular. Additionally, it meant that the Khitans, and later the Jurchens, and then the Mongols would wield the strategic initiative.

This meant that in north China the position was one of military instability, especially in respect to K'ai-feng—the capital considered to be vulnerable to attack (it was seized by the Khitans in 946–947 and by the Jurchens in 1126). But the situation was different in the south. A saying of the times went: "go by boat in the South, take a horse in the North" (Shiba 1970, 4). Cavalry, the key to land power and to the north, was of lesser value in the south and could be offset by substantial naval power—the factor that assured the survival of the southern Sung for 150 years after they were expelled from the north (see the data on the Sung navy in table 9.3).[4] Only when the Mongols mobilized the naval resources of north China and Korea to their advantage after 1250 did they succeed in conquering the south.

In evaluating the Sung, we find for the first time, on a scale that moves toward global significance, evidence of the basic strategic tension of modern world politics: that between land and modern sea power, or better still between continental and oceanic power. This makes the relationship between the Sung and the Liao—and especially that between the Sung, the Chin, and the Mongols—prototypical in at least some respects to later strategic contests between world powers and their challengers that we know about from the unfolding of long cycles.

This also makes it less surprising that processes of rise and fall of the world powers that are the substance of long cycles, may, in their prototypic form, be observed in the Sung era. We might regard the Sung as forerunners of later oceanic world powers, and the Mongols as a short-lived and failed attempt to organize the world on a continental basis. As will readily be noticed in table 9.4, the northern Sung, the southern Sung, and the Mongols each had one term of office of somewhat over a century. In fact, as we look at this matter more closely, we notice that each of those three might also be thought of as having passed through a political learning cycle that lasted about 120 years.

Table 9.4

Global Politics Process: A China Perspective

Agenda-setting	Coalition-building	Macrodecision	Execution (long cycle)	
		Eurasian Transition Era		
930	960 Sung founded at K'ai-feng	990 1005 Peace with Liao	1030 Northern Sung	
				LC1
1060 Wang An-shih reforms	1090 Reformers versus Conservatives	1120 Chin wars; Capital to Hangchow	1160 Southern Sung	
				LC2
1190 Genghis ruler of Mongols	1220 Chin conquered	1250 Kublai conquers Southern Sung	1280 Mongol world empire	
				LC3
1300	1320	1355 Ming dynasty founded in Nanking	1385 Venice	
				LC4
		West European Era		
1430	1460	1494	1516 Portugal	
				LC5
1540	1560	1580	1609 Dutch Republic	
				LC6
1640	1660	1688	1714 Britain I	
				LC7
1740	1763	1792	1815 Britain II	
				LC8
		Post-West European Era		
1850	1873	1914 World Wars I & II	1945 United States	
				LC9
1973	2000	2026	2050	
				LC10

Note: The Chinese perspective emphasizes the Mongolian role in the thirteenth century. A European perspective would highlight the Genoese role. For our theoretical purposes, Genoa remains the prototypical long-cycle leader. Yet Genoa's western maritime position depended a great deal on Mongolian territorial domination in the east.

As in the more familiar long cycles of the West European era, the China-centered patterns also focus upon periods of decisive warfare (that is, macro-decision) where the successful outcome gave definition to the three dynastic systems by which this period of Chinese history has usually been ordered. Table 9.4 suggests that the process of structural change outlined there is the initial manifestation of long cycles in global politics. By establishing this linkage with the global level, we wish to avoid entering the debate on the role of the dynastic cycle in Chinese history.

Defined as the recurrent pattern of the rise and fall of major dynasties (Reischauer and Fairbank 1960, 114 ff; Yang 1961; Meskill 1965), the dynastic cycle has long been familiar to historians of China because the continuity of that history over several millennia inevitably invited reflection on patterns that might characterize it. But the dynastic cycle was also sometimes thought to represent a repetitive rhythm of a static political system. While in Chinese commentaries much stress was laid on the role of personalities, more recent work sees it mainly as an economic-administrative process.[5]

More specifically, we might refer to the classical philosophy of the "five elements"—a comprehensive theory to explain change in the cosmos known as a "theory of the cyclical evolution of history" (Chan 1984, 26ff; Henderson 1984). This theory was first formulated by the cosmological school of Tsou Yen (-305–240) who maintained that the principal mechanism of all change came from the cyclical rotation of the basic cosmic forces of wood, metal, fire, and water in relation to Earth which was central. From the Han to the Sung, this theory was further elaborated on and employed in debates concerning the legitimation of successive dynasties that were thought to be under the auspices of one of these elements.

However, the proto-long cycle presented in table 9.4 is seen in the first place only as a pattern characterizing the early stages in the evolution of the global political system. We begin this schematic summary of China's part in global structural politics not with 960, the date of the founding of the Sung dynasty, but somewhat earlier when the forces that would create the new structure began to nucleate—about 930. We agree with Wang (1963, 4) that the transition from the T'ang to the Sung can be "better understood in terms of the important changes during the first half of the Wu-tai period."

The first three decades of the new dynasty may then be regarded as a period of coalition-building during which several other members were added to the nuclear grouping in a process more akin to confederation than conquest: "the rapid and almost bloodless reunion of the independent parts of the empire" (Fitzgerald 1950, 383). It was not until 1005 and the conclusion of peace on terms of equality with the Liao empire, which meant a clear renunciation of imperial aspirations (terms of the treaty, Rossabi 1983, 68), that the Sung dynasty might be said to have achieved definition by consolidating its rule.

The war with Chin (after 1120) brought the loss of K'ai-feng and the transfer of the capital to Hangchow, thus inaugurating the period of southern Sung. The conquest of the south by Kublai Khan after 1250 marked the end of the Sung and the peak of the Mongol world empire. The expulsion of the Mongols from China by the Ming, one hundred years later, was the tail end of this particular round of globally linked changes in China's political structures.

Thus, not only the economy, but also the politics of Sung China were linked to worldwide processes. We notice, too, that at least two of the macro-decisions of the Chinese era—the Sung-Chin War (in the second cycle) and the Sung-Mongol War (in the third cycle)—each involved crucial naval elements (see also McNeill 1982, 44–4). The celebrated seven Ming expeditions to the Indian Ocean (1404–1434) were no more than the last stirrings of a naval power that was crucial at an earlier stage of the Chinese political process.

A PATTERN OF FOUR K-WAVES

World-Significant Innovations

It has long been a commonplace observation that certain innovations have been basic to modernity. Francis Bacon put it succinctly in *Novum Organum* (circa 1620):

> It is well to observe . . . the force and virtue and the consequences of discoveries. These are to be seen nowhere more conspicuously than in those three which were unknown to the ancients, and of which the origin, though recent, is obscure and inglorious; namely, printing, gunpowder, and the magnet. For these three have changed the whole face and state of things throughout the world . . . whence have followed innumerable changes. (Needham 1969, 62)

We now know that all three innovations, and others, derive from the Chinese experience during the Sung era.[6] The work of Joseph Needham and his collaborators has been to explicate these origins in great detail on the basis of exhaustive documentation. In the series *Science and Civilization in China,* the story of paper and printing forms one entire volume; the "gunpowder epic" forms another volume; and navigation forms the third. Even if Needham's research focuses more on the fact of invention than that of economic application through innovative production, the research does form a compelling account of a much ignored process.[7]

K-Waves in Sung China?

We have shown earlier that a growing body of scholarly opinion now supports the view that the evolution of the global economy might be seen to take the form of the rise of successive leading sectors. Over a period of some fifty to sixty years, sectors that arise on the basis of basic (Schumpeterian) innovations experience at first slow, and then gradually accelerating growth, such that they come to exert significant impact on the world economy. In time, that growth levels off, and other sectors take up the leadership.

We have identified such processes of rise and decline of leading sectors as K-waves. The existence of K-waves since the Industrial Revolution is now quite well established. In part 3 we have extended this claim all the way back to the mid-fifteenth century. This chapter addresses the question of whether the developments in Sung China might be seen as a series of K-waves that serve as the first intimations of a process that has since characterized the emerging global economy.

The question before us is not the occurrence of these innovations and the significance of the industries which they spawned in the Sung era. As already shown, that position is well established. Equally well established is the shift in the center of gravity of the Chinese demography and economy from north to south (see, for example, Hartwell 1982).

The question that now arises is: can a temporal sequencing of innovations be established such that it might be interpreted as a pattern of K-waves, and can this pattern of K-waves be seen as the onset of the process of evolving a global economy? On general grounds, if we have basic innovations or clusters of such innovations that spawn major new industries, then we would also expect K-waves.

More specifically, we expect to find a number of K-waves in the evolution of the Chinese economy arranged on the same pattern as that later found in other regions of the world system, especially after 1430. In particular, we would expect to find a pattern of coordination (or coevolution) between the political and the economic process. Corresponding to each (political) long cycle in table 9.4, we would expect to find two K-waves. The first of these (the odd-numbered one) would lay out the conditions for the establishment of a political order to be validated by a macrodecision. In plain words, the first K-wave helps to win the big war. The second K-wave (the even-numbered one) follows up that victory (or macrodecision) and consolidates an economic order based upon it.

In other words, we seek to elucidate the connections between structural processes in economics and politics. Jacques Gernet's (1982, 323) observation that the political history of the Sung was "dominated by this close relationship between defense problems and economic problems, which combined to form a sort of vicious circle" lends additional interest to such an investigation.

Global Economy Aspects

Embedded in our approach is an additional hypothesis: a sequence of bursts of innovative growth is more than a form of alternation between K-waves that support a rising political structure and other waves that create an economic order. We also hypothesize that the entire sequence of four K-waves constitutes an experiment in the search for building a world market, and that the Sung sequence constitutes an initial breakthrough in that direction (just as the Sung political process did for the evolution of global politics). This would be an experiment creative not only of the world's most active economy of its time, but also constitutive of the basis for a global economic system.

One aspect of such a sequence is its internal structure. For a market economy takes shape not in a random fashion, but in some meaningful order. We have already hypothesized that the order follows that of other processes of structural change, and for the global economy it consists of this sequence: base-building, networking, breakthrough, and payoff. In the case of the Sung we might posit that it begins with an informational phase, and goes on to establish a network within which transactions can occur. It then confirms, reforms, or consolidates that network in a political process, and ends up by reaching out through market operations toward a global system. In other words, it goes through the phases of an evolutionary learning process that builds up and gradually restructures the economy of world trade.

We may formulate our hypotheses about the existence of K-waves in Sung China in the following manner (as also summarized in table 9.5):

1. The breakthrough to a world market economy took the form of four K-waves, each with its own specified time frame and locational focus.
2. Two K-waves coevolved with one long cycle.
3. The four K-waves formed one phase of the global economy process.

Table 9.5
K-Waves in the Sung Era: Breakthrough to Global Economy

Long Cycle	K-Waves	Predicted K-Wave Characteristics	Predicted High-growth
LC1			
Northern Sung			
	K1	Informational	960–990
	930–960	(Base-building)	
	K2	Network-building	1030–1060
	990–1060	(Networking)	
LC2			
Southern Sung			
	K3	Political Framework	1090–1120
	1060–1120	(Breakthrough)	
	K4	Global Trade	1160–1190
	1120–1190	Expansion (Payoff)	

K-WAVES IN THE SUNG ECONOMY

The Data

Students of this subject usually demonstrate the existence of K-waves by means of statistical analyses of economic time series. The tradition that examines price series goes back to the late nineteenth century. In recent decades, though, other sorts of economic data have become available and have made possible extended trend analyses of output and production statistics. Even sectoral analyses are increasingly being aided by quantitative work on data drawn from the entire modern period.

Quantitative economic data on Sung China are scarce. The best of the relevant series—such as those on population (Hartwell 1982), iron output (Hartwell 1966), government cash income (Worthy 1975, 112), or on the military (cited in table 9.3)—give data for only a few points in time or a few annual averages, despite the fact that Chinese historical records are of high quality. One laudable exception is the list of all tribute missions to the northern Sung assembled by Hartwell (1983). As a fuller utilization of the existing stock of sources along with an analysis of pertinent questions is set in motion, more data series will undoubtedly become available. In the meantime, we have to make do with what we have.

For the time being, the right approach must be qualitative, with emphasis on asking the right questions for available data collections. We must be able to show from the relevant sources and commentaries that certain lines of activity that we know were based on significant innovations experienced substantial surges in volume in the relevant time frames. Not only must the growth spurts be seen as significant, but other industrial or commercial sectors must not be experiencing a similar expansion or must be expanding in different periods. The reported location of such activities must be identifiable in some meaningful manner from the predicted sequence, and their importance for the building of a world market economy must also be arguable.

FOUR K-WAVES IN SUNG CHINA

We shall endeavor to show that four sectors of economic activity prominent in the Sung economy—printing and paper; formation of a national market; fiscal and administrative framework; and expansion of maritime trade—did not expand all at once or at random, but rather followed each other roughly between the years 930 and 1200 in the order just indicated.

In each of these cases we shall also first endeavor to show that an expansionary burst on the basis of an innovation, or a bunch of innovations, occurred in the Sung era; on this, the authorities generally do concur. We shall then try to demonstrate that such activity centered on a particular period and a particular locale or region, and that each such expansionary wave was a precondition of the next. These latter points are not usually brought out clearly in the existing literature.

Printing and Paper (930–990)

The launch of printing as the first great innovation of the modern era is now rightly attributed to Sung China. It marks a turning point in world system evolution not unlike that of the invention of writing four thousand years earlier in the Middle East. Printing is not only a significant turning point in cultural history, but also constitutes a process of economic significance and, as argued earlier, one of worldwide repercussions.[8] Without the foundation of a printing industry and papermaking, further global systemic development would have been hindered.

These innovations concerned methods that permitted large-scale printing of books; the introduction of these methods was in fact gradual. The use of paper for writing began at the end of the Han era. According to Shiba (1970, 103), ''in the Sung era the paper industry took a great leap forward'' with the widespread use of paper made from bamboo and mulberry, and the development of new types of fine papers. In the form of wood-block printing, this development dated from the late T'ang era (being used in Buddhist monastic communities for the production of religious texts), but it received a great boost under the Sung. This was later followed by the development of movable-block techniques. "From the T'ang to the Sung, . . . ink-stick manufacturing, paper-making, and book printing developed into brand-new industries" (Liu and Golas 1969, 44–55).[9]

As general propositions, these facts are familiar and incontestable. What remains to be clarified is the question of timing. Our hypothesis suggests that these developments focused in particular on the years 930 to 990. What is the evidence?

For instance, Jacques Gernet (1982, 333) makes clear the popular and commercial basis of the application of wood-block printing as early as the eighth century in the lower Yangtze (and in Szechwan, in particular). But it is the printing of the classics at K'ai-feng by the imperial command at the suggestion of scholar-official Feng Tao between 932 and 954 that established book printing. Another edition of the classics was later printed by private industry in Szechwan, and the Buddhist canon was printed between 972 and 983. The center of official publishing in K'ai-feng was the National Academy—a large-scale government printing project started in 988 which produced one hundred thousand woodblocks with each block capable of producing up to fifteen thousand copies (Tsien 1985, 370). Thus "wood-block engraving, which made it possible to reproduce accurately the calligraphy and illustrations of texts, became part of ordinary life in the course of the tenth century" (Gernet 1982, 335).

Let us return briefly to the circumstances that led to the initiation of the government printing of the classics. The date, 932, is of some significance because it is in the decade between 926 and 936 during the reign of late T'ang emperor Li Ssu-yuan. According to Wang (1963, 171, 174), during this time the foundation was laid for the ultimate consolidation of imperial authority under the Sung—the "recovery of the bureaucracy" in fact occurred and "the ideal of a bureaucratic empire received further recognition."

Li Ssu-yuan (926–933), along with his predecessor Li Ts'un-hsiu, was a Sha-t'o Turk tribal aristocrat and army leader from Ho-tung (Shansi). Since 915 Li Ssu-yuan had maintained an alliance with military and administrative personnel of Hopeh (where Peking is now situated). By 923 the Ho-tung forces were the senior partners in that alliance, but the relationship gradually reversed as the Hopeh men acquired considerable power at court and came to dominate palace commissions (Wang 1962, 208–15). After the execution of the barely literate, but powerful, military secretary from Ho-tung in 931, a clear shift in the power balance may be observed. During the following year a Hanlin academician from Hopeh, Feng Tao, obtained authorization to print the classics. In the event, the classics became the intellectual basis of the influence that (Chinese) scholar-officials came to wield at the expense of (tribal aristocratic) military leaders. The classics consolidated the power of the men from Hopeh out of whose ranks eventually emerged the Sung regime in 960.

We do not have statistics that show the economic importance of printing and papermaking even though we know that it was also a prosperous private industry—indeed, books commanded good prices and were eagerly sought for export (Hartwell 1989, 485). Our evidence suggests that printing and paper did in fact move into the position of lead industry, and we know of no other industry holding that position in the tenth century.

The consequences of the entrenchment of books and paper were pervasive and affected both the economy, society, and political system. Gernet's (1962, 128) work stressed that printing went hand-in-hand with the rise of the merchant class and the rapid development of regions with the highest density of urban populations. Printing and paper became the infrastructure of the commercial revolution (as it did with the issuance of paper money in the next K-wave). Elvin (1973, 178–84) observes that printing helped to nourish scientific and technical progress.

For society, books and writing served to also nourish a class of scholars. "For the first time, the supply of books became cheap and abundant" (Fitzgerald 1950, 360). This supply provided a means toward a modern "learning society" whereby "ever-widening sectors of society sought to improve themselves by learning" (Gernet 1962, 128). Paper—together with ink stick, ink slab, and brushpen—had become "one of the four treasures of the scholar's studio" wrote Su I-chien in 986 (Tsien 1985, 48).

The most significant effect of printing was seen in the political realm. The classics, as reinterpreted by scholars, became the foundations of Sung legitimacy and the rule of scholar-officials. A significant proportion of officials were chosen by means of competitive examinations based upon classical texts, and these scholars soon became the backbone of the regime while military men receded into the background. The administrative system, the pride of Chinese civilization, reached its perfection during the Sung period—in synchronization with the expansion of official printing. Whereas in the 970s and 980s twenty to thirty candidates were awarded the doctorate (chin-shih), by 992 353 passed at K'ai-feng out of a total of 17,300 candidates (in 1124 the number of passes reached 806) (Ma 1971, 112). The officials who served at the capital (three-quarters worked in the provinces) also became the network undergirding the emerging national economy. "By 1004 . . . the administrative structure had settled into a pattern that was to remain with little basic change until a fundamental reorganization was undertaken in 1080'' (Kracke 1953, 27).

Formation of a National Market (990–1060)

We know that ''in the course of the later part of the T'ang dynasty, and the Sung dynasty, a nation-wide market was formed in China'' (Shiba 1970, 45). A complex phenomenon of this kind must obviously be the result of a cluster of factors and a number of crucial innovations, but it is also worth noting that a national market, for an economy of this size, was in and of itself a major innovation of global significance. The basic features of a market economy (population movement across borders, property rights in land, social division of labor, local markets, and prices) could be found, according to Kang Chao (1986, 2–4), as early as the period of Warring States. The present argument is intended to clarify the process of forming a national market economy which, in turn, was a precondition of sustained external trade.

But can we place this crucial development in our predicted time frame, which is between 990 and 1060? How do we conceptualize the various factors involved? Let us propose that a national market achieves formation when significant agricultural and industrial surpluses are exchanged via a functioning system of transportation and finance.

The basic industry was, of course, agriculture, and it is now well established that a significant agricultural expansion occurred in Sung China. The key to this expansion was the double-cropping system (already underway in the second half of the T'ang era; see, for example, Cartier 1991 reporting on the work of Li Bozhong) in which early ripening rice became a central feature.[10] A drought-resistant variety obtained from Champa, by means of what might have been an early form of technology transfer, proved to be particularly significant. According to a Buddhist monk (writing between 1068 and 1077; Ho 1956, 206–7), it was the second Sung emperor who, about the year 1000, dispatched special envoys ''bearing precious things'' to Champa and saw them return with twenty bushels of rice ''which have since been grown almost everywhere.''[11] Another mission, sent to India, brought back green lentils.

These and other innovations must have been instrumental in bringing about a large increase in the area of land under cultivation.[12] If the data reported in Ma (1971, 13) are trustworthy, the cultivated area of northern Sung rose by 69 percent between 996 and 1021, as compared with an increase of only 6 percent in the early Sung era, between 975 and 996.[13] This would tend to confirm that the decades after 990 witnessed a surge of agricultural production linked to population growth and concentrated in the middle and lower

Yangtze region which provided large surpluses. In the eleventh century, as much as one-quarter of the rice and grain output of that region was moved north along the canal system (see Gernet 1982, 320).

Equally striking was the rise in industrial output. According to Gernet (1982) "all manufactures expanded rapidly." Especially striking were the large-scale developments in the production of iron and coal. These were based on improvements in technology in the first decades of the eleventh century that included the use of coke in blast furnaces and the use of hydraulic machinery for working the bellows. Large-scale enterprises employing hundreds of full-time workers arose in Honan and southern Hopeh. China's iron production rose dramatically between 998 and 1064 (from 32,500 to 90,000 tons) and apparently peaked at about 125,000 tons in 1078.[14] As Hartwell (1966) has pointed out, as late as 1788 British output of iron was only seventy-six thousand tons. The price of iron (in terms of rice) fell quite rapidly, by 1080, to about one-third of its price in 997 (Jones 1988, 76). The government and the capital city of K'ai-feng were principal customers for the products of that industry—especially in respect to weapons (which supplied the huge armies of that period), coinage, and materials for construction. "In a general way, all mining production increased rapidly in the eleventh century" (Gernet 1982, 321).

The specialization, and hence the trade permitted by such surpluses—both agricultural and industrial, in turn propelled what some have called a transportation revolution: "for the first time in its history, China took full advantage of (its) immense network . . . of navigable waterways formed by the Yangtze and its tributaries and extended by canals . . . traversed by the biggest and most various collection of boats that the world had ever seen until then" (Gernet 1982, 321).

The final element in the formation of the national market was the monetization of the economy. This was based in part on a substantial expansion of the coinage, especially after 1000, and in part on the institution of paper money. The world's first experiment with paper currency occurred in Szechwan in 1024 when paper notes were issued for a limited period (valid for only two or three years) and for certain areas; by the next century paper "became the principal kind of money" in Sung China (Gernet 1982, 325). In turn the state derived an increasingly large portion of its revenues from cash payments.

Overall, the evidence is good that the principal surge toward the formation of a national market occurred in the predicted timeframe (990–1060). Champa rice was introduced around 1000. Northern Sung land cultivation soared between 996 and 1021. Iron production tripled between 998 and 1064. These agricultural and industrial production increases were accompanied by a more efficacious use of transportation and the expanding monetization of the economy, especially after 1024.

Fiscal and Administrative Framework (1060–1120)

We hypothesize that the third K-wave stemmed from innovative changes in the government's relations to the economy. A series of reforms undertaken by Wang An-shih changed the traditional tribute system and lightened the government's heavy hand on trade and commerce. This amounted to the consolidation, on the political-economic interface of the system, of the transformations wrought in the economy by the two previous K-waves.

Wang An-shih, a southerner from Kiangsi, was a scholar-official and holder of a doctorate. He first assumed high office in 1069 and he left in 1076, but his reforms continued until the death of the emperor. A backlash followed after 1085, but by 1094 the party of ''innovators'' was back in power and continued the reforms—although in a weakened form until 1125.

The principal problem confronting the Sung must have been the size of government and the rising burden of military expenditures. In the 1040s, during the war against the Hsi Hsia, the army reached the unprecedented strength of close to 1.3 million soldiers—nearly four times that of the early Sung armies. The army still exceeded one million in the 1060s, during peacetime, when an official calculation revealed that 80 percent of government income was needed to support them (McNeill 1983, 40). The budgetary and logistical problems of supplying such a huge force must have been a tremendous strain on government administration and the economy.

The extent of the burden is shown in the proportion of Sung national income absorbed by public expenditures. Recent estimates, that deal with the period of around 1080, put that share at rather high levels—high by the standards of early societies and even high by modern standards. These range from 10 percent (Hartwell 1988, 78), to 13 percent (Feuerwerker), to 24 percent. The author of the latter estimate, Peter Golas (1988, 94), feels that the results of his calculations ''severely strain credibility.'' Yet if we bear in mind the size of the military forces we have just considered, then the figures appear less surprising, even if they could stand refining and additional confirmation. This is one more illustration of the difficulties experienced by the Sung (circa 1080).

It is therefore no surprise that Wang An-shih's reforms centered on the fiscal problem, even though it was a measure of his modern vision that he was able to see budgetary questions in the broad context of economic growth. The most important of his measures for our purposes concerned changes in the tribute system of payments in kind.

The Sung authorities, as those of the T'ang before them, met their revenue needs through a system whereby "the whole empire forwarded vast quantities of grain and produce to the capital, a system that was widely regarded as oppressive, and a source of provincial grievances under the T'ang." Wang An-shih attempted to make it less burdensome to the provinces, and the first of his laws, called "Equalization of Loss," was directed precisely to that end: "tribute was no longer forwarded to the capital to be stored in state granaries, and sold at a low price" which produced a glut in the capital and scarcity elsewhere. "Wang An-shih arranged that the produce of one province should be exchanged against the produce of some distant region. Tribute grain and silk could now be sold locally for the profit of the treasury rather than transported to the capital where it would fetch only a very low price. Prices were kept even, gluts and famines were avoided, and the peasantry assured of a steady demand for their crop." (Fitzgerald 1950, 397–98)

The new system demanded much of the Sung public official, but a strong public service was already in place and new officials were being recruited.[15] These and other measures tended to make the state an active participant in more markets, but they also tended to strengthen the national market system and promote monetization of the budget and the economy. The market was also strengthened by such measures as the abolition of state monopolies (for instance, on tea in 1059) and relaxation of restraints on commercial activities (when the curfew was abolished in K'ai-feng in 1063).

The other part of Wang An-shih's project concerned military reform, and thus lessened the strain on resources from the demand side. The size of the military forces was reduced and a regime of rural militias substituted for much of the prefectural armies. A horse-breeding scheme was intended to lessen China's dependence on the import of Mongolian-bred horses for its cavalry.

In sum, the reforms streamlined the Sung administration, confirmed the trend toward the abandonment of the command mode of supplying its needs, and invigorated the national economy at its interface with politics. The reforms did not prevent the loss of the north in 1126, but they may have made it possible for the Sung to have another lease on life in the south.

Maritime Trade Expansion (1120–1190)

Our fourth hypothesis concerns seaborne commerce, and proposes that after 1120, and with a peak at about 1190, maritime foreign trade became the leading sector of the Sung economy. Moreover, viewed from a global perspec-

Table 9.6

Number and Value of Tribute Missions

Tribute Missions Arriving	Number	Missions per Year	Total Value in Silver Kilos per Year	Percent Value from the South
1010–1019	89	8.9	6,972	22.8
1070–1089	93	4.65	3,050	34.1

Source: Hartwell 1989

tive, this fourth K-wave would constitute the culmination of the entire Sung experience for it would show how that sequence would be crowned by the coupling of the world's largest national economy with an emerging global process.

Let us first observe the distinction between overland and seaborne trade. China had, of course, been a center of trade of both kinds for at least two millennia. But it could be argued that the major part of that trade occurred in the immediate neighborhood (with Korea and Japan) or, as in the case of the Silk Road, passed over long overland distances through several intermediaries. For instance, the lists of tribute missions published by Hartwell (1983; 1989, 465–70) show that in the eleventh century roughly two-thirds of the traffic, by number and value, came from points west and northwest—presumably overland. That is, too, where the Sung's own tribute commitments were directed (to Liao, Hsi Hsia, and later Chin). Up until the T'ang era, the southern maritime traffic was in non-Chinese hands.

This brings us to the second distinction—between tribute and trade. The overall trend throughout is what Shiba (1983) has referred to as an "eclipse of the tribute missions by trade." If the tribute system (in a sense, an extension of domestic pre-market arrangements), a feature of China's external relations since the Han, was in part a mechanism of trade, then its weight as a factor in the organization of global trade was bound to be gradually eroding. The list of tribute missions published by Hartwell (1983) shows a steady decline in frequency from a peak in 960–990 (some eleven missions per year) to a low in 1060–1119 (two missions). Hartwell (1988, 30) believes that once the new dynasty no longer needed foreign tribute for its symbolic value or legitimation, the emperor would restrict new missions to special occasions only. The trend toward decreasing frequency and intensity of such exchanges might be further illustrated in table 9.6.

Tribute missions are not the optimal device for conducting world trade. We would therefore expect a diminution in their role and a surge in nontribute trade if there is to be a significant expansion in maritime interchange. Hence the expansion in seaborne, mainly nongovernmental commerce in the postulated timeframe is not really surprising. Even in the eleventh century, a shift in the value of tribute missions toward the south may already be observed, as shown in table 9.6. Following the loss of the north (and the consequent shift of the center of gravity of the Sung domain to the south, to the Yangtze Valley, and to the coastal provinces), an increase in (southern) maritime traffic is only to be expected. That same process also meant decreased reliance on the (northern) Silk Road caravan traffic to Central Asia. A surge in sea power would further augment these trends, as would other measures of official support prompted by the prospect of new sources of revenue. In turn, making such a large, productive, and innovative economy face toward the ocean would tend to lay the foundations of oceanic trade.

The hypothesis, then, seems inherently plausible. What is the evidence that might confirm or deny it? One type of evidence would be a good series of foreign trade statistics. Without these, what do we have?

We know from the testimony of Arab and European travelers of the thirteenth and fourteenth centuries that the activity of the southern Chinese ports was on a scale far larger than that of European ones. While the T'ang had just one port open for foreign trade, Sung China had nine. Ch'uan-chou in Fukien, the leading seaport and shipbuilding center, was reported in 1120 to have links with thirty-six overseas countries (Elvin 1973, 208). The junks of this Sung age—with four or more masts, twelve big sails, and four decks—were formidable sailing machines and were preferred by foreign travelers because of their superiority to Arab or European ships of that time. Large seagoing junks carried several hundred men, and the small ones carried more than a hundred. The junks were products of a lengthy evolution—the most recent stage of which might have been the transportation revolution that occurred in the eleventh century as part of the formation of the national market.

But what was probably decisive for oceanic sailing was the application of the compass—an innovation of global significance. A work dating from 1119 records its use at the end of the eleventh century.[16] Studies of magnetism had by then a long background in the history of Chinese science, but the changing conditions experienced by southern Sung would have made a wide use of this innovation a necessity.

The compass was reportedly used by Chinese shipping on the Canton-Sumatra route where pepper and nonalimentary spices were major trade items.[17] This spice trade, which two to three centuries later helped motivate Portuguese operations in the Indian Ocean, reached China much earlier and more easily. By at least the tenth century Chinese junks began to trade to the south. Eventually this trade expansion produced what Fairbank (1992, 191–95) has labeled the active outer fringe of maritime China that "countered the land-based and agrarian-centered style" of the traditional empire: the thriving network of overseas Chinese communities throughout Southeast Asia (whose principal entrepot on the China coast became Amoy, in Fukien).

According to Jacques Gernet (1982, 324) government receipts from maritime customs duties went up from one-half million strings cash in the early years of the dynasty to sixty-five million strings cash in 1189.[18] Robert Hartwell (1989) maintains that in the late 1100s Sung seaborne trade was valued at more than 520,000 silver kilos per year, thus constituting a substantial proportion of the nonagricultural domestic product.[19] If we set this figure against the annual value of tribute missions in the eleventh century, we deduce that a drastic expansion in the role of nongovernmental trade must indeed have occurred in the twelfth century. Hartwell also argues that toward the end of that century, public support for foreign trade began abating—another piece of evidence that would argue for the validity of expecting a plateau around 1190.

The last piece of evidence concerns the Sung navy. While a naval force was founded in 957, just before the Sung took power, Lo (1969) claims that it soon became no more than ornamental. We note, though, that in 987 the emperor ordered four naval missions dispatched to buy foreign products and to encourage foreign rulers to send tribute (Lo 1969; Hartwell 1988, 29, 35). There was a reorganization in 1069, probably part of Wang An-shih's reforms, but the war with Vietnam (1077) brought little success. After 1228, however, the Yangtze campaigns against the Chin who crossed the river and held Nanking marked a turning point in the Sung attitude toward the navy. What Lo (1969, 82) called "a High Sea Fleet" (the military commission for coastal defense) was founded in 1132, separate from the river squadrons, and was soon equipped with larger ships. The new Sung navy achieved some key defensive successes against the Chin invasion attempt, including the destruction of the Chin fleet off the coast of Shantung in 1161. Piracy was brought under control which provided a security blanket for maritime activities. According to Lo, the zenith of sea power was reached between 1161 and 1204.

The zenith of Sung sea power coincided with the ascendancy of the Tairas in the politics of Japan (1156–1185). The Taira clan was then based on western Japan where they had cleared the Inland Sea of pirates and made it a secure route between Kyoto and China. The clan encouraged trade with Sung China and derived great wealth from it. Their final defeat occurred in a naval

fight at Dannoura, at the western end of that sea. The victors were the Mina-
motos who proceeded to establish the Shogunate at Kamakura near (today's)
Tokyo—the first in a series of military governments, built upon the support of
the *samurai* warrior caste, which would rule the country until 1868 (Sansom
1978, 270, 274).[20]

In the absence of evidence to the contrary, the case is quite good for placing
the surge in foreign trade between 1120 and 1190. That surge would account for
the high level of commercial and maritime activities that so impressed the travelers of the thirteenth and fourteenth centuries such as Marco Polo (1280s) and
Ibn Battutah (1340s). The level thus reached was then maintained for another two
to three centuries—until and including the time of Columbus—at which time the
Chinese market still served as the magnet for world trade.

THE COEVOLUTION OF ECONOMICS AND POLITICS

Let us summarize briefly the findings on the coordination of economics
and politics. We have postulated that each of the two long cycles—that for the
northern Sung (LC1) and that for southern Sung (LC2)—would match two
K-waves. By long cycles we mean the learning cycles shown in each row of
table 9.4, and not the reign periods of the respective dynasties. The learning
cycles account for the rise of an (actual or potential) world power, and that is
why our analysis of the rise of northern Sung starts in 930 and the rise of
southern Sung starts about 1060.

Table 9.7 shows how the two processes—the long cycles and the
K-waves—are thought to be related. For the first process, the printing and paper wave (K1) provided the material infrastructure for the political and ideological consolidation of the entire Sung era on the basis of an effective public
service oriented to a nonmilitary agenda. The second wave (K2) consummated
the Sung success in stabilizing a political structure for most of China by surg-
ing to form a national market economy and expanding it in a number of crucial
sectors. The reforms of Wang An-shih in turn adjusted the political framework
to the burgeoning new economy by fiscal and administrative changes (K3),
and laid the foundation on which the Sung could reestablish its rule in the
south. The expansion of seaborne trade (K4) was the great payoff of the entire
process, and produced, for the south, a strong entry into a newly emerging
global market economy.

We notice that the entire process is punctuated by a series of transition
crises. Above all, it is sandwiched by two major developments: (1) the disintegration of T'ang rule and the ushering in of the period of Five Dynasties; and
(2) by the crisis heralded by the rise of the Mongols from 1190 onward and

Table 9.7

Testing Sung K-Wave Predictions, 930–1190

K-Waves	Leading Sectors/ Innovations	Locational Focus	Coordination with Politics
Northern Sung K1 930–990	Printing and paper industry/woodblock book printing	K'ai-feng	Via scholar-officials
K2 990–1060	National market: Wet cultivation: Champa rice Iron casting: coke paper currency	Lower Yangtze Honan, Hopeh Szechwan	Settlement Government supply
Southern Sung K3 1060–1120	Public finance/ tribute system reformed (Wang An-shih)	Lower Yangtze	Fiscal framework
K4 1120–1190	Maritime trade/ use of compass	Kwangtung Fukien	Naval expansion High sea fleet

Genghis Khan's ascension to ruler of the Mongol federation in 1206 (a crisis that ended in the fall of southern Sung in 1276–1279).

The second process consisted of K-waves (see table 9.8) with an onset marked by a period of instability and disorder—both political and economic. The Sung-Liao War of 979–1004 did not restore all of China proper to Sung rule, but the settlement of 1005 consolidated the system and formed the foundation for a burst of economic growth. The war against the Tunguts (Hsi Hsia) placed a considerable strain on the economy which demanded a great mobilization of military strength. The fighting against the Jurchens, who first destroyed the Khitans in alliance with the Sung and then turned on the Sung, brought severe devastation to the Yangtze Valley. In the end, the devastation allowed the southern regime to reorient in a maritime direction.

Loss of flexibility, loss of adaptability, and incapacity to learn were clearly seen in Sung political reactions, or rather in the lack of them, to the emerging threat of the Mongols. In the same year that the Mongols were brought together in a powerful new political structure, the Sung launched a futile attack against the Chin empire; two decades later they joined the Mongols in destroying the Chin.

Table 9.8

Sung Long Cycles, K-Waves, and Transition Crises

Long Cycle	K-Waves	Transition Crisis
		Disintegration of T'ang
LC1		Five Dynasties
Northern Sung		
	K1	
	Printing and paper	
		Sung-Liao War, 979–1004
	K2	
	Formation of national market	
		Sung-Hsi Hsia War, 1038–1043
LC2		
Southern Sung		
	K3	
	Fiscal framework	
		Sung-Chin alliance, 1120
		Sung-Chin War, 1125–1141
	K4	
	Seaborne trade expansion	
		Kamakura Shogunate, 1192
		"False learning," 1194–
		Decline in revenues,
		Sung-Chin War, 1206–, 1212–
		Mongol federation, 1206
		Sung-Mongol alliance, 1231
		Chin destroyed, 1234
LC3		
Mongol world empire		
and ascent of Genoa		
in West		

In doing so they repeated the disastrous strategy pursued one century earlier against the Khitans, with even more disastrous results.[21] This political learning failure was representative of a more general Sung inability to launch a new agenda or address emerging problems. The difficulties encountered in dealing with new problems were also indicated by the campaign against false learning during which Chu Hsi, the greatest of the neo-Confucians, suffered banishment (in 1194). When after his death the policies of his opponents (and the attack on the Chin) collapsed in abject failure, neo-Confucianism (as transmitted in his teachings and commentaries on the classics) surged to new heights, but soon froze into the role of dominant orthodoxy which it retained until well into the twentieth century.[22]

Gunpowder and Firearms

As just discussed, major warfare shaped the Sung era. The degree of mobilization for military purposes greatly exceeded anything else in world politics of that time. Military campaigns of great size and complexity were mounted, and great cities of over one million people (such as K'ai-feng) were subjected to sieges. No wonder military technology made great strides and military innovation flourished at such times, especially during transition crises. McNeill (1982, 39) cites rewards offered in 969 to a general and his officers for suggesting a new model of ''fire arrow.''

We need to distinguish stages in the development of gunpowder, its incendiary and explosive properties, and its propellant characteristics. According to Needham (1969, 65–69), the first reported use of gunpowder mixtures to ignite flamethrowers dates to 919, and a ''fire arrow'' (a rocket) was developed ''by the early eleventh century.'' By the time of the Hsi Hsia War, the first mention of the formula for gunpowder appears in a work on military strategy (in 1044). The range of firearms available includes smoke-producing incendiary grenades, catapults for launching incendiary bombs, and explosive grenades. By the time of the Chin invasion (in 1161) catapults which hurled explosives (standard equipment on all warships since 1129) secured victory for the defenders.

The transition to the barrel gun begins with experiments in the use of a fire lance—a tube filled with rocket material, but not allowed to get loose (a primitive form of flamethrower). The fire lance was employed in city defenses in the 1130s. The Chin employed ''iron fire bombs'' to shatter city walls. But it is the Mongols that made use of great explosions in their campaigns (about 1230). The barrel gun, the employment of mortars (or bombards) with a metal tube of iron and bronze, dates from the final stages of their campaigns against the Sung (before 1280) (Needham 1969; Gernet 1982, 311–12; Elvin 1973, 88).

The evolution of gunpowder arms parallels the time path of the Sung cycles, but also extends into the Mongol era. The technology first developed and refined in the wars fought among the Sung, the Khitans, and the Jurchens was put to use throughout the Eurasian continent by the Mongols, and formed one of the foundations of their world empire.

These radical transformations in military technology, which continue to exert a profound impact upon the entire world system to this day, undoubtedly

Table 9.9

High Price Periods as an Indicator of Sung Transition Crises

Peaked Observed	Type	Source
1004	Tea certificates in terms of grain	Lamouroux (1991, 999)
1048–1051	Tea certificates in terms of cash	,,
1101–1107	Devaluation of paper money	Lo (1969, 61–64)
1134	Inflation restarted	,,

involved considerable industrial activity—most obviously so in the coal and iron industries already mentioned under the K2 wave. Unfortunately, we do not have the data to pinpoint, with greater precision, the extent, duration, or location of these activities. We might add, though, that foreign trade must have been involved given the import of sulphur from Korea in 1080, or the presence of "Greek fire" from Champa or Muscat (a forerunner of black powder).

Price Trends

Statistical information describing trends in general price levels has traditionally been given careful scrutiny by students of K-waves. Periods of high prices are likely indicators of transition crises. We have no systematic information on price trends in Sung China. But scattered information makes it possible to argue the existence of spurts in prices at intervals that, in more recent times, have been associated with K-waves—namely those of some fifty to sixty years. This data is summarized in table 9.9.

The peaks observed coincided in three of the four cases with major military campaigns and corresponded to the transition crises earlier named. The fourth case (1101–1107) is less clear.

CONCLUSION

This chapter embodies a number of conjectures about the relationship between critical political developments of the Sung era and the beginnings of an oceanic economy of global trade. For instance, the Sung expansion constituted the first sustained thrust toward a world market economy, built upon the creation of a national economy in China. This thrust consisted of four related bursts of globally significant innovations based on a succession of leading sectors.

The data now at hand lend support to these hypotheses. The four expansionary surges are quite well documented; together these form a sequence of

K-waves that might also be interpreted as an evolutionary one. As more evidence becomes available from original sources, the hypotheses may need to be retested and reexamined. But it is also worth noting that, in the first place, the hypotheses concern the operation of a global process that had its beginnings in the Sung era. In the second place, these hypotheses concern an era of Chinese history—even if it is an era known to have had profound global repercussions.

One insight yielded by this study is the close degree of interdependence of economics and politics demonstrated here. We know that Chinese history was written by scholar-officials who would tend to give weight to political processes and therefore understate and underreport problems of the economy or the activities of merchants. They also may have underwritten the military history of the age and the exploits of generals. Even so, the lines of interaction between economics and politics emerge clearly from our study.

Most of all, this analysis of a turbulent yet innovative and productive period also suggests some answers to questions that have puzzled observers: why have growth and the spirit of innovation (that reached such a high level in twelfth-century China) ceased after 1190. Why has the active zone of global innovation in the next century decisively shifted westward?

One line of answers to these questions becomes clear as soon as we realize that, in the experience of the world system, zones of innovation invariably do shift in the long run. By long run we do mean, of course, time spans approaching a quarter millennium. Such a "good run" in the game of solving global problems makes it less likely that another cluster of superior solutions will emerge from the same context (if only because the best solutions to old problems are the enemies of best solutions to new problems). In the evolution of the global economy over the past thousand years, we have no instance of a series of more than four K-waves centered upon one major region.

The mere fact that the focal zone of innovation shifted around this time from southern China (along the Silk Roads, both northern and southern) to renaissance Italy may not in and of itself be surprising to students of innovation. The active zones of the world, over the long run, have been shifting regularly among the world regions. The China that in the thirteenth century was part of the Mongol world—devastated by sustained warfare and mass epidemics, and subject to ruthless exploitation for the benefit of one clan ruling over a vast empire—became a different country and an unlikely home for new bursts of innovation. When the Ming expelled the Mongols, China turned in upon itself and shut itself off from the outside world—an understandable reaction, but hardly a recipe for fostering adventures of ideas or enterprise. What could be more surprising is the regression that followed under the Ming and the failure to keep up with developments elsewhere. We have already noted that the ending of Sung innovation coincided with Japan's turn toward military rule.

In a global perspective, the experience of Sung China is not really surprising. While it lasted, the world system benefited hugely from the injection of its pioneering practices and more spacious institutions, and their effects are still around us. Once its capacity for innovation was exhausted, the challenge was taken up by other hands in a process that continues to pass the leadership of change to new generations.

After Sung China, the leadership of change shifted to Genoa and Venice before moving farther west to Portugal and more recent global system leaders. To continue our argument for a millennium of K-wave continuity, the next chapter focuses on the commercial political economy of the eastern Mediterranean in the thirteenth through fifteenth centuries.

Chapter Ten

Renaissance Italy
Thirteenth to Fifteenth Centuries, K-Waves 5–8

The K-waves beginning in the late fifteenth century were marked by their relationship to attempts to discover new routes from Europe to Asia. The urge of Europeans to go east is well known in the annals of world economic history. Yet that same world economic history did not begin in 1494 or even 1415 when the Portuguese began to move down the Moroccan coastline. Our thesis is that the Chinese developments in the eleventh and twelfth centuries can be linked both directly and indirectly to Portuguese activities in the fifteenth and sixteenth centuries. The Portuguese efforts to reach Asia were preceded by several hundred years of variable levels of economic interdependence between Asia and Europe and attempts to improve the degrees of interconnectivity. We are certainly not the first to suggest that medieval Europe operated as a regional subsystem within a larger economic system stretching from England to China. Still, the story is not that well known, just as parts of the story remain unclear due to the shortage of documentation.

We are well aware of the difficulties associated with advancing precise generalizations about international economic transactions in the twelfth through fifteenth centuries. Nonetheless, we contend that four K-waves (K5–K8), centered in the trading operations of the Italian city-states (especially Genoa and Venice), maintained the continuity of the K-wave chain from its initial stimulation in Sung China to the dramatic expansion of European actors throughout the globe. How and why the continuity was maintained is complex and involves the coming together of a number of factors—including, but not limited to, demographic and economic expansion in Europe beginning in the tenth century, probable Chinese innovational diffusion to the west, Genoese and Venetian commercial leadership, geopolitical changes originating in Central Asia in the twelfth and thirteenth centuries, and consequent transformations in the volume and flow of east-west trade. We need to outline the nature of these changes and their interrelationships. We also need to explore the limited empirical evidence that is available to assess whether fluctuations in Italian innovation and leading economic activities conformed to the hypothesized K-wave shape and rhythm in the 1190–1430 period.

THE HISTORICAL INGREDIENTS

An Expanding Europe, Trade, and the Diffusion of Chinese Innovations

One specialist on medieval Europe (Lopez 1987, 379) has suggested that the European "dark ages" were due to incessant wars and invasions, scourging taxation and inflation, recurrent major epidemics, serious ecological damage, unfavorable climatic changes, and a reversal from demographic growth to demographic decline. By the tenth to eleventh centuries these influences had begun to weaken or disappear. European development and population growth was once again expanding. The demand for, and the ability to pay for, luxuries from Asia (spices and silks) expanded as well. No doubt, the taste for Eastern commodities was whetted by greater exposure to them in the twelfth- to thirteenth-century Crusades, another manifestation of European expansion.

One should also keep in mind that the medieval usage of the term spice could be highly elastic. An early fourteenth-century inventory of spices (Lopez and Raymond 1955, 109–14) lists 288 commodities encompassing almost all of the possible raw materials imported from outside Europe. In this list some discrimination is made between general spices and "minute" spices (commodities sold in small quantities at high prices). Even so, there are still twenty-nine different minute spices discernible in the list. The implication is that the spice trade was more complicated than may be conveyed by imagining sacks of pepper on an Italian wharf.

Trade, no matter how small its overall value may have been in comparison to later trade values or some calculation of trade as a proportion of medieval gross domestic product, was also critical to the continued expansion of the European economy:

> In the middle ages only trade, and the financial activity which was closely allied to it, could offer a man the opportunity for enrichment and for rapid social promotion. In this way, it introduced change and movement into an economy and a society which were above all rural, and as such endowed with a great force of

inertia. Links with the outside world more over, the very essence of commerce, were in themselves powerful contributors to progress. (Bernard 1976, 274)

At the same time, the monetary value of trade was not necessarily all that minuscule. Lopez (1987, 355) estimates, for example, that the value of taxed Genoese trade in 1293 was roughly seven times the income of the French monarchy.

Paralleling this early phase of European expansion, as we have seen in the preceding chapter, Sung China was also in a phase of economic innovation and expansion—one that was even more spectacular and radical, and presumably stimulating to trade throughout Asia. It is sufficient for our purposes to note that the west began seeking an increased flow of eastern goods after hundreds of years of decline in east-west trade (since the time of Rome), roughly at a time when the east was stimulating maritime trade (twelfth century). General supply and demand conditions were definitely propitious for increased east-west transactions.

It may be that much more was involved than simply increases in commodity trade at both ends of a reemerging Eurasian trade network. The extreme position is represented by arguments that a good proportion of European innovations can be traced directly to earlier Chinese innovations. Table 10.1 offers one example of this type of argument which, if the path of diffusion could be substantiated, would provide us with an extremely direct link between K-waves 1 through 4 and 5 through 8, to say nothing of some of the K-waves that we examined in chapters 5 to 7. The problem is that while some of these innovations probably did migrate from east to west, we have little in the way of specific corroborating evidence. There is also evidence to suggest that some of the types of claims advanced in table 10.1 may be exaggerated. Landes' (1983) argument for the separate European development of modern clocks along different lines than the Chinese models is a case in point.

Discretion and an appreciation for the possibility and probability of independent inventions advises against arguing that all of the innovations that we will analyze in the Italian renaissance period must have some Chinese roots. But we will show that the ones we think are most important concern how best to move Asian goods from east to west. In this sense, the links to the Chinese growth surges in the eleventh and twelfth centuries are minimally indirect, but still very real. At the same time, we are in no more of a position to rule out the direct diffusion of technological innovation, via such well-known transmission belts as the Silk Roads and other more numerous and more obscure points of contact, than we are to accept them without reservations.

Table 10.1

Selected Chinese Technical Innovations and Their Appearance in Western Europe

Selected Chinese Technical Innovations	Appearance in Western Europe	Implications
Sternpost rudder	Circa 1190	These four innovations were critical to the development of European discoveries and subsequent maritime supremacy.
Magnetic compass	Late 12th/13th centuries	
Multiple masts with multiple sails	14th/15th centuries	
Lug sail	16th century	
Gunpower formula	first mention in 1285	By escalating the costs of war, European state expansion and consolidation was strongly encouraged. Naval artillery proved critical to the subsequent development of maritime supremacy.
First military use of gunpowder	second half of 14th century	
First paper made in Italy	end of 13th century:	Foundation for printing and book production.
Printing with movable type	1430–1460	
Modern clocks	late 13th/early 14th centuries	Heightened awareness of time with multiple implications for society and economy.
Blast furnace	late 14th century	European iron production almost doubled between 1350 and 1500. The principles involved were fundamental to the metallurgical half of the 18th-century Industrial Revolution.
Waterpowered machinery for textile production	late 14th century	Prototype for all later developments in powered textile machinery to 1790 and the textile half of the 18th-century Industrial Revolution.

Source: Based on the discussion in Adshead 1988, 155–62, and Gernet 1982, 378.

The Champagne Fairs

The Champagne Fairs consisted of a sequential circuit of six fairs in the French provinces of Champagne and Brie (see figure 10.1). Each fair lasted about two months which made the circuit a year-round affair. They were able to emerge and prosper in part because the territory involved enjoyed a degree of autonomy from royal and papal authority. The local counts provided protection and dispute resolution in exchange for transit and trading fees. The predictability of the fairs facilitated the development of credit arrangements which expanded the volume of transactions that could be handled. Gradually, the protection offered to traders was extended to French territory outside the immediate fair's locale, which encouraged increased regional involvement.

As the fairs became the central market for regional European transactions, as well as the money market of Europe, they also helped to facilitate the interregional transfer of commodities from the Middle East and Asia to Europe. Textiles from northwestern Europe could be exchanged through this market for spices and other eastern luxury goods. As a consequence, Italian traders, led by the well-placed Genoese, assumed the role of principal intermediaries in these interregional exchanges. Italians could deliver the eastern goods because they controlled a number of Middle Eastern enclaves in Crusader-held territory (Abu-Lughod 1989, 108). This advantage gave them control over the flow of eastern goods into Europe and the fairs' circuit. Van der Wee (1990, 16) also noted that Italian traders gradually penetrated into the northwest European area giving them some degree of control over all intra-European transactions as well.

The fairs operated in the twelfth, thirteenth, and early fourteenth centuries before being replaced by a succession of other central markets in western Europe. A variety of factors came together in the late thirteenth century to decrease the attractiveness of the Champagne circuit. Increasing political interference by the French monarchy and the eventual assumption of royal control in 1285 led to increasing restrictions on the participation of non-French traders. At the same time, the Crusader enclaves in the Middle East were diminishing in number. Probably more significant was the development of the Atlantic route by the Genoese following the conquest of Andalusia by Castille. By breaking the Moslem stranglehold on the Straits of Gibraltar traffic in the early 1290s, a new route was created which began to be used regularly by the end of the thirteenth century to circumvent the need for more expensive and less safe overland transactions.[1]

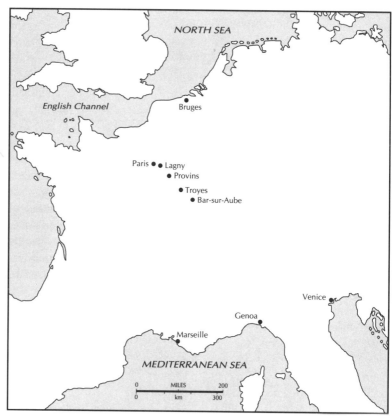

Figure 10.1. The Champagne Fairs

Shifting East-West Transaction Routes

Having previously introduced the Silk Roads in chapter 8, it remains to point out that the political-economic significance of the east-west transaction routes lay in their vulnerability to disruption by war. Only rarely were the several routes open simultaneously. Hence, whoever enjoyed the best position on the routes that were open when the others were closed was in a position to exploit its trade advantage and, quite often, restrict its rivals from equal access to the route. As a consequence, the twelfth through fifteenth centuries, from a Eurocentric perspective, can be seen as a sequence of oscillating monopolistic positions as first Venice, then Genoa, and then Venice again enjoyed relative edges in access to the operating east-west routes. A good deal of the oscillation must be attributed not so much to Italian ingenuity, but to actions and events over which the Italians frequently had little control.

From an Asian-centered perspective, the principal driving force of this period was the Mongol world empire. Once fully in place, after 1250 (figure 10.2), Mongol imperial rule made the routes of the overland Silk Roads secure. This lowered the costs of land transport which meant that the northern route to the West, opening on the Black Sea, was favored (see also table 8.2).

The thirteenth century Mongols offered neither strategic cross-roads location, unique industrial productive capacity, nor transport functions to the world economy. Rather their contribution was to create an environment that facilitated land transit with less risk and lower protective rent. By reducing these costs they opened a route for trade over their territories. (Abu-Lughod 1989, 154)

In actuality, the Mongols did more than merely eliminate the multiple and commercially predatory sovereignties through which the caravan routes had customarily run. From the outset, Mongol policy promoted trade in general as an important source of wealth creation and Mongol elite syndicates, recycling booty from Chinese raids, invested in caravans. While this preference for trade may seem unremarkable, it should be considered in the context of traditional East Asian insularity policies and the Mongols' own initial strategic preferences (Barfield 1989, 197–206).

Before the death of Genghis Khan in 1227, the usual interaction between nomadic warriors of Central Asia and neighboring agrarian states had been one of extortion and appeasement. The nomadic tribes would threaten more urbanized societies who, in turn, would prefer to buy off the raiders as the least costly route to security. The expansion of the Mongol Empire under Genghis Khan pursued this conventional strategy as well. The problem was that the military prowess of the Mongols—based on the development of new organizational principles, well-coordinated and highly mobile cavalry forces, psychological terrorism, and the opportunistic absorption of any innovations in military technology that were encountered—worked too well. Opponents were beaten too decisively to be extorted. Gradually, the Mongols became reluctant imperial administrators by default.

Temujin became a Mongolian leader as early as 1190 but did not begin his series of successful attacks on non-Mongol groups until 1204. Before that time, he had succeeded in uniting the Mongol tribes and had developed an army that was not organized around undependable tribal or family command structures. Instead, commanders were chosen on the basis of their demonstrated personal loyalty to Temujin—known as Genghis Khan after 1206. Within two decades, the Tanguts (Hsi-Hsia), the Jurchen Chin, the Kara Khitai, and the Persian Khwarezm had been conquered. In the following decade (the 1230s) attacks were launched against Korea, Sung China, Russia, and eastern Europe (early 1240s).

In some cases, the devastation wrought by Mongol attacks was quite intentional. Extortion works best when its victims do not resist. Resistance, therefore, needed to be punished severely. The early size of the Mongol armies was an additional restraint. Genghis Khan's armies grew to roughly 125,000, but in the face of even larger opponent armies, there was little temptation to siphon away troops for garrison police duties. Destroying offending cities thus killed two birds with one sword. Object lessons were made obvious and scarce troops were preserved for more mobile purposes.

There also seems to have been some early disputes and disagreements on the part of the Mongols on how best to maximize wealth. As they conquered more heavily populated areas of China, there was an initial instinct to simply eliminate peasant farmers in large numbers as a military nuisance and return their land to pasture. It required some persuasion to point out the enormous tax potential of permitting the peasants to cultivate their land. Eventually, and certainly by the time of the rise of Kublai Khan (a grandson of Genghis Khan named as grand khan in 1260) and the conquest of the southern Sung (1261–1279), Mongol policy had switched its wealth creation preferences from extortion to territorial expansion and domination.

Putting all of these ingredients together led to the creation of a world empire that stretched from the Pacific to eastern Europe and parts of the Middle East, as shown in figure 10.2. The spinal column of that empire was the Silk Road in its overland variant that had been in place for over a millennium. Even though the Mongols had destroyed much of the productive potential of large parts of Eurasia, and created no leading sectors of their own, they did encourage east-west trade via Central Asia. Huang (1990, 144) also claims that the maritime traffic of southern China peaked under their rule, but the subsequent repeated and massive diversion of shipping to unsuccessful expeditions against Japan and Java in the last third of the thirteenth century had to have taken its toll. According to Lewis (1988, 178), the scale of Chinese maritime trade after 1261 did not retain the levels recorded in the period immediately before then. When Mongol rule began to disintegrate, both the northern and the Persian Gulf routes suffered great disruptions, thereby decisively favoring those who plied the Red Sea branch of the maritime route.

In the eleventh and through the early twelfth centuries, Venice possessed a strong edge at the northern route's terminus (Constantinople) thanks to Venice's proximity and the naval services it provided to the Byzantine Empire. In exchange, the Venetians were granted substantial tax benefits (1082) that positioned them ahead even of Byzantine traders, but still excluded all foreign traders from the Black Sea. In 1204 the Venetians consolidated their favored position by leading the Fourth Crusade that attacked and seized Constantinople. From 1204 to 1261 the Venetians monopolized Black Sea trade. However, in 1261 a new Byzantine dynasty reconquered Constantinople with Genoese assistance (Treaty of Ninfeo) which helped to replace Venice with Genoa as the lead Italian city-state operating in this area—just as the Mongols were opening up the northern Silk Roads.

The European thrust south against Moslem controlled territories from about the eleventh century on was manifested differently in various parts of the Mediterranean. In the Iberian Peninsula, for example, it set in motion renewed efforts at *Reconquista* (the defeat and absorption of the Moorish kingdoms). In the Syrian-Palestinian sector, it resulted in the forceful creation of several Christian kingdoms that managed to survive through the twelfth and most of the thirteenth centuries. Facilitating these European incursions into the Middle East were several Italian city-states—Amalfi, Pisa, Genoa, and Venice—that provided maritime transportation and naval support. In return for their services, they were granted control over commercial enclaves in Palestinian and Levantine ports through which they were able to meet the rising demand for eastern goods in Europe which, in turn, was in part due to the expanded exposure to the luxury commodities afforded by participation in the Crusades.

In the second half of the thirteenth century the Mongol attack on Baghdad (1258) destroyed much of the utility of the Persian Gulf route. The eviction of the Europeans from their Crusader enclaves first by Saladin and then the Mamluks (1291) further depreciated the value of this route to Genoa and Venice. However, the Mongol peace in Central Asia made the northern route much more viable and lucrative after about 1250. The Genoese commercial ascen-

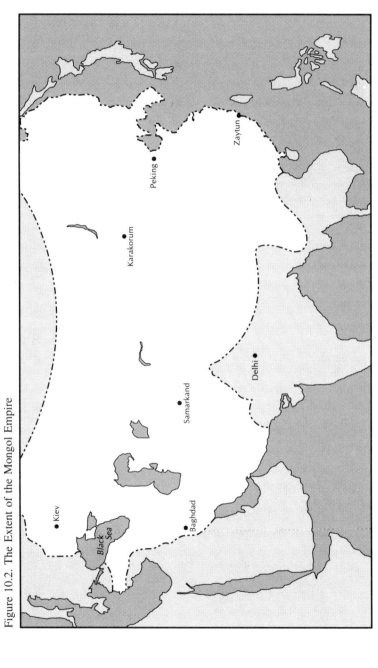

Figure 10.2. The Extent of the Mongol Empire

dancy in the Black Sea area (after 1261) meant that Genoa benefited dispro-
portionately, in comparison to its Italian rivals, from the newly established
security of the Central Asian route.

Dislodged from their commercial niches in Constantinople and Palestine,
the Venetians sought to make trade arrangements with the Mamluks who controlled the southern Red Sea route. Even here, the Genoese held an initial advantage due to their supply of Circassian slaves from the Black Sea area which
were needed to renew the Mamluk military slave caste in a period of major
battle casualties. As the military threat from the Mongols and the Christians
receded toward the end of the thirteenth century, so too did the need for Genoese slave replacements—replacements that could once again be secured
through overland routes. This development may help to explain the timing of
the burst of unsuccessful Genoese attempts to break the Mamluk control over
the Red Sea route in the 1290s.[2] In the same decade, a large contingent of
Genoese were building galleys in Persia so that the Mongol ruler of Persia
might interdict the Indian-Egyptian trade by blockading the Red Sea entrance
(in 1290). At the same time, a much smaller contingent, the Vivaldi brothers,
sailed down the northwest African coastline reportedly in an early attempt to
circumnavigate Africa (in 1291).

But then this same decade also witnessed Genoese penetration into the
African interior in search of gold (1291), the opening of the Straits by a Ge-
noese-Castilian fleet (1294), the second Venetian-Genoese War (1294–1299),
and the regularization of the Atlantic route to Bruges and Southampton
(1297). Scammell (1981, 165) may have the best systemic explanation. He argues that the improved Genoese position in the Black Sea generated an increasing supply of eastern goods that required payment in terms of bullion (the
search for African gold) and Flemish textiles (the opening of the Atlantic route
to Bruges), as well as more market outlets. Thus, Scammell interprets the
1290s as a period of economic reorganization on the part of the Genoese. Even
so, the Genoese trade network, shown in figure 10.3, effectively linked Asia,
Africa, and Europe.

Italian trade with the Middle East in the last quarter of the thirteenth and
first half of the fourteenth century was complicated by Papal bans on trading
with the enemy. The Italian trading states more or less respected the bans on
direct trade and instead resorted to indirect trade through intermediaries in Cyprus, Armenia, and even North Africa. Venice reestablished its Mamluk ties as
early as 1302, even though it did not resume direct trade with Alexandria until
the 1340s after Papal approval for its resumption was finally secured in 1344.
(The Venetian petition for a papal license claimed that the whole system of
world trade was threatened by the ban.)

Figure 10.3. The Genoese Network

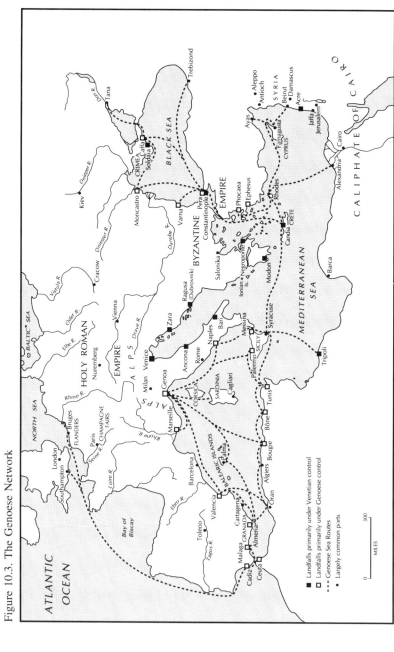

Landfalls primarily under Venetian control
Landfalls primarily under Genoese control
Genoese Sea Routes
Largely common ports

0   300
MILES

The 1340s ushered in a new era of change with the spread of the Black Death/bubonic plague throughout Eurasia. Just as the Mongol Empire had been an important agent in increasing Eurasian economic interdependence in the second half of the thirteenth century, it was an equally important agent of the rapid erosion of that interdependence a century later. Incubated in Central Asia around 1338 and spread initially by Mongol troops, the plague demonstrated the extent of world economic interdependence by spreading to China, India, Italy, Egypt, and Portugal within ten years (Lopez, Miskimin, and Udovitch 1970). The consequent loss of life—as much as 30 to 60 percent in Venice, Genoa, and Cairo—also encouraged the outbreak and/or persistence of depression and war from China to France. Civil war characterized the areas earlier conquered by the Mongols and ensured the diminished flow of trade through the northern and central routes. The rise of Timur in the late fourteenth century continued the turmoil surrounding the northern route. The southern, almost exclusively maritime, route controlled by the Mamluks was the main beneficiary as the routes requiring land movements became too insecure.

Yet one of the ironies of the devastation inflicted by the plague was an apparent increase in the per capita wealth of the European survivors and an inclination, among the elite at least, to spend more on luxuries (including spices). So, while the security of the land routes was disintegrating and the European population size was decreasing rapidly, the European demand for spices may actually have been increasing or not declining much.

In the two wars (1350–1355 and 1378–1381) between Venice and Genoa in competition over the remaining trade, Venice won the last war. While Genoese traders continued to compete with Venetians in Egypt, Genoa was unable to resume its eastern Mediterranean rivalry with Venice after 1381.[3] Between 1400 and the end of the fifteenth century, the Venetian-Mamluk connection intensified as Venice increased its control of the spice flow to Europe from less than 45 percent to between 60 and 70 percent (Scammell 1981, 104; Wake 1979, 1986).

The Commercial and Nautical Revolution

The last quarter of the thirteenth and the first quarter of the fourteenth centuries encompassed a period of rapid change in maritime technology and techniques that facilitated the expansion of Mediterranean trade by lowering transaction costs. The introduction of the compass made navigation possible in the winter when the stars were often obscured by clouds and storms. Improved charts with compass bearings became possible. New developments in steering (stern rudders), sails (square sails with reef points), and rigging made the construction of larger and more productive ships conceivable.[4] Lane (1987b, 240) described the typical Venetian galley before 1300 as consisting of a crew of 140 to 220 men with a carrying capacity of 20 tons. By 1320 the largest galleys carried 150 tons of cargo with a crew of about 150. A greater than sevenfold increase in cargo capacity with about the same or less labor input in a relatively short time must be viewed as an impressive productivity revolution.

In conjunction with the increasing interdependence of markets from the Black Sea area to northwest Europe, the Venetians are credited with developing a new approach to maritime commerce during this period. Taking advantage of the changes in nautical technology, the Venetians developed specialized, state-built, and state-owned merchant galleys by converting biremes into triremes between 1294 and 1318 (McNeill 1974).[5] Although these vessels were actually sailing vessels with multiple masts, galley oars were useful backup devices in case the wind died or the shore was too close to maneuver. Dedicated largely to conveying low-bulk, high-value goods such as spices, the galleys were leased each year to the highest bidder; they continued to be subject to state regulations on sailing times, fleet size, freight prices, the need to operate in convoys, and the requirement that all trade transit through Venice.[6] By the 1330s, this state-directed enterprise, which was concentrated on the most lucrative sector of Venetian trade, had become institutionalized and persisted for the next two centuries.

Through the mechanism of the galley line, Venice was able to manage intra-Venetian competition over the most profitable trade, develop a reputation as the most dependable and well-protected carrier of goods in the Mediterranean, establish itself as the primary European entrepot for spices and, eventually, establish a commercial hegemony in the eastern Mediterranean. The initial focus of these galley lines was in the Black Sea (Romanian) area and Cyprus. The principal focus shifted to Alexandria in the mid-fourteenth century. For instance, Scammell (1981, 104) notes that 60 percent of the state galley leases in the 1332–1345 period involved Black Sea destinations. In contrast, some 80 percent of the leases between 1410–1412 and 1443/1456 were linked to Levantine traffic.

A separate line to Beirut was added and the links to Flanders were also resurrected later in the fourteenth century. Lines to Naples/France/Barcelona (Aigues-Mortes) and North Africa (Barbary and Trafego) were added in the fifteenth century. As Lane (1973, 337) put it, the Venetian galley lines, sketched in figure 10.4, eventually covered all of the shores of the Mediterra-

Table 10.2

The Hypothesized Relationship Between the Italian Learning Long Cycle and
Lead Industries in the Twelfth Through Fifteenth Centuries

Learning Long Cycle	Lead Industries	Predicted "Start-up"	Predicted "High-growth"
Genoese			
K5	Champagne Fairs	1190–1220	1220–1250
K6	Black Sea trade	1250–1280	1280–1300
Venetian			
K7	Galley fleets	1300–1320	1320–1355
K8	Pepper	1355–1385	1385–1430

nean and the Straits of Dover.[7] Venice was not the only state to use galleys for commercial purposes in the Mediterranean. Other Italian states, including Genoa, used them as well. But Venice developed the most successful system and reaped the maximum advantage from its innovation until galleys became increasingly obsolete in the sixteenth century and the European significance of Mediterranean commerce declined in face of the increasingly favored Atlantic routes.

THE K-WAVE HYPOTHESES

We have two sets of hypotheses with four bursts of innovation between the end of the twelfth and the middle of the fifteenth centuries. These innovations were centered first on Genoese and then on Venetian trading operations with the geographical locus of the most important activities shifting from northern France to the Black Sea to Egypt. Yet throughout these shifts in location, the ultimate focus of leading sector trade for the European subsystem was the reordering of the flow of high value goods from Asia to Europe. Who carried the goods and which routes were used shifted from time to time; yet the identity of the goods—mostly spices—remained consistent.

Table 10.2 summarizes both sets of hypotheses. As in earlier chapters, we distinguish between a start-up and high-growth period essentially by dividing each Kondratieff period in two. We also advance a specific focus for leading sector activity in each period. Thus, we should expect to find the various types of transactional activities, beginning with the Champagne Fairs and moving to the Romanian and Levantine emphases, peaking in the twenty-five- to forty-year intervals specified in table 10.2.

Figure 10.4. The Venetian Network

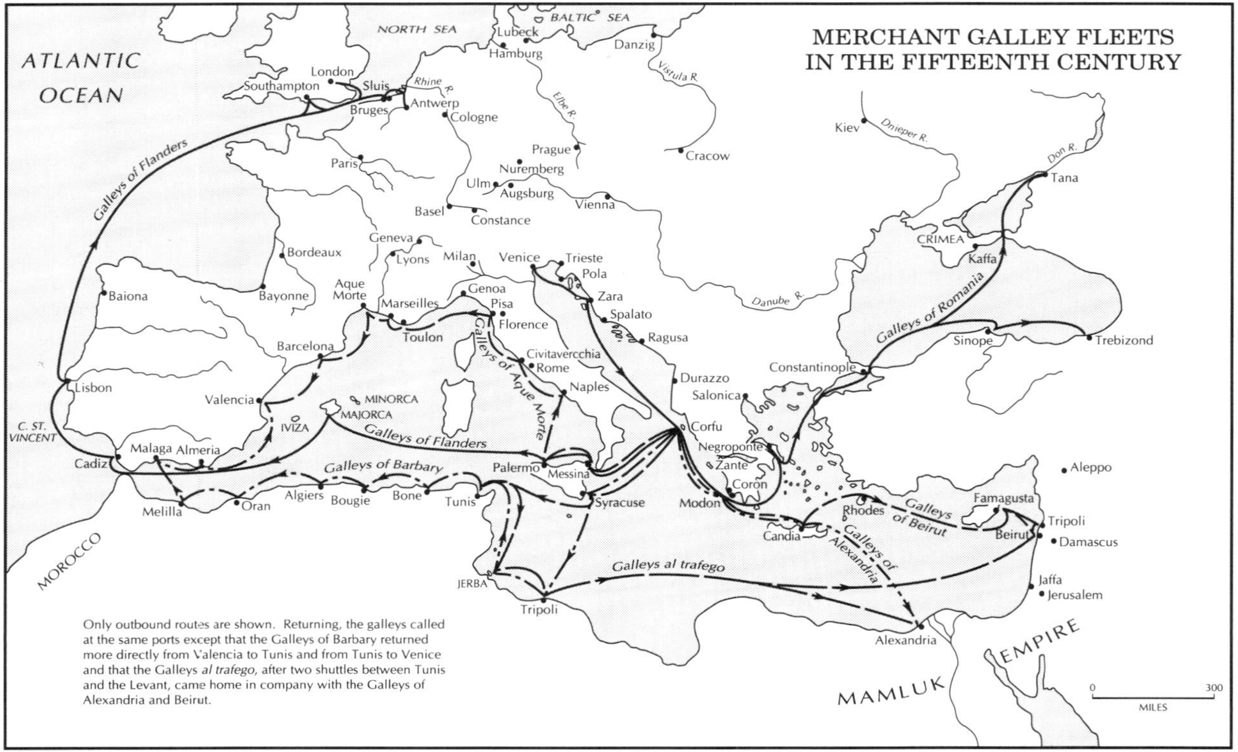

MERCHANT GALLEY FLEETS
IN THE FIFTEENTH CENTURY

Only outbound routes are shown. Returning, the galleys called at the same ports except that the Galleys of Barbary returned more directly from Valencia to Tunis and from Tunis to Venice and that the Galleys al trafego, after two shuttles between Tunis and the Levant, came home in company with the Galleys of Alexandria and Beirut.

The Question of Leadership

It is not absolutely crucial that we demonstrate the respective leads of Genoa and Venice. We might have simplified the hypotheses by referring more vaguely to the Italian city-states as a collective. But they did not operate as a collective and, while several states played prominent roles at different times (namely Amalfi, Pisa, and Florence), the primary action revolved around the rivalry of Genoa and Venice. Recognition of this armature for political-economic conflict in Mediterranean commerce also helps to justify the postulated shifts in leading sector activity.

Ideally, we might turn to series on the relative proportion of trade carried by the two Italian rivals to assess which city-state led and when. We do not have access to such information and even if it were available, it is quite likely that aggregate data would be misleading. While both states competed in the spice carrying trade, Genoa developed an affinity for bulkier, lower profit commodities such as alum. In contrast, the Venetians consistently specialized in luxury commodities. Consequently, an examination of the aggregate value of goods carried without considering differential profits might suggest a Genoese lead longer than was appropriate.

Unfortunately, we also lack series on commercial profits or sectoral dominance which would make comparisons more meaningful. Instead, we have culled a set of observations by several authorities on the economic history of southern European/Mediterranean trade that are displayed in table 10.3. The leadership picture outlined is not subject to much dispute. Genoa attained a political-commercial lead in the thirteenth century and maintained it into the next. The fourteenth century was one of economic-leadership transition with Venice catching up to and eventually surpassing Genoa's control of the spice trade around the last quarter of the century. Venice's great political and commercial ascendancy was won in the third and fourth wars with Genoa (which ended in 1381), peaked in the second decade of the fifteenth century, and persisted until disrupted by the Portuguese at the turn of the sixteenth century.

Ashtor (1983) provides some useful information on the number of European merchants operating in Alexandria in the first half of the fifteenth century. Table 10.4 summarizes some of his data by eliminating information on merchants from other Italian city-states, Marseilles, and Barcelona and focusing only on the Venetian-Genoese transition. At the turn of the century, Venetian merchants were still outnumbered by their Genoese counterparts. By a decade or two later, the ratio had changed decisively in favor of Venice.

Table 10.3

Literature Indications of Italian Leadership Shifts

In the mid-1100s Genoa was equaled in Italy only by Pisa and Venice; by 1200 Pisa had been surpassed and Venice overtaken (Scammell 1981).

Genoa sent 63 galleys and 163 other vessels against Spanish Saracens in 1147–1148. In 1242 83 galleys, 13 "tariden," and 4 great cargo ships were sent against the Pisa-Sicilian fleet (Sombart 1924, 349).

After 1250 the Venetian control of routes and its maritime supremacy was fiercely contested by Genoa; before 1250 their rivalry had been muted by a mutual concern for Pisa (Lane 1973).

By the Treaty of Ninfeo (in 1261) with the new ruler of Byzantium, Michael Palaeologus, Genoa attained "maritime primacy in the Mediterranean" (Negri 1974, 381).

In 1263 Genoa was maintaining 60 war galleys in Greek waters; twenty years later (in 1283) as many as 199 galleys were in service in various theaters (Sombart 1924, 349).

Genoa defeated Pisa decisively at sea off Meloria in 1284 when a Genoese fleet (88 galleys commanded by Oberto Doria and Bernadetto Zaccaria) routed the Pisan navy (72 galleys commanded by Alberto Moresini and Ugolino della Gherardesa, all but 20 of which were lost) (Negri 1974).

In 1285 Genoa had 12,085 men in service with the fleet out of Riviera: 9,991 oarsmen, 2,615 soldiers, and 279 mates (*nauclerii*) working 65 galleys and 1 galleon (Sombart 1924, 349).

Genoa maintained supremacy in European trade with the Levant during the second half of the thirteenth century and peaked at the end of the century (Ashtor 1983).

A Genoan fleet under Lamba Doria (78 galleys) inflicted defeat upon the Venetian fleet under Andrea Dandolo (98 galleys) at Curzola in 1298 (Negri 1974).

Gold coinage appeared at Genoa in 1252, the first gold coin in Western Europe (Negri 1974, 366); also at Florence in 1252 and Venice in 1284 (Lane 1973, 148).

In the middle and second half of the fourteenth century, Genoa was still the most important actor in trade between Europe and Egypt; after 1370 Venice took over the lead (Ashtor 1983).

The Mediterranean trade in very valuable commodities was contested between Venice and Genoa throughout the 1300s, but in the 1400s this trade became the exclusive preserve of Venice (Scammell 1981).

By the end of the fourteenth century Venice had the greatest share of southern European-Middle Eastern trade, but it still had not gained supremacy in Levantine trade. Catalonia was in economic decline from about 1412 on (Ashtor 1983).

Venice became the leading commercial and financial center of Europe from the second quarter of the fifteenth century (Van der Wee 1990).

In the second half of the fifteenth century the supremacy of Venice in the Levantine trade was almost crushing (Ashtor 1983).

Table 10.4

Venetian and Genoese Merchants in Alexandria

Years	Venetian	Genoese	Total	Venetian Proportion
1400–06	178	197	375	.475
1415–22	246	69	315	.781
1426–28	130	52	182	.714
1434–35	70	25	95	.737
1455–56	61	19	80	.763

Data source: Ashtor 1983, 142, 229, 242, 253, 359.

The Rhythm of Economic Expansion and Contraction

While we lamented the absence of serial information on the question of commercial leadership, we actually do possess serial information on some aspects of the timing of economic expansion and contraction in Italian commerce. Regrettably, these series do not encompass the heyday of the Champagne Fairs. Once again, we are forced to rely on various clues found in the economic history literature. The clues listed in table 10.5 are not numerous and are more specific on the decline of the fairs than they are on their rise. The fairs gradually took shape throughout the twelfth century. The flow of north European textiles to Genoa as early as the mid-twelfth century suggests the east-west linkage function began equally early. The advent of the Italians in an organized fashion in the last quarter of the century, in step with the extension of the safe conducts throughout France, suggests that the essential ingredients for a centralized marketplace were fully in place by the second quarter of the thirteenth century.

The increasing politicization of the fairs in the second half of the thirteenth century signaled the increasing decline of their utility. The fairs had been able to perform their central market function in part because they enjoyed some degree of insulation from political interference. As the insulation eroded, especially in conjunction with the opening of the Black Sea and Atlantic trade routes, other venues would become more attractive.

Thus, we can bracket the likely peak of the Champagne Fairs activity as occurring sometime after the first quarter (when its structural features were still coming together) and some time before the third quarter (when the local politicization was beginning and, not coincidentally, when alternatives were emerging) of the thirteenth century. This bracket points to the second quarter (1225–1250) as the most likely peaking period. The predicted interval was

Table 10.5
Literature Clues on the Rise and Fall of the Champagne Fairs

Italian new wall construction peaked in 1150–1200; northern European new wall construction peaked in 1200–1250 (Lopez and Miskimin 1962).

Some semblance of the Champagne Fairs can be dated at least from 1114 with the basic institutional patterns begin established by the middle of the twelfth century. By the middle of the thirteenth century, the Fairs were fully operative (Abu-Lughod 1989).

In 1191 Henry of Champagne became "virtual ruler of Outremer" (Kingdom of Jerusalem, Acre, and Cyprus); when he died, Tibald III, his younger brother, launched the Fourth Crusade in 1197 but died in 1202 before it started; the marshall of Champagne negotiated the logistics of the campaign with Venice (at a price of 84,000 silver marks) (Norwich 1983).

"The Champagne Fairs . . . reached their height in the second half of the 13th century . . . they became . . . the money market of Europe" (Pirenne 1937, 102, 101).

Flemish cloth was arriving in Genoa in large quantities via the Champagne Fairs by the mid-twelfth century; as early as the late twelfth century caravans of Italian merchants were attending the Champagne Fairs (Abu-Lughod 1989).

Safe conducts associated with trading at the Champagne Fairs became increasingly nationalized (throughout France) between 1180 and 1223 (Miskimin 1975).

The Central Asian trade route was opened in 1250 (Abu Lughod 1989); By 1277 Genoa had reached the English Channel and began to open a new and revolutionary commercial route (Scammell 1981).

The Champagne Fairs increasingly became politicized after 1262 due initially to Franco-Flemish tensions. They began to lose their competitive edge in 1285 when French royal jurisdiction was assumed (Abu-Lughod 1989); The Champagne Fairs had begun to decline after the end of the thirteenth century (Van der Wee 1990); The Champagne Fairs were in rapid decline after the beginning of the fourteenth century (Bernard 1976).

1220–1250. While the evidence is neither direct nor compelling, the predicted fit, at least, seems quite good.

Fortunately, we have more direct evidence for the other hypothesized innovational peaks. We have good reason to believe that Black Sea trade expanded in the second half of the thirteenth century. The *Pax Mongolia* facilitated the increased overland flow of goods from the east after 1250. The ascendancy of the Genoese over the Venetians at Constantinople after 1261 positioned the Genoese to take the utmost advantage of the Black Sea opening to the east. During the same time, they were also pioneering a new route to northern Europe through the

Table 10.6
Literature Indications of Economic Expansion and
Contraction in the Second Half of the Thirteenth Century

The Central Asian trade route was opened in 1250 (Abu Lughod 1989).

In Florence the entire 1250–1320 period was a period of economic expansion (Verseth 1990).

In southern Europe the period of 1248–1254 was a period of economic upswing while 1255–1262 was a period of downswing (Lopez 1987).

Although Venice began to expand the Black Sea trade in 1204, the trade underwent a large scale expansion only after 1261 (McNeill 1974).

By 1277 Genoa had reached the English Channel and began to open a new and revolutionary commercial route (Scammell 1981).

Both Venice and Genoa experienced commercial expansion in the 1270–1290 period (Lane 1973); Between 1214 and 1274 the volume of Genoese trade doubled, but between 1274 and 1293 the volume quadrupled (Scammell 1981); Genoese trade probably reached the peak of its rapid rise in the last ten years of the thirteenth century (Luzzato 1961).

In southern Europe 1280–1298 was a period of economic upswing while 1299–1320 was one of contraction (Lopez 1987).

Straits of Gibraltar to Bruges and Southampton. Table 10.6 is supportive of these generalizations and takes us one step further in pinpointing the last quarter of the century as the peak of Genoese trade expansion.

As it happens, it is possible to be even more specific about the Genoese trade peak. While data on the Black Sea trade per se does not appear to have survived, we do have serial information on the anticipated volume of trade entering the Genoese port (Kedar 1976; Lopez and Miskimin 1962), which is plotted in figure 10.5. Corroborating the information provided in table 10.6, figure 10.5 highlights the 1290s as the peak Genoese decade over some two hundred years. Other peaks are suggested (for example, the 1370s and 1400s), but these subsequent spikes in trading activities tend to be related to temporary postwar expansions. There is also the problem of Genoese currency devaluation that makes longitudinal comparison trickier. Lopez and Miskimin (1962) calculated that the value of the Genoese pound had declined some 75 percent between 1288 and 1509. This means that the peaks after the 1290s would be reduced substantially if the data were corrected for currency debasement. For our purposes, the main implication of these considerations is that we need to look elsewhere for innovational peaks in the fourteenth century. Only the

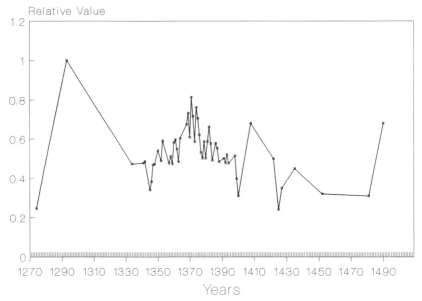

Figure 10.5. Estimated Value of Genoese Trade Indexed as a Proportion of 1293 Values

1290s peak is truly impressive in figure 10.5. Genoese trade through the end of the fifteenth century seems to have been on a consistent downward spiral relieved only by temporary upswings.[8]

According to table 10.7, the last quarter of the thirteenth and the first quarter of the fourteenth centuries was a period of major maritime and commercial revolution in the Mediterranean theater. Still, this same period does not appear to have been an era of consistent economic expansion. The economic history literature suggests a period of upturn in the 1280s and 1290s, followed by some level of contraction in the first two decades of the fourteenth century and then another upswing in the quarter century (1320–1346) immediately preceding the arrival of the Black Death. Although there may have been a brief respite in the 1350s, the period from the late 1340s to the early 1380s is described as a long downswing. A new upswing, at least for Venice, is supposed to have begun in the 1380s and may have continued more or less uninterrupted through about 1430. Ashtor (1983), however, does state that the Levantine trade boom peaked in the 1390s.

One of the more significant expressions of the changes in which maritime commerce was conducted in the general Mediterranean was the development of the Venetian galley lines. Ashtor (1983) provides a good deal of informa-

Table 10.7

Literature Indications of Economic Expansion and
Contraction in the Fourteenth and Fifteenth Centuries

In sourthern Europe 1280–1298 was a period of economic upswing while
1299–1320 was one of contraction (Lopez 1987).

The principal impact of the commercial revolution was experienced between 1275
and 1325 (Bernard 1976); between 1280 and 1330 Mediterranean ship design
underwent fundamental changes; a series of innovations drastically cheapened
transportation costs (McNeill 1974).

The 1320–1346 period was among the most prosperous in Venetian commercial history
(McNeill 1974); the commercial revolution crested before 1346 (Lopez 1987).

Italian economic contraction began after the 1330s (Bernard 1976); in Florence the
1330s to 1340s were a period of contraction, famine, financial collapse, crop
failures, famine, and plague (Verseth 1990).

Venice experienced a period of plague, war, and depression that began in 1347; the
levels of population and trade reached before that data were not reached again until
1420 and perhaps not even then (Lane 1987a); Venice was an exception to the
general malaise of post-plague trade and industry (Bernard 1976).

The 1350–1369 period in Florence was characterized by economic stabilization and
rising wages for workers (Verseth 1990).

There was a shortlived sharp increase in Italian demand after 1355 (Lopez 1987).

The 1370s in Florence were characterized by recession, war, famine, and plague
(Verseth 1990).

After decades of hard times, the end of war in 1381 marked the beginning of a
Venetian upturn (Lane 1987a); a period of Venetian commercial prosperity
comparable to the decades prior to the Black Death began after 1381 (McNeill
1974); the late 1380s were relatively prosperous in Florence (Verseth 1990).

The Levantine trade boom peaked in the 1390s (Ashtor 1983).

Around 1409 Venetian trade and wealth had recovered—if not to the levels
preceding the Black Death then at least to the range and volume prior to the onset
of the Venetian-Genoese war ending in 1381 (Lane 1973); in Florence the
1413–1423 years were relatively prosperous ones (Verseth 1990).

The second quarter of the fifteenth century was the period of greatest growth in
Venetian trade with the Levant (Ashtor 1983); all aspects of Venetian maritime life
expanded until about 1430 (Lane 1973); in Florence, the 1434–1464 period was
marked by intermittent growth and relative prosperity (Verseth 1990); the luxury
market seems to have weakened by the middle of the fifteenth century making it a
bleak period for Venice (Bernard 1976).

Table 10.8

Selected Venetian Galley Sailing Activity, 1328–1498

Years	Romania	Cyprus-Armenia	Alexandria	Beirut	Joint Alexandria-Beirut
1328–1330	24	24			
1331–1340	88	75			
1341–1350	48	44	16		
1351–1360	19	20	20		
1361–1370	46	26	28		
1371–1380	26	8	20		
1381–1390	23		14	35	
1391–1400	21		29	46	
1401–1410			30	28	
1411–1420			34	37	
1421–1430			23	31	7
1431–1440			25	24	13
1441–1450			34	27	
1451–1460			33	36	
1461–1470			30	35	
1471–1480			39	32	
1481–1490			46	33	
1491–1498			32	24	

Data Source: Ashtor 1983, 55, 79, 116–17, 318, 474.

tion on the frequency of galley traffic in the lines that were most critical to the transportation of spices between Asia, the Middle East, and the Venetian entrepot. Table 10.8 summarizes the shipping activity for four lines: Romania (Black Sea), Cyprus-Armenia, Alexandria, and Beirut. The Romanian and Cyprus-Armenian lines did not disappear completely toward the end of the fourteenth century as the table suggests, but the traffic level did decline precipitously reflecting a transition in favored trade routes from Asia Minor to the Middle East and especially Egypt.[9]

It would be a simple matter to test the literature's upswing/downswing schedule with the galley traffic level data if the ships had remained the same size throughout the fourteenth and fifteenth centuries—but they did not. Lane (1987b, 240) states that the cargo carrying capacity of the galleys was roughly 20 tons prior to 1300 and expanded to about 300 tons in the second half of the fifteenth century. More specifically, he gives the following cargo expansion schedule:

pre-1300:   20 tons of cargo

post-1300:   50 tons of cargo
by 1320:   150 tons of cargo
after 1450:   300 tons of cargo

Obviously, a focus on shipping frequency would understate changes in shipping volume. Thus, some adjustments or weighting of the frequency data is necessary. Lane's cargo expansion schedule, regrettably, is less than precise and therefore requires some interpretation. For instance, it is doubtful that all galleys carried 150 tons by 1320. Rather, we interpret Lane as noting that some ships had attained this size by that date. We also have the impression that galley shipping on the Asian Minor lines tended to be consistently smaller than those utilized on Levantine lines. Both of these considerations suggest a conservative weighting scheme. Accordingly, we have adopted the following schedule:

1320–1370:   100 tons
1380–1420:   150 tons
1420–1460:   200 tons
1460–1500:   250 tons

Applying these volume weights to the galley traffic frequency summarized in table 10.8 and merging the two eastern and southern lines yields the estimated galley shipping volume data reported in table 10.9 and plotted in figure 10.6. At least three peaks are evident in figure 10.6: the first one is associated with the Romanian galleys in the 1330s and the second one is found in the Levantine traffic in the 1390s. A very brief downturn is recorded in the 1400s, followed by further expansion that stagnates slightly in the 1430s and 1440s. A long expansion begins after 1450 peaking (for the third time) in the 1480s.

The peaks in the 1330s and 1390s correspond to the upswings postulated in the economic history literature (see table 10.7). More to the point, they also correspond to the K-wave predictions advanced in table 10.2. K7 was predicted to peak between 1325 and 1350 and K8 was predicted to peak between 1390 and 1430. Both predictions prove quite accurate.

But what about the third peak in the 1480s? Is this one peak too many which thereby dilutes the success of the first two predictions? Two features of the fifteenth century suggest that this is not the case. First, prices and profits in the spice trade need to be taken into consideration. Evidence of the price of spices suggests that it fluctuated, but tended to decrease in the fifteenth century. From this, one may assume that profits declined—at least in comparison to earlier decades. Scammell (1981, 104) notes a fifty-percent drop in pepper prices between 1420 and 1440, and even further decreases by the end of the century.

A second consideration is that the first Portuguese K-wave was found to peak in the 1480s as well. When we are examining our selected indicators of

Table 10.9

Venetian Galley Traffic and Estimated Volume

Years	Romanian Galleys		Levantine Galleys	
	Number	Volume	Number	Volume
1328–1330	48	4,800		
1331–1339	163	16,300		
1341–1349	112	11,200	16	1,600
1351–1359	39	3,900	20	2,000
1360–1369	72	7,200	28	2,800
1370–1379	34	3,400	20	2,000
1380–1389	23	3,450	49	7,350
1390–1399	21	3,150	75	11,250
1400–1409			58	8,700
1410–1419			71	10,650
1420–1429			61	12,200
1430–1439			62	12,400
1440–1449			61	12,200
1450–1459			69	13,800
1460–1469			65	16,250
1470–1479			71	17,750
1480–1489			79	19,750
1490–1499			56	16,800

Note: The volume estimates are predicted on the following cargo weighting schedule: 100 tons through the 1370s; 150 tons from the 1380s through the 1410s; 200 tons from the 1420s through the 1450s; and 250 tons from the 1460s through the 1490s. Romanian galleys include those sent to Cyprus and Armenia as well as the Romanian line. The Levantine galleys column combines the Alexandrian and Beirut lines.

K-wave activity, we need to keep in mind the likelihood that these innovational surges are likely to be reflected elsewhere. Since our argument is that lead economy innovations periodically stimulate the world economy, we would be surprised if we did not find similar upswings in other parts of the system. In this particular case, the connection is not difficult to fathom. The Portuguese search for gold reflected a more general European balance-of-payments difficulty in importing Eastern luxury commodities, especially spices. An increase in the stock of European precious metals, to which the Portuguese made some contribution, would permit some increase in European spice consumption—a phenomenon to which the Portuguese made an even greater contribution in the early sixteenth century.

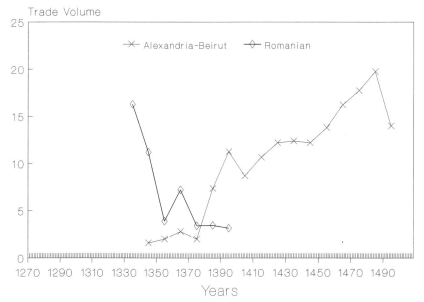

Figure 10.6. Estimated Venetian Galley Trade Volume on Selected Lines

In sum, we have postulated four Italian K-waves—two Genoese and two Venetian. We have not argued that these K-waves were exclusively Genoese or Venetian in nature, but that each respective wave was led by one or the other city-states, in competition with each other and with other Italian, French, and Catalonian rivals. In each case, we have predicted periods of start-up and high growth and have attempted to find evidence that pertinent economic activities peaked in the appropriate intervals. Table 10.10 summarizes the outcome.

Table 10.10 indicates that our predictions have been successful in four out of four trials. Admittedly, the data are less than perfect and in the first case (the Champagne Fairs) nonexistent. In each case, the evidence that can be mustered appears to bear out the K-wave chronology with very little in the way of qualification being necessary. Moreover, the linkages to the preceding Chinese economic innovations and the later West European innovations can be made without stretching credulity. Even if there was no diffusion of innovations from China to the Mediterranean, there was at least an increase of Chinese production that could be sent to the west, and there was very clearly a Mongolian facilitation of the movement of these goods. Each of the four Italian K-waves concerned innovations in the ways in which east-west commerce could be conducted. Portugal and its successors merely continued the trend or

Table 10.10

Predicted Versus Observed Growth Peaks in Italian Lead Industries

Learning Long Cycle	Leading Industry Indicators	Predicted "High-growth"	Observed Growth Peak
Genoese			
K5	Estimated rise and decline of the Champagne Fairs	1220–1250	second quarter of the 13th century
K6	Estimated Genoa trade volume	1275–1300	1290s
Venetian			
K7	Romanian galley fleet traffic	1325–1350	1330s
K8	Levantine galley fleet traffic	1390–1430	1390s

perturbations originally set in motion by northern and southern Sung innovations.

One last interpretive issue remains. How should we interpret the macrodecision/global war phases in the Italian cases? Should we expect to find full-fledged global wars as in the modern era? And if we do not, does it suggest that the periodicity schedule is a figment of our analytical imagination? Perhaps not surprisingly, our answer to both questions is negative. While the global wars of the modern era were quite destructive affairs, they did not begin in the late fifteenth century as bloody as they were to become in the twentieth century. Therefore, the considerable evolution and escalation in global war lethality over the last five centuries suggest we need not be looking for the direct equivalents of a World War II in the thirteenth and fourteenth centuries.

However, what we should expect to find in 1250–1279 and 1350–1384 are periods of crises that lead to something resembling the resolution of contested systemic leadership—albeit on a more constrained geographical scope than is customary after 1494. In the first macrodecision period of this era (1250–1279), the competition between Genoa and Venice escalated considerably after 1250. Their first war was fought, appropriately enough, between 1257 and 1270. Although none of the Genoese-Venetian regional wars were all that decisive from a military perspective, Genoa clearly gained the upper hand in the Black Sea theater by supporting the winning side in a Byzantine internal struggle while Venice backed the losing side. During this same period, Genoa's commercial edge throughout the eastern Mediterranean, which was what the two city-states were fighting about, became readily apparent.

Concurrently, the conquests of Baghdad in West Asia and the southern Sung in East Asia gave the Mongols uncontested control over the bulk of Eurasia. These were military operations of global significance deserving the appellation of proto-global wars. Symbolically, they marked the high-water point of Mongol rule and its impact on the trade routes. It would be inaccurate to place that impact solely within the 1250–1279 phase. The Mongol conquests began in earnest in the second decade of the thirteenth century. Yet their full impact upon Mediterranean trade was not realized until after 1261 and the ascent of Genoa at Constantinople.

Thus, it seems appropriate to argue that Genoa moved significantly ahead of Venice in the Eastern Mediterranean region roughly between 1250 and 1279. In that sense, what we are calling the macrodecision phase (see table 10.11) is associated with the clear emergence of Genoese leadership that aligned itself with the Mongols in the Black Sea area. Much the same happened in the 1350–1385 macrodecision phase, except that it was now the Venetians who pulled ahead of the Genoese, and they did so in part because the Mongols were now in an advanced stage of disintegration—a condition to which Timur (d. 1405) made a particularly significant contribution.

The third and fourth Venetian-Genoese Wars (1350–1355 and 1378–1381, respectively) were fought within this 1350–1385 interval. Again, the wars were less than decisive from a military perspective. Yet it was equally clear that Venice survived the fourth war while Genoa virtually collapsed due to a number of factors including Venetian naval prowess. After the 1378–1381 war Venice was faced with significantly less competition in the Eastern Mediterranean. Venice's political-commercial leadership had been established.

Just as the Genoese-Venetian competition of 1250–1279 took place within the larger context of Mongol expansion, so too did the Italian conflict of 1350–1384. But where the thirteenth-century development led to a Mediterranean economic upswing, the fourteenth-century developments created an economic environment characterized by general depression. The primary causal agent was the transmission of the Black Death, probably initiated in campaigns in Burma, that was carried to the Black Sea by Mongol troops and then diffused throughout the Mediterranean by Italian commercial interactions. The resulting level of societal crisis was so great that one analyst (J. W. Thompson 1921), writing in the 1920s, argued that only the ravages of World War I approximated the impact of the plague in the late 1340s.

Table 10.11

Italian Long Cycles, K-Waves, and Transition Crises

Long Cycle K-Wave	Transition Crises in the Mediterranean	in the Mongol World
	1204 Constantinople falls to Fourth Crusade	1206–1226 Wars of Genghis Khan
LC3 Genoa K5 Champagne Fairs 1190–1250		
	1250– Genoa-Venice wars 1284–90 Pisa routed	1258 Mongols sack Baghdad 1268-79 Mongols conquer Southern Sung
K6 Black Sea Trade 1250–1300		
	1291 Mamluks seize Acre 1309 Popes to Avignon	
LC4 Venice K7 Galley Fleets 1300–50		
	1343–54 economic depression 1346 Black Death 1353–81 third and fourth of Genoa and Venice wars	1367 Mongols expelled from China 1381 Timur conquers Persia
K8 Pepper 1350–1420		
	1423–54 Venice, Florence wars with Milan 1453 Ottomans seize Constantinople	
LC5 Portugal		

Predicted periods of macrodecision: 1250–1280, 1350–1385.

This comparison to global war is most interesting and reminds us that major societal crisis can come in a variety of forms. The question is whether the outcome is similar. In this case, it is similar because the Black Death played an important role in once again realigning east-west trade routes and promoting the ascent of Venetian commercial leadership over Genoa. At that time, Genoa was beset by plague from the East, bitter conflict with Venice, depressed trad-

Table 10.12
K-Waves and Innovations in the Commercial-Nautical Revolutions

K Wave	Innovations
K5 Champagne Fairs 1190–	Map out West European economic space; Create European money market; gold coinage in Genoa and Florence (1252); Double-entry bookkeeping.
K6 Black Sea, Atlantic trade 1250–	Pioneering East-West and North-South shipping around the coasts of Europe; charts, compass; Transmission of innovations from China via northern Silk Roads.
K7 Galley fleets 1300–	Regular Venetian merchant galley convoys after 1320.
K8 Pepper 1350–	Institutionalization of pepper trade with Mamluks at Alexandria.

ing conditions in general (especially in nearby France thanks to the Hundred Years War), and intense domestic political turmoil.

The Italian macrodecision phases, as a consequence, differ not so much in the presence or absence of significant warfare from the macrodecision phases that preceded and followed them. Warfare played a major role in every macrodecision. However, the difference is that the Genoese-Venetian wars cannot claim all the credit for the specific outcomes in leadership transition. The respective Genoese and Venetian ascents were assisted greatly by the outcomes of warfare outside the Eastern Mediterranean subsystem—especially so by developments in the Mongol world. As we move away from the early Eurasian transition era and into the West European era (see table 9.4), the locus of leadership transition conflicts gradually became less sensitive to external warfare impacts.

The movement certainly was not immediate. The Portuguese search for a route to the East was influenced by the effects of Ottoman expansion on Venetian commerce. In a different sense, the Portuguese movement down the African coast and into the Indian Ocean was greatly influenced by the innovations associated with the commercial and nautical revolutions summarized in table 10.12, and, of course, their political-economic consequences. The Portuguese did not discover Asia; they developed a new route in order to better control a trading system that had been revitalized, as far as western Europe was concerned, in the twelfth through fourteenth centuries.

The slow development of effective resistance to the Portuguese in the Indian Ocean may also have been influenced by Venetian-Ottoman-Mameluke conflict in the first twenty-five years after the Portuguese arrival. Along related lines, the timing of the late-sixteenth-century global war was affected by the relative conclusion of Spanish-Ottoman conflict in the Mediterranean after Lepanto. Increasingly, though, the macrodecision phase became more intensely concerned strictly with the devastation wrought by its own agents in struggles over the leadership of the global system.

We now have a cohesive argument and considerable documentation that K-waves, global wars, and nationally based global system leadership have been interdependent for some time. Should we assume that they will continue to be equally interdependent in the future? What leading sectors will carry the next K-wave? Will innovation continue to be a national monopoly? Should we expect another global war to follow the next K-wave? Our answers to these questions must be less than definitive. We do not claim any unusual access to a crystal ball. What we do have, however, is an empirically supported theory and a thousand years of historical experience to guide our speculations about the near future in the next and final chapter.

Part Five

LOOKING AHEAD

Chapter Eleven

The Nineteenth K-Wave
and No Global War?

Table 8.1 has shown a K-wave starting in 1973 and reaching peak performance in the years after 2000. That is the estimate inferred from the postulated phasing of the long cycle, but it is also close to the consensus of K-wave studies of the past decade. This means that the start-up portion of a new K-wave is now underway, the early shape of the leading sectors of the near future should now be visible, and the probable shape of the new technological paradigm could now be estimated.

What are the emerging lead industries of the K-wave that will reach a plateau at about 2030? This is an important question. Good answers to it should enable us to pick the winners—those industries that would be not just the national champions of the coming decades, but also the core of global economic leadership. Such knowledge would surely be important for public policy.

THE NUCLEAR POWER AND SPACE INDUSTRIES

Over the course of the Cold War, now ended, industrial competition between the United States and the Soviet Union prominently centered on two sectors: nuclear power and space. In both countries these two industries enjoyed generous public support. Both had obvious and urgent military applications in the present, but both also appeared at various times as possible leading sectors of the future.

The developmental potential of nuclear energy has been clear at least since August 1945. In that year, President Harry S Truman, in his statement announcing the use of the first nuclear weapon at Hiroshima, declared that atomic energy may, in the future after "a long period of intensive research," supplement "the power that now comes from coal, oil, and falling water"—becoming "a powerful and forceful influence towards the maintenance of world peace" (Truman 1961, 197–200). Intensive research brought forth experimental power reactors in the 1950s and commercial nuclear power in the 1960s. Half a century after World War II, nuclear power stations are a familiar, if sometimes feared, part of the industrial landscape.

Close to 20 percent of U.S. electric power now comes from more than one hundred power reactors that constitute the world's largest nuclear power industry (followed by the former Soviet Union and France), but they still only supplement—and do not supplant—the more conventional forms of energy. Fusion power, once thought just over the horizon, but still absorbing large research funds, is now expected by the mid-twenty-first century. In the meantime, and in the wake of the oil shocks and widespread public concern, attention has shifted to alternative sources of energy (such as solar). Important as cheap energy is to modern society, nuclear power does not appear to be delivering it at this time or serving as the defining element of a new sociotechnical paradigm.

The rapid expansion of the space industry is another product of heavily subsidized cold-war competition. Aided by military demand for large missiles and observation satellites, space was a $40 billion industry in the late 1980s. In the west, the United States accounted for 80 percent of the space industry. The main commercial thrust of that industry is, of course, not outward toward the stars, but rather earthward toward telecommunications where it plays an important but not irreplaceable part (because optical fiber and cellular telephone systems might soon substitute for some of its functions). Though it is unlikely to serve as the defining element of a new paradigm either, it might constitute some part of it.

We might add that in the past half-century the former Soviet Union had acquired, at great expense, both a large nuclear industry and a substantial space program. The power industry, after Chernobyl, appears to be operating below world standards. The Russian space program still executes frequent launches and operates a space station, but its status and future appear uncertain. Joint projects with the United States are the path for the next decade or so.

A heavy investment in what, to many theorists, appeared to be leading sectors does not seem to have yielded substantial rewards; it did not give the old Soviet Union a vibrant or even moderately successful economy and yielded no global economic leadership. It appears that attempting to pick winners—without reference to broader factors, or lacking other supporting conditions such as a market economy, open society, or free polity—does not really work.[1]

Table 11.1

Leading Sectors in the Current K-Wave

Mensch (1979, 203): A "hard" transition toward "hyperindustrialization" is more likely than a nontechnical, "soft" transition toward a post-industrial society with a "participative economy."

Kurth (1979, 33): "An obvious candidate for the next great leap forward is the telecommunications industry."

Timbergen (1983: 19): "Attention is focussed on microprocessors."

Ray (1983, 188): Not microprocessors but energy, food, and environment.

van Duijn (1983b, 23): Microelectronics is a sector that is growing during this depression.

Hall (1985, 16): Future industrial growth lies in "computer applications, information systems, and automatic control (robotics)."

Bruckmann (1987, 3): New K-wave carried by "microelectronics, robotics and bioengineering."

Yakovets (1987, 290): Major breakthroughs possible in microelectronics and biotechnology.

Freeman (1987, 302–3): New paradigm of information technology most apparent in electronics, and especially in computer and electronic component industries. Also in scientific instruments, telecommunications, and watch industries.

Goldstein (1988, 353): "The next leading sector might most plausibly be the information sector in telecommunications, computers, and biogenetics."

Thompson (1990, 232): "Biotechnology, computers, robotics, lasers, and new sources of energy will lay the leading sector foundation" into the twenty-first century.

K-WAVE EXPERTS AND THEORETICAL PREDICTIONS

Expert Opinion

If nuclear power, or space, are not the basis of a new paradigm, what might it be? On this subject, for nearly two decades the K-wave experts have provided some fairly clear answers. Table 11.1 presents a sampling of their views by means of excerpts from their writings.

Gerhard Mensch (1979) was probably the first to identify the recent condition as the end of one paradigm and the takeoff stage of another. He called this condition a technological stalemate, but did not really specify the industrial sectors expected to form the core of the new paradigm—beyond maintaining, pessimistically, that a hard transition toward "hyper-industrial-ization" was the more likely course.

Without being unanimous, K-wave writers seem to have been converging on the view that information technology (IT), as illustrated in table 11.2, is beginning to form the basis of a new sociotechnical paradigm. Of the ten quotes following Mensch in table 11.1, all but one mention either microelec-tronics, computers, telecommunications, or information systems as the core elements of the new K-wave. Biotechnology, too, might be regarded as based in information sciences as it is founded on the breaking of the genetic code. Mensch's pessimism about the possibility of a soft transition does not seem to have worked out. But does that mean that we have to take such a consensus as the basis of our analysis?

The identity of the new leading sectors has not really remained a secret. Pub-lic and private organizations in a number of countries—including France, Korea, and Taiwan—have been compiling lists of emerging technologies around which critical industries might coalesce. Japan is reported to have executed a strong move into high technology by greatly enhancing its research and development capacity in these fields starting in the 1970s and peaking in the late 1980s; some writers have described the Japanese as "the electronic tribe." By 1991 the U.S. Office of Technology Assessment observed that there is general agreement that technologies involving electronic components and information systems were key drivers of future industrial performance.[2] Support for information industries was one of the issues raised by the 1992 Clinton presidential campaign, and by 1993 the information superhighway, promoted by Vice President Al Gore, became one of the buzzwords of the new era.

In other words, the leading sectors of the current K-wave have now be-come a matter of common knowledge—not just in one country, but in the en-tire global economy. We might suppose that in earlier K-waves, too, the launching of new sectors was a competitive process involving more than one city or country. The Portuguese undertakings in West Africa, and later in the Indian Ocean, were keenly followed in Genoa and Venice; and developments in the British cotton industry were not unknown in France of the 1780s. After 1850 the reach of such knowledge has increased vastly, and now travels worldwide without much delay.

Analytical Prediction

At this point we might compare this (inductive) consensus of experts and public knowledge with predictions that might (deductively) be derived from our (tested) theoretical framework. Such predictions may be derived from an

Table 11.2

Information Technology Functions and Applications

Function	Application	Hardware/Software
Data collection	weather forecasting	radar, infrared detecting devices
	medical diagnosis	CAT-scanners, ultrasonic cameras
Data input	word processing	keyboards, touch-screens
	flexible manufacturing systems (FMS)	voice recognizers
	mail sorting	optical character readers
Data storage	accounting	floppy disks
	archives	magnetic tape and bubble devices
	libraries	hard disks
	cartography	video disks
Electronic data processing	FMS	robotics, artificial intelligence
	inventory control	microcomputers, application software
	CAD/CAE	microcomputers, application software
	medical diagnosis	expert systems software
	scientific computation	supercomputers, application software
	traffic control	minicomputers
	unemployment/welfare payments	mainframe computers, application software
Data output	word processing management/administration	PCs, printers, CRTs, computer graphics
Communications	international financial transactions	integrated services digital networks
	office systems	LAN, PBX, application software
	teleconferencing	satellites, fiber optics
	vehicle dispatch	cellular mobile radios

Source: based on Todd 1990, 16.

evolutionary conception of the global economy and global polity, both also responding to common global problems.

What is the cluster of global problems to which the K-wave and the long cycle might seem to be responding? Let us hypothesize that since about 1850, having moved beyond preconditions and nucleation, the global system has entered into a long-term phase of organization (that should last some four long cycles). That is, we see the beginning of a prolonged process of explicit organization having reference to the entire global system in the form of world organizations, of which the most obvious current example is the United Nations and its family of functional agencies. These have grown as part of the global leadership system that we have followed and are animated by it, but they also supplement it at the margins and gradually accrete new functions. At present, these organizations primarily serve to collect information, and also in some degree as foci of global solidarity, but have little autonomous executive power.

Let us postulate further that this evolutionary process of global system organization is, in its current long cycle, in the phase of democratic transition: the formation of a global democratic community on the basis of the close to one-half of humankind that now live in democratic societies. Such a democratic community is a necessary counterpart of a functioning market economy and a viable "zone of peace."

What kind of innovations are called for by the formation of a global democratic community? What might be the leading sectors that would best respond to such a challenge? Obviously, these would be those sectors of the global economy (manufacturing or service oriented) that promise to help integrate the global community on a democratic basis—most generally, information systems that provide the capacity to create the "global village" of Marshall McLuhan. One such basic sector is telecommunications that holds out the possibility—through the application of computers, space satellites, and fiber optics—of knitting together the human race (via multimedia) in a dense network of voice, video, and data links (giant computer pathways serving as the technical infrastructure of global solidarity). Computer hardware and software industries; electronic equipment industries; and information services and their respective research and development establishments would seem to be the sectors of the economy most likely to succeed in response to such demand. We might be reaching the point where, over the next two to three decades, the exchange of information will be instantaneous and worldwide, and will raise global networks to higher level, thereby creating something like a central nervous system for human organization.

In this way, a new K-wave would be responding to exogenous demand for its innovative products. It would also be responsive to the dynamic of its own (endogenous) development. If there is merit to the portrayal of the path of the global economy in table 8.1, then the current K-wave, building on the development of electric power and electronics in the previous two phases (K17 and K18), has reached the stage when the creation of an information society worldwide is now within reach.

THE INFORMATION AGE

In table 8.1 we designated the entire period of the global economic process since 1850 as the "Information Age." This is intended to highlight the truly novel feature of economic transformation in the most recent K-waves. Conventional observers have been impressed by the enormous expansion, in the late nineteenth century and after, of the heavy industries (iron and steel industries, in particular). While their growth was impressive, we need to remember that iron and steel technology have been with us for centuries since the onset of the Iron Age some three thousand years ago, and that Sung China in particular experienced a memorable burst of productivity in the eleventh century.

The truly novel features of late-nineteenth- and twentieth-century economic expansion have been in electric power generation (K17) and in electronics (K18), previously documented in some detail. They also provided the broad framework within which several additional trends occurred that heralded the onset of the Information Age. In the K17 wave, starting in 1850, path-breaking developments arising from basic research on electromagnetism occurred in telegraphy and telephony. Telegraphy first grew alongside railroads in the 1840s; the Western Union Telegraph Company was founded in 1851, and by 1866 a transatlantic cable connection was operating between Ireland and Newfoundland. Telephones became widely available in the 1880s.

The K18 wave (that we date from 1914) was the era of radio, film, and television. Transport ships and navies began using radio communications in the 1910s, and speech signals were first broadcast across the Atlantic by American Telephone and Telegraph Company in 1915. The first regular broadcasting system started operations in Pittsburgh in 1920 and the practice immediately spread rapidly worldwide. The motion-picture industry began in California after 1910 and soon assumed a global role. Television broadcasting began in the 1930s (Germany in 1935, Britain in 1936, and the United States in 1941), but did not really establish itself until after World War II (in the 1950s). Also notable was the role of electronics in this global war period: radio came to be essential to military communications; radar played a crucial part in submarine and air warfare; and the interception and decoding of enemy communications became the major focus of greatly expanded intelligence operations.

In that light, the current K19 wave is but a culmination of a series of developments that, extending over several phases, gave shape to an information age that is putting in place an infrastructure of knowledge for a new world economy.

LOCUS OF THE NINETEENTH K-WAVE

Which country might be the locus of the leading sectors of the information industries' K-wave? We know that this is likely to be the first K-wave (of a pair) that leads the new cycle of global leadership. As we have shown, knowing this locus gives us one of the necessary conditions of future leadership.

If information industries define this K-wave and its new sociotechnical paradigm, then the strength of the information sector in country and global proportions is a good clue to its standing in the competition for future global leadership. The U.S. strength in information technology has been quite substantial in this century as it was built on early leadership in the telephone, radio, film and television industries, and in recent decades in the computer and allied industries. Equally to the point, the United States has a strong comparative advantage in this area derived from its long history as an open society based upon freedom of speech.

In recent years, though, Japanese firms have made significant advances in electronics and computer equipment, and in research and development related to these fields.[3] The speed of Japanese gains is illustrated in figure 11.1 which plots the two industrial rivals' positions on their share of world high-technology exports. Between 1970 and 1989 the United States lost about 9 percent of the world share; Japan gained about 9 percent in the same period. However, examinations of high technology production indicators face the same problem as the ones we have looked at for leading sectors. What are the best indicators?

Laura Tyson (1992, 18) defines high-technology industries as those in which "knowledge is a prime source of competitive advantage for production" and those that invest heavily in knowledge creation as indexed by above-average research and development expenditures and employment of scientists and engineers. In the case of the positions plotted in figure 11.1, high technology encompasses chemicals, pharmaceuticals, power-generating machinery, data processing and electronic office machines, telecommunications, electronic components, aircraft, and scientific instruments (Tyson 1992, 20–21). Some of these products are directly related to information technology

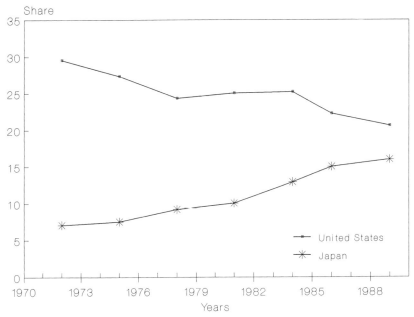

Figure 11.1. U.S.-Japanese Shares in High Technology Trade

while others are only related indirectly. In some cases, figure 11.1 may even be mixing eighteenth and nineteenth K-wave products. Without the benefit of hindsight, it is always difficult to know what should be excluded or included.

The approach that we have preferred in this study is to be as selective as possible in choosing the most appropriate indicators. If one accepts the proposition that microelectronics is a critical foundation of information technology, then microprocessor production can be advanced as a highly attractive focus. As summarized by Slomovic (1991, 181): "a microprocessor is a microelectronic device which can perform a variety of arithmetic and logic tasks specified by software. Microprocessors generally perform the following functions: read and decode programs, read data and programs stored in memory, perform operations on data, store data for later processing, and communicate with the outside world."

The history of microprocessors is one of learning how to place more components and functions on a single computer chip. The more successful the outcome, then the greater the processing speed and the greater the number and complexity of applications in industry—ranging from personal computers to

machine controls to telecommunications. The first microprocessor was introduced in 1971 by Intel, somewhat ironically, in response to the demands of a
new Japanese programmable calculator. Product improvements by Intel (8080,
8086, 8088, 80186, 80286, 80386, 80486, and Pentium) and other firms have
appeared every few years since then.[4] However, Intel's industrial coup took
place in 1979 when the 8088 was adopted as the IBM personal computer central processing unit. Software compatibility concerns and subsequent investment patterns meant that clones of the IBM PC also had to use Intel
microprocessors, which allowed Intel the privileged position of setting industrial standards for the bulk of the world's personal computers (the other main
competitor is Motorola, which supplies Apple) as long as it managed to maintain its lead in producing new generations of chips.

As shown in table 11.3, in 1990 U.S. firms controlled three-quarters of the
world microprocessor market and Japanese firms controlled about 10 percent.
Intel alone controlled one-half of that market. Three years later, in 1993, the
world microprocessor market was even more firmly in the control of U.S.
firms—especially Intel. Thus the microprocessor production indicator paints a
more positive picture of the U.S. competitive position than is evoked by figure
11. 1. However, we hastily add that much different proportional distributions
which strongly favored Japanese firms are associated with other computer
components such as RAM, DRAM, and EPROM peripherals (Borrus 1988). If
U.S. manufacturers lost their initially commanding position in constructing
computer memory devices to Japanese firms, they may also lose their lead in
other areas. On the other hand, U.S. firms have managed to retain their lead in
software. For example, in 1993 Microsoft alone supplied some 80 percent of
the operating systems, and 50 percent of applications software worldwide.
They also regained some of their lost position in overall semiconductor production in the early 1990s.

The London *Economist* thus summarized the outlook for the near future
in ''Who's Sharper Now?''—an editorial dated 15 January 1994:

> American leads in most of the young industries likely to grow fastest in the
> future—from multimedia and all things digital to biotechnology and all things
> scientific. American firms have lost their lead in the manufacture of commodity
> chips and computers, but enhanced it in more profitable areas such as micropro-
> cessors. They have slipped in consumer electronics but strengthened their domi-
> nance in entertainment. Much of this creativity has manifested itself in services
> rather than in manufacturing, a fact that was once decried as a weakness yet now
> makes America look less vulnerable than its rivals to competition from low-cost
> manufacturers in Asia and Latin America.

Table 11.3

World Microprocessor Market Shares, 1990 and 1993

Company	Headquarter's location	Market Share 1990	1993
Intel	United States	53.2	74.1
Motorola	United States	13.3	8.0
Advanced Micro Devices	United States	5.1	5.8
Hitachi	Japan	3.6	
NEC	Japan	3.5	
Texas Instruments	United States		2.2
National Semiconductor	United States	2.7	
SGS	Italy-France	2.3	
Toshiba	Japan	2.1	
Others		14.3	9.9*
U.S. headquartered companies		74.3	90.1
Japanese headquartered companies		9.2	

Sources: Tyson 1992, 127; *New York Times*, 20 February 1994; F13; value of world microprocessor market in 1993: $8.9 billion.
*No single company with more than 2 percent of the 1993 market, including U.S. companies.

Leads in microprocessors and software, as well as the overall positional improvement, are not coincidental. These leads reflect U.S. firms' historical edge in establishing what Ferguson and Morris call industry architecture. Writing about the rise and decline of IBM:

> The secret of IBM's dominance, as IBM understood better than anyone, was that it had created, and owned, a pervasive industry *architecture*. All the competitors were playing by IBM's rules—making devices, writing software, manufacturing clones, running time-share centers—all within a computing environment that IBM defined and that only IBM had completely mastered. The confidence of IBM customers was so great, their commitment to the 360/370 architecture so deep, that no competitor had a chance of replacing it. It would mean throwing out too much investment built up over too long a time. (1993, 15)

This strategy for dominance applies equally well to microprocessors, software, and other IT sectors. Establishing industry standards gives a firm a sustained competitive advantage because it is producing technologically superior products to which others must respond.[5] But the strategy also means that dominance can only be maintained as long as the firm stays at least one product generation ahead of the competition. If it allows its lead to be leapfrogged, its market position is likely to decline.

The rate of technological change in the computer industry remains astonishingly high. Some observers now contend that the personal computer, which in the past dozen years has surged ahead of mainframes, might soon be supplanted by the "consumer computer" that is evolving out of the video-game players of today. New machines due in 1995 are expected to be not only faster, but also significantly cheaper than even the most powerful of the current generation of personal computers. But they also portend a shift toward a new wave of computing marked by user-friendliness, new mass-marketed consumer products, and communications. Japanese companies—including Nintendo, Sega, and Sony—have been leaders in the video-game field, and the strength of their manufacturing base in electronics means that global competition in this rapidly changing area will remain fierce (Markoff 1994, 13).

Overall, the leadership in producing the architecture of specific IT product lines continues to be contested, which suggests either that the issue of leadership is not yet resolved or, possibly, that it may be unlikely that a single national leader can or will emerge in the nineteenth K-wave's constantly evolving IT paradigm.

Transition Crisis

A transition is the interval between two bursts of innovation and growth while the crisis is the product of the difficulties that economic and other social systems experience in managing innovation and in transiting from one economic (or political) paradigm to another. We have already noticed the patterning of transition crises in the Sung Chinese and in the Italian cases, as summarized in tables 9.7 and 10.12. We have documented, moreover, the regularity with which global wars have paced the transitions between (odd- and even-numbered) K-waves since the mid-fifteenth century. In the twentieth century the interval between K17 and K18, the period between 1914 and 1945 that included severe global warfare as well as the Great Depression, was particularly memorable. That is why we have reason to believe that the current era, the start-up time for K19 (and the phase of delegitimation and agenda-setting by the long-cycle calendar), is a time of transition and bears the characteristics of transition crisis.

We have postulated in chapter 5 that each K-wave may be partitioned into start-up and high-growth portions. The high-growth phase generally is a time of prosperity and expansion, and short-term business cycles within it tend to be shallow. But start-up is beset with greater problems. The leading sectors of the last K-wave have reached maturity and have ceased to be the motors of growth. Competitive pressures from newcomers erode the position of former innovators who face bankruptcy unless they drastically restructure their operations. Formerly active regions of lead economies experience both unemployment and disruption. All of this occurs while the new industries are taking shape elsewhere, but they have not yet moved into high gear and their new productivity is yet to be widely felt. The order of the day is change, oftentimes failure, and much disarray.

The result is economic slowdown, an air of depression, high structural unemployment, political turmoil, and the surfacing of fundamentalist ideologies. For the difficulties are not only endogenous to the lead economies, but they also coincide with political uncertainty at the global level. Every other (odd- to even-numbered) K-wave transition has synchronized with macrodecisions that rearrange the global political structure and select new leadership. The current period, the transition to an odd-numbered (nineteenth) K-wave, does not carry the potential for global war, but it does evince the political dislocation attendant upon a period of delegitimation—in which the status quo of existing political arrangements begins to be questioned, and the debate opens about new global agendas which create a feeling of loss of values and of the moral compass.

We know that the period since 1973, and lasting in our analysis until about 2000, is one of transition. The industries that have been the bearers of post-World War II prosperity—the "auto-industrial" complex (including oil) and electronics (even including mainframe computers)—have become mature industries. They are no longer sources of rapid growth and major innovation. These are also precisely the industries that have suffered from competition with Japanese and other East Asian producers. This competition has brought unemployment, restructurings, and shocks to world trade balances. Those economies that failed to restructure, in particularly those of the former Soviet Union, have suffered most of all. In the meantime, the information industries have been slow in making their impact felt. The large investment in the new technologies has not yet had noticeable effects on productivity. This is a "lag" that is characteristic of paradigmatic shifts in industrial organization. Early in this century, a similar delay, on the order of two decades, was seen in the impact of strong commitment to electric power equipment.

On the political front, dislocations have been equally severe. The global leadership of the United States, strong after 1945, has now come under question. Flagged in the 1970s, its weakening was relatively manageable as compared to the sudden collapse of the Soviet Union and its worldwide and regional East European enterprises in 1989 to 1991. This collapse left not only a political, but also a huge ideological void. The filling and repair of that void may be the stuff of new agendas for decades to come.

It might be that the period of 1989 to 1994 will be remembered as an equivalent to the Great Depression of 1929 to 1933—only in a minor way. Severe unemployment, reaching double digits in Europe, and dramatic declines in output, comparable in scale to the Great Depression, in Russia and elsewhere in Eastern Europe have occurred during this period. In addition, a surge of political extremism occurred to the degree that a "Weimar hypothesis" is now being considered as a possibility in relation to Russian political development. These events call for economic and political readjustments that might be slow in coming to place. And the benefits of the new technologies and the new industries have yet to be seen.

THE NINETEENTH K-WAVE AND
THE LIKELIHOOD OF GLOBAL WAR

As we look further ahead, beyond the year 2000, it is also possible, and in fact increasingly likely, that the global leadership function in the long cycle now unfolding will assume a more complex, more collective, and possibly even less prominent character—it is likely to be overlaid, to a greater degree than in the current cycle, by elements of global organization. Over the past several centuries (since 1500), one nation-state has served as the vital center of the global economy. The more complex economy of the next century—more complex substantially because of the information revolution now underway—might accommodate innovative industrial sectors led by multinational firms (such as Intel or Microsoft, Sony or Hitachi, or Siemens) linked through strategic alliances which operate in all the principal zones of the world economy. Such a dispersal would also tend to lend substance to the evolutionary tendency toward a form of global political structure less centered on a nation-state.

Among students of industrial organization, Kenichi Ohmae espouses the concept of *The Borderless World* (1990) ordered by transnational business alliances and constituted by what he earlier called the triad of Japan, the United States, and Western Europe. Others, such as Michael E. Porter (in *The Competitive Advantage of Nations,* 1990) insist on the crucial role of national advantage, especially in relation to innovation and the formation of new firms. Both are tapping important dimensions of the problem.

A combination of the inherent characteristics of information industries, expanding international organization powers, and the genuine dispersal of leading sector production might be important movers in reducing the probability of global war in the next macrodecision phase. Global wars are not inevitably linked to this leadership crisis resolution period. We have seen earlier prototypical macrodecision phases without global war (but involving considerable warfare) as exemplified by the Italian renaissance era. This era immediately predated the emergence of nation-states and the eventual development of their ability to mobilize resources and people on a scale increasingly necessary for global war. Yet the potential destructiveness of another global war, thanks to the lethality of current weaponry—one outcome of the information revolution in science and technology—could literally destroy the entire system if actually employed. Acute conflicts over the national control of commercial and industrial leading sectors and their implications have also been increasingly prominent in the factors leading international tension and armed conflicts.

It is conceivable, as many scholars argue, that some combination of weapon systems lethality, denationalized industrial production, increased political management capacities on the part of international organizations, and the continuing diffusion of democratic institutions might offer a way out of the primitive leadership selection process developed, and relied upon, over the past five hundred years. The most pertinent questions are two-fold: (1) are these trends and processes necessary and sufficient to manage global problems without recourse to global war; and (2) if they are necessary or sufficient, can these trends come together in time to preclude the perceived necessity of still another descent into the maelstrom of global war?

At the time of this writing, only one process—weapon system lethality and its correlate of national mobilization potential—has clearly attained a level that could be judged necessary to deter the attractiveness of major power warfare. By itself, however, it is doubtful that the fear of the outcome of total or nuclear war is sufficient to deter action. At the very least, we have little or no evidence that it is sufficient (Modelski and Morgan 1985). The other possible factors are still emerging. How fast they will continue to emerge—assuming that they will continue—and how far they have to go are not subject to precise prediction. Our analysis suggests that we might have as many as three decades in which to seek substitutes for global war. For we can only reaffirm that there are other ways to resolve conflicts over whose policies will prevail in shaping the global order. Given a conducive environment, decision makers may yet opt for one or more of these alternative approaches to global macrodecision.

CONCLUDING REMARKS

We have presented empirical evidence for the existence of coordination between two basic structural processes at the global level: K-waves and long cycles. We have shown that over the past thousand years, two K-waves, viewed as a bunched group of basic innovations, have matched each long cycle of the rise of world powers. The first of these, an odd-numbered

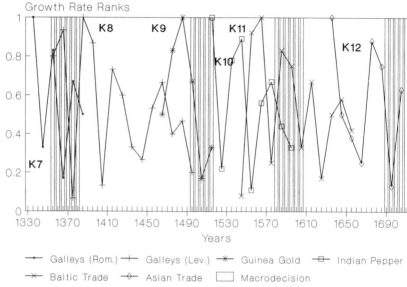

Figure 11.2. K-Waves 7–12

K-wave, anticipates global leadership; the second, an even-numbered K-wave, follows it.

This argument might be pursued in a number of directions, but we shall point to only the three most important:

1. There are a large number of ways to imagine the linkages among long-term economic growth, war, and global leadership. We have developed a set of criteria that can be used to evaluate the adequacy of the available set of arguments. We have also advanced a cohesive theoretical argument that satisfies the seven critical criteria of chapter 3 that is empirically testable.

2. Retracing the past, this analysis extends the empirical study of K-waves to the fourteenth century and, in the context of the evolution of the foundations of the global economy, to Sung China (circa 1000). Figures 11.2 and 11.3 present a summarized empirical perspective on the continuity of these K-waves. The interdependence of long-term economic growth, radical innovation in commerce and industry, nationally based economic and political leadership, and even global war are given stronger empirical foundation. The overlapping and sequential pattern of their timing has been clarified further.

3. Looking to the future, if the first of a pair of K-waves anticipates changes in political structure (and, conversely, world politics at such times lags global economics), then the status of and prospects for the information sectors (including computers, telecommunications, and electronic components) offer important

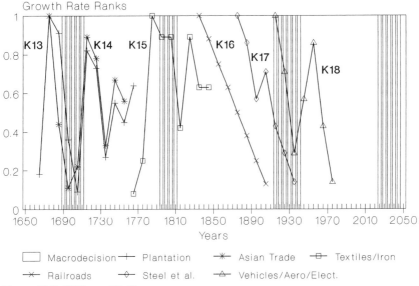

Figure 11.3. K-Waves 13–18

clues to the locus of global leadership in the next century. A contest over the control of these sectors and their implications for national autonomy and economic growth is currently ongoing. The Japanese-U.S. dispute over trade deficits is one manifestation. The disintegration of the Soviet Union and the 1992 watershed in European integration, in part, are two other manifestations of this same phenomenon. But there is more at stake than trade deficits, the disintegration of a tottering empire, or the accelerated movement toward the unification of an important region. These closely related developments, in turn, all share a close relationship to the timing, location, and dislocations associated with repeated surges in leading sector innovation. How the nineteenth K-wave works itself out, and how policy makers respond (and intervene in its workings), is very likely to be crucial to what happens in the world politics of the first half of the twenty-first century.

Finally, we should emphasize that, despite what may appear to be an overly neat and deterministic argument, we do not view the coordination of the long-cycle and K-wave processes as particularly deterministic. There is nothing inevitable about one K-wave following another. Nor is it inevitable that a new world power will emerge to fill the gap left by a predecessor in relative decline. Before the Sung period, for instance, the shape of the patterns that we see in later centuries is uncertain. And we have already suggested that we may not see the coevolution of world politics and the world economy continue forever along the lines of previous centuries. Global war, for example, need not follow the first of a pair of K-waves the next time around.

Rather than a deterministic inevitability, what we see are clusters of strong probabilities. Invention and routine innovation may be more or less continuous processes in economic activities. Radical innovation is neither inevitable nor continuous. Yet once spurts of radical innovation begin, there is some probability that they will continue because other actors will perceive new opportunities and new necessities as the payoffs of the previous spurt erode. Some actors may also be in an improved position to engineer new ways of doing things thanks to the advances associated with the previous spurt of radical innovation. In commerce, this has meant the discovery of new routes, new markets, and new modes of transportation. In industry, this has meant new ways of creating products that improve productivity and perform tasks that could not be performed as efficiently and quickly as before.

Once there are major spurts of economic growth that define the prospects for long-term growth, it is difficult to imagine how the impacts of such change might be isolated to the purely economic sphere. Uneven economic growth is a fundamental destabilizer of an international political status quo that emerges in an environment characterized by an increasingly dated distribution of resources and capabilities. As long as there is an important linkage between the ability to act beyond domestic borders and the economic resource base to pay for such acts, changes in economic and technological pecking orders imply changes in political pecking orders. Even so, the interaction is not only one way. Political hierarchies can also work to reinforce economic hierarchies for a time. That is one reason K-waves come in pairs.

In any event, there is a strong probability that spurts of growth will alter the structure of economic leadership which, in turn, affects the probability that major powers will feel it necessary to contest claims to political leadership. Once resolved, political leadership facilitates or increases the probability of a second growth spurt, but it need not enhance the probability of a third spurt. In some circumstances the primary beneficiary of a pair of K-waves becomes too complacent and overly committed to increasingly obsolete ways of doing things to maximally exploit the opportunities associated with the next K-wave. The next K-wave may also demand resources, markets, and locations that simply are not available to the previous economic leader. Thus, there is some probability that economic leadership will move from one place to another.

All of these probabilities can be exploited or resisted successfully or unsuccessfully. Human agency definitely plays an important role in these processes. We have stressed systemic patterns because we feel that the larger picture first needs to be established. But it is people who invent, innovate, and make war decisions. It is people who must respond to the changing incentive structures associated with the patterned periodicity of political and economic fluctuations. It is people who must suffer the sometimes painful transitions between K-waves and the always painful costs of global warfare. That we have chosen not to deal with micro-considerations at this time, as opposed to the macropatterns on which we have concentrated, is simply a matter of analytical strategy and not a matter of implicit theoretical neglect.

We have focused on what we regard as the bigger picture, to the detriment of more microconcerns, because we believe that is where major answers to the puzzle linking war and long-term economic growth are located. Too often, both war and economic growth, whether examined separately or together, are viewed from short-run perspectives. As a trio of economists have commented on their own discipline (but in a way that has pertinence for the study of war as well):

> Productivity growth is a vital subject that has, unfortunately, fallen into the hands of macroeconomists. . . . For productivity growth is essentially a long-run issue. . . . Yet macroanalysts have been shaped by their training to a short-run orientation, which suits them poorly to the study of what may well be the most important implications of productivity. Until the Keynesian revolution, preoccupation with the long run was the hallmark of academic economists. . . . The economic literature was framed in terms of long-run tendencies, long-run equilibria, and what one of us once called "the magnificent dynamics," which encompass the secular expansion or decline of entire nations and societies over protracted periods. (Baumol, Blackman, and Wolff 1989, 1)

We, too, have a preference for focusing on long-run tendencies in which the rise and decline of certain national polities and economies figure quite prominently. We contend that one of "the magnificent dynamics" is the K-wave/global war/K-wave sequence and its profound implications for the long cycle of global politics and leadership. If we are right, we need to rethink our fundamental approaches to explaining war, economic growth, and, most critically, their interaction.

NOTES

CHAPTER ONE: PROBLEM AND PREMISES

1. Recent discussions of this topic include Modelski 1981, 1987; Thompson and Zuk 1982; Vayrynen 1983; Freeman and Perez 1988; Goldstein 1988, 1991; W. R. Thompson 1988; Chase-Dunn 1989; Berry 1991; Beck 1991; Thompson and Vescera 1992; Sayrs 1993; and Williams 1993.

2. A bibliography of Kondratieff's writings may be found in van Duijn 1983, 71–72. Nikolai Kondratieff (1892–1938) was one of the outstanding Russian economists and statisticians of the 1920s. Founder and director of the Moscow Business Conditions Institute during its entire existence from 1920 to 1928, he was arrested in 1930 and executed in 1938. Manuscripts written by him while in prison are being prepared for publication.

3. For a recent review of the "new growth" theory, see Romer 1994; Grossman and Helpman 1994; R. H. Solow 1994; and Pack 1994.

4. Table 1.1 shows a total of eighteen long-cycle phases when counted between 1494 and 1973. The phases are deductively derived from the conception of long cycles as a four-phased, evolutionary learning process, and verified by tests of seapower concentration. A comparable list, Goldstein's (1988, 67, 246) series of alternating upswings and downswings of the "long wave," is inductively derived from changes in price levels between 1494 and 1980 (and from writings of scholars), and shows twenty such phases. Between 1732 and 1975 Goldstein's world industrial production series leads prices by about ten to fifteen years (Goldstein 1988, 216). Goldstein's upswings and downswings are not to be confused with start-up and high growth periods in the analysis presented here.

5. The "learning" mode may be thought of as accounting for the inner dynamic of the long cycle: spelling out its character as a recurrent (or repetitive) evolutionary process (see Modelski 1990b).

CHAPTER TWO: THE CONFUSED STATE OF THE LITERATURE

1. See W. R. Thompson 1982 which finds little systematic support for the idea that there is a relationship between short-run business cycles and the outbreak of major power war.

2. Imbert apparently died shortly after publishing his ambitious study.

3. Earlier Goldstein analyses examine series beginning in 1495.

CHAPTER THREE: A CRITIQUE OF THE LITERATURE

1. The reference to cumulative literature refers to one in which later works build upon earlier studies.

2. World War II ended a downswing and preceded an impressive upswing which contradicts a good number of the fourteen clusters.

CHAPTER FOUR: LONG CYCLES, WAR, AND LONG-TERM ECONOMIC GROWTH

1. The stress on global warfare often causes leadership long-cycle theory to be inaccurately pigeonholed as a theory of war.

2. Empirical evidence for global war impacts may be found in Thompson and Rasler 1988 and Rasler and Thompson 1989.

CHAPTER FIVE: DO K-WAVES AND LONG CYCLES COEVOLVE?

1. Table 5.1 supersedes the list of leading sectors in Modelski 1981, 69.

CHAPTER SIX: LEADING SECTORS IN THE GLOBAL ECONOMY

1. The following indicators are not utilized in the present analysis: the frequency of Portuguese shipping to Asia; the estimated frequency of royal Portuguese ship construction; the volume of Spanish Indies shipping; bullion imports from America; Hondschoote cloth production; Venetian cloth production; the volume of Dutch Baltic grain shipping; Leiden cloth production; the volume of Dutch East Indies Company ship construction; nitrogen fertilizer production; plastics/resins output; and synthetic fiber production.

2. See Boyajian 1993 for a recent study of the post–1580 fate of Portuguese commerce and one that argues that its decline was slower than conventionally thought.

3. Solow (1987) pointed out that the plantation techniques employed in America could be traced to similar techniques adopted by Portugal and Venice in the cultivation of sugar on Mediterranean and Atlantic islands.

4. In previous examinations, the semiconductor and aerospace indicators were not looked at separately but in aggregation with the first K-wave (of the U.S. pair) indicators. One of the consequences of disaggregation is that the principal peak is now associated with the 1950s. In earlier analyses, only a 1940s peak appeared.

5. Relative leading sector shares data are reported in W. R. Thompson 1988, 1990 for the Britain I and U.S. long cycles.

6. It was not until the seventeenth century that Dutch and English control of Asian spice flows to Europe finally put an end to the Mediterranean role in the spice trade.

7. Boswell and Misra (forthcoming) first used the slave trade indicator to measure Dutch commercial hegemony. We employ it instead to tap into the relative position of the successors to the Dutch. It should not be surprising that the successive chain of leaders in the slave trade were first Portugal, then the Dutch, and then Britain.

8. For comparative purposes, the railroad track laid indicator is modified by the use of a second indicator (railroad track laid per square kilometer) to control somewhat for different country sizes. The railroad construction index is calculated by adding both indicators and dividing by two. Lest the reader think too much measurement emphasis is placed on railroad track, Landes (1969, 221) provides data on total steam engine capacities for the period 1840 to 1896. It shows a later peak in the growth of this series (1850s), but also a discernible slippage in the British position. In 1840 Britain possessed roughly 38 percent of the world's steam engine capacity. This figure dropped to 32 percent in 1850, 26 percent in 1860, and about 22 percent in 1870.

9. However, Vescera (1994) has found a positive Granger relationship between a spliced British/American leading sector growth series and world industrial production since the mid-eighteenth century.

10. The dispute over whether Portugal or Spain should provide the center of sixteenth-century attention often neglects Portugal's global economy lead in the first half of that century (before 1540) and lays stress on Spanish gains in the second half.

11. This issue is explored more fully in W. R. Thompson 1992b and Rasler and Thompson 1994.

CHAPTER SEVEN: TESTING FOR COEVOLUTION

1. The problem of whether the oscillations of these data resemble K-waves has received attention in W. R. Thompson 1990 and 1992a and need not be repeated here.

2. In cases where the second K-wave (of a pair) series is much shorter than the first K-wave series (thereby involving smaller ranks), the second K-wave series rank orders have been inflated by a constant (2) to better facilitate first K-wave/second K-wave visual comparisons.

3. These links are hardly coincidental. The first wave's innovations make the second wave more probable in a variety of ways. In some cases, we also think that the cumulative outcome of the two waves makes the next K-wave more likely to happen somewhere else.

4. However, the Granger causality findings on the Britain II and U.S. relationships among leading sector growth, leading sector share, and naval share reported in Rasler and Thompson 1991 suggest strong evidence for systematic connections.

5. Successful debt strategies have played a role as well but these too depend on the image of a prosperous, growing economy or, in other words, a good credit risk (see Rasler and Thompson 1989, chap. 4).

6. See as well the analysis of the national origins of discoveries and innovations in Freeman, Clark, and Soete 1982.

7. Of the four hundred Nobel prizes in physics, chemistry, and medicine/physiology awarded in 1901–1989, 39 percent were in the United States; in Japan, less than 1 percent. In 1901–1973 26 percent of the Peace Prizes went to Americans, but 70 percent of the prizes in economics were awarded to Americans during the same time period.

CHAPTER EIGHT: AN ENLARGED FRAMEWORK

1. In his latest (1990) work Douglass North lays out a broadly evolutionary framework that is "a necessary first step in evolving a theory of institutional change" of societies. The history he provides is "illustrative" but "far from providing for the kind of hypothesis testing that must ultimately be done." For North, the "central puzzle of human history is to account for the widely divergent paths of historical change"; for us, the central puzzle is to account for the convergence of a spectrum of processes upon the building of today's world economy and polity.

2. Joseph Schumpeter's *History of Economic Analysis* (1954) is a story of economic theories viewed as continuously evolving over time in a cumulative fashion, much in the same way as natural science theories. The author (J. Schumpeter 1954, 435–46) discusses five types of "evolutionism" in the sense of confidence in the progress of reason as having reached a high-water mark in the nineteenth century.

3. Freeman (1983, 245) points out that some authors prefer the term "wave" for the Kondratieff phenomenon because wave has less of a mechanistic or deterministic connotation than cycle.

4. The speed of diffusion of K-waves to other economies depends on the degree to which such conditions prevail elsewhere in the world economy.

5. We leave aside for the time being the broader aspects of global coevolution, those involving the two other global processes of global community formation and social movements, and of global opinion formation and structural-cultural change.

6. Christiaan Huygens, the Dutch mathematician and astronomer, observed in 1665 that two pendulum clocks placed in proximity synchronized their movements.

7. Steven Strogatz and Ian Stewart (1993) review recent research on "Coupled Oscillators and Biological Synchronization" in *Scientific American.* Our discussion of coupled oscillators draws its terms from this account.

8. Our (Modelski and Thompson 1988) measurements of seapower concentration over the shorter period of one-half millennium (1494–1993) show average periodicity (between five peaks) of 108 years.

CHAPTER NINE: SUNG CHINA AND THE EVOLVING GLOBAL ECONOMY

1. On the spelling of names and places: the usage here follows the system of Romanization employed by *Encyclopedia Britannica* (15th edition), described therein as "Western conventional," except for bibliographical references to authors and titles that are reported without change. The *Encyclopedia* also lists the Pinyin equivalents.

List of place names and proper names:

Western Conventional	Pinyin
Sung	Song
Hanlin Academy	Han-lin Yuan
Hsi Hsia	Xi Xia
Su Shih	Su Shi
Chu Hsi	Chu Xi
K'ai-feng	Kaifeng
Hangchow	Hangzhou
Yangtse	Chang Hang
Szechwan	Sichuan
Shansi	Shanxi
Hopeh	Hebei
Honan	Henan
Kiangsi	Jiangxi
Fukien	Fujian
Amoy	Xia-Men
Nanking	Nan-Jing
Hainan	Hainan

2. Kang Chao (1986, 60) estimates the ratio of Sung urbanization as 21 percent in 1221. Elvin (1973, 176) puts the ratio for the year 1100 as "at least ten percent for the nation as a whole." He places the peak population of K'ai-feng at 1.4 million circa 1100; Hangchow at 2.5 million circa 1220; and Soo-chow and Hu-chow at probably more than 350,000 each. A comprehensive listing of the world's largest cities may be found in Chandler 1987. Chandler's lists for 1100 do not include the other major city of the Liao empire—the southern capital (today's Peking)—and might also under-report cities in the Sung realm. According to E. A. Kracke (in Liu and Golas 1969, 11), by the year 1100 "at least four urban areas far surpassed the capital area" with at least one million living within the borders of their prefectures.

3. Reischauer and Fairbank (1960, 202) estimate this tribute to account for about 2 percent of Sung revenues. See also data in Hartwell 1988. Comparing the costs of keeping the peace or fighting the war with Liao, Sung officials were satisfied that the payments to Liao could easily be afforded—they amounted to less than 1 percent of the cost of military operations (Lebadie 1981, 206–7).

4. In 1713 the British navy had a strength of thirteen thousand "naval personnel," and reached fifty thousand for the first time in 1756 (Modelski and Thompson 1988, 30). But the Byzantine navy at its peak, in 600–1000, might have numbered some forty thousand sailors (Dupuy and Dupuy 1977, 221).

5. Even though they view the dynastic cycle as having been "a major block to the understanding of the fundamental dynamics of Chinese history" because it down-played the role of change and highlighted simple repetition, Reischauer and Fairbank (1960, 114) also admit that the concept has "considerable validity" as long as it is

understood as a "somewhat simplified pattern that overlay[s] the more fundamental technological, economic, social, and cultural developments." The dynastic cycle is, of course, a political process that has to be seen in its proper relation to economic and other processes, but also in an evolutionary framework.

6. S. A. M. Adshead (1988, 155) distinguishes five elements in this "package of superior Chinese technology" that were crucial for Europe's takeoff: nautical, metallurgical, mechanical, chemical, and horological. On the last, see the critical comments in Landes 1983, chap. 1.

7. That is why Reischauer and Fairbank's (1960, 211) comment that the Sung commercial revolution showed "no spectacular industrial innovations" needs to be qualified.

8. Joseph Needham (1969, 65) is satisfied that Johannes Gutenberg knew of Chinese movable-block printing.

9. The author reports that more than sixty northern Sung families became famous for ink-stick manufacture, and mentions the case of forgery of trademarks of one of these families that, he argues, showed the existence of a "national market" for this product. Elvin (1973, 134) acclaims the official gazette issued by the Sung government as "the world's first national newspaper."

10. Already underway in the second half of the T'ang era; see, for example, Cartier 1991, reporting on the work of Li Bozhong.

11. According to Hartwell (1989, 458) Champa rice might have been introduced by refugees settling on Hainan and near Canton. We know that around 1000 Champa, located in what is now central Vietnam (the only Asian mainland culture with oceanic features), was under pressure from Vietnam, which had regained independence from China in 939, invaded Champa in 980, and sacked its capital. Champa's appeals for help from China proved unavailing. By 1000 the capital was transferred south to Vijaya.

12. Kang Chao's (1986, 195) data show that the Sung era witnessed a great surge of innovation in respect to farm implements: thirty-five cases in the Sung era, twenty-six cases in the preceding millennium, and only seven cases since.

13. But Ma's table also shows a precipitous and unexplained drop around 1051, largely restored in about 1066. For comments on the uneven quality of the acreage data, see Kang Chao (1986, 79–80), who noted that the human-land ratio declined between 976 and 1072 from 7.96 *mou* to 5.50 *mou* (one *mou* = 666.5 square meters).

14. Whereupon decline set in; some attribute it to government price controls, others to the high sulfur content of the coal and a consequent loss of quality. The area soon came under Chin control.

15. Hartwell (1982, 400) argues, on the basis of a study of the career patterns of fiscal officials from 960 to 1165, that the administrative reforms of 1082 marked a "symbolic turning point." At that time, "inter-regional career patterns in specific branches of the bureaucracy" tending to favor centralization were replaced by "intra-regional ones in diverse fields of administration," more responsive to local interests and presumably more conducive to freer trade. Authority shifted from the 306 prefectures (*chou* or *fou*) (circa 1100) to the 1207 districts (*hsien*) and to large regional administrations (provinces, or *sheng*).

16. This is based on Gernet 1982, 326–29. Needham (1969, 73–74) contends that the "first use" of magnetic compass in Chinese navigation "must have started as early as the tenth century."

17. See, for instance, Adshead (1988, 152–55) who sees it as the product of the "peak of consumerism" reached by Chinese society in the late Sung age which manifested itself in a shift to the consumption of protein—hence butcher's meat and spices.

18. A sign of the importance attached to maritime trade by the southern Sung was the official recognition, by the emperor in 1156, of the cult of Ma Zu—patron goddess of fishermen, sailors, and sea merchants. Later known as the Empress of Heaven, she became in effect the patroness of "Maritime China" (Fairbank 1992, 157).

19. This appears to be an extrapolation from the estimated revenues of the superintendencies of maritime commerce that levied a tax on all imports (Hartwell 1988, 30).

20. The reversal in the fortunes of the Tairas, and the consequent militarization of Japanese politics after 1192 (further reinforced by the threat of Mongol invasions in the next century), made Japan's turning into a market economy that might have served as an alternative center of innovation in East Asia even more difficult. It strengthened the impending shift of the active zone of the world system westward.

21. Charles Peterson (1983, 230) doubts that there ever was a genuine choice.

22. Another vivid facet of the loss of flexibility was the practice of female footbinding (Fairbank 1992, 175) that began at court in the ninth century and then gradually spread throughout the country. It was commended by the neo-Confucian poet Su Shih (d. 1101), but it is disputed whether it was backed by Chu Hsi (d. 1201) who was no champion of women's rights according to Fairbank.

CHAPTER TEN: RENAISSANCE ITALY

1. Apparently, it was overland trade through France that was too expensive and unsafe for the Venetians who developed an alternative land route to Germany through Verona and the Brenner Pass in the fourteenth century.

2. See Phillips 1988, 146, for a brief summary of European designs on Egypt in the thirteenth and fourteenth centuries.

3. The Genoese decline was probably due to a combination of intra-elite conflict in Genoa and the collapse of the important French markets due to the Hundred Years War. Another factor may have been a difference in style. The Venetian approach to dealing with the Mamluks was usually one of appeasement while the Genoese (and Catalonian) interactions were much less centralized and more conflictual in style. Presumably, the Mamluks would have preferred to deal with the Venetians in maintaining the Red Sea monopoly.

4. Moreover, the Venetian Arsenal (the model for Dante's Inferno), where standardized galleys were constructed along an assembly line, can probably claim to be one of Europe's first modern industrial factories.

5. Actually, the galleys comprised only a small portion of the Venetian fleet. A 1423 inventory by Doge Tomaso Mocenigo (McNeill 1974, 258; Modelski and Modelski 1988,

30–31) counted 3,000 small vessels (with 17,000 crew members), 300 large sailing vessels (with 8,000 crew members), and 45 galleys (with 11,000 crew members). Of the 45 galleys, 25 were heavy (merchant) galleys, 15 were light (war) galleys, and 5 were used for carrying mail and passengers. The number of galleys could be more than doubled in times of crisis by utilizing a reserve maintained at the Venetian Arsenal.

6. The Venetians had begun using seasonal sailing caravans to Romania and Crusader enclaves in the thirteenth century, but some credit for the high degree of organization demonstrated in the Alexandrian line should also go to the Mamluks who insisted that European traders arrive at the same time and on a regular schedule.

7. See Tenenti and Vivanti 1961 and Braudel 1972, 392, for visual displays of the traffic frequency and routes used. 8. Another supporting piece of evidence (Scammell 1981, 169) was the 700 percent fall in value of Genoese customs at Pera (near Constantinople) over the 1334–1423 period. Of course, this evidence is also an indicator of the switch from Romanian trade to the Egyptian route.

9. Kedar (1976) and Abu-Lughod (1989) are mistaken in using the declining size of Venetian convoys to the Black Sea area as an indicator of general contraction in maritime trade.

CHAPTER ELEVEN: THE NINETEENTH K-WAVE AND NO GLOBAL WAR?

1. What happens to challengers (for global leadership) is not uniform. Sometimes they are important innovators, as in the case of the Germans. In other instances, such as immediately prior to the French Revolution, they may simply appreciate how much they are falling behind. In either case, though for different reasons, the circumstances may make major conflict more probable.

2. A concrete index of rapid sectoral ascent is the estimate (*Electronic Business* 1985, 66) that electronics production as a proportion of total industrial production in the United States has doubled every ten years since 1975 (1975: 7.5 percent; 1985: 15 percent; 1995: estimated 31 percent).

3. According to information made available by the World Intellectual Property Organization (*World Industrial Property Rights Statistics,* multiple volumes), the United States accounted for the largest share of worldwide patent activity during 1981 to 1988. The Japanese share was the second largest and is rapidly converging toward the American level.

4. The 8086 chip had 29,000 transistors; the 80486 has 1.2 million and the Pentium has 3.1 million.

5. Ferguson and Morris stress that it is not specific products that represent industry architecture. Products only reflect the prevailing architecture. Rather, it is the complex network of proprietary and nonproprietary standards that "define how programs and commands will work and data will move around the system—the communication protocols that hardware components must follow, the rules for exchanging data between application software packages and the operating system . . . and so forth" (Ferguson and Morris 1993, 120).

BIBLIOGRAPHY

Aakerman, J. 1932. *Economic Progress and Economic Crises.* London: Macmillan.
_____. 1944. *Ekonomisk Teori.* Vol. 2, *Kausalanalys Av Det Ekonmiska.* Skeendet-Lund: Gleerup.
Abu-Lughod, Janet L. 1989. *Before European Hegemony: The World System, A.D. 1250–1350.* New York: Oxford University Press.
Adshead, S. A. M. 1988. *China in World History.* London: Macmillan.
Aerospace Facts and Figures. Multiple volumes. Los Angeles: Aero Publishers.
Angell, Norman. 1933. *The Great Illusion.* New York: Putnam.
Ashtor, Elyahu. 1983. *Levant Trade in the Later Middle Ages.* Princeton, N.J.: Princeton University Press.
Banks, Arthur S. 1971. *Cross-Polity Time-Series Data.* Cambridge, Mass.: MIT Press.
Barfield, Thomas J. 1989. *The Perilous Frontier: Nomadic Empires and China, 221 B.C to A.D. 1757.* Cambridge, Mass.: Blackwell.
Baumol, William J., Sue Ann Batey Blackman, and Edward N. Wolff. 1989. *Productivity and American Leadership: The Long View.* Cambridge, Mass.: MIT Press.
Beck, Nathaniel. 1991. ''The Illusion of Cycles in International Relations.'' *International Studies Quarterly* 35: 455–76.
Bergesen, Albert. 1985. ''Cycles of War in the Reproduction of the World Economy.'' In Paul Johnson and William R. Thompson, eds., *Rhythms in Politics and Economics.* New York: Praeger.
Bernard, Jacques. 1976. ''Trade and Finance in the Middle Ages, 900–1500.'' In Carlo M. Cipolla, ed., *The Fontana Economic History of Europe: The Middle Ages.* New York: Barnes and Noble.
Bernstein, A. M. 1940. ''War and the Pattern of Business Cycles.'' *American Economic Review* 30: 524–35.
Berry, Brian J. L. 1991. *Long-Wave Rhythms in Economic Development and Political Behavior.* Baltimore: Johns Hopkins University Press.
Blainey, G. 1973. *The Causes of War.* New York: Free Press.
Borrus, Michael G. 1988. *Competing for Control: America's Stake in Microelectronics.* Cambridge, Mass.: Ballinger.

Boswell, Terry, and J. Misra. Forthcoming. "Cycles and Trends in the Early Capitalist World-Economy: An Analysis of Leading Sector Commodity Trade, 1500–1600.50–1750." *Review.*

Boswell, Terry, J. Misra, and J. Brueggemann. 1991. "The Rise and Fall of Amsterdam and Dutch Hegemony: Evidence for the Baltic Sound Tolls, 1550–1750." In R. Kasaba, ed., *Cities in the World-System.* New York: Greenwood.

Boswell, Terry, and Mike Sweat. 1991. "Hegemony, Long Waves and Major Wars." *International Studies Quarterly* 35: 123–49.

Boxer, C. R. 1957. *The Dutch in Brazil.* Oxford: Oxford University Press.

Boyajian, James C. 1993. *Portuguese Trade in Asia Under the Habsburgs, 1580–1640.* Baltimore, Md.: Johns Hopkins University Press.

Braudel, Fernand. 1972. *The Mediterranean and the Mediterranean World in the Age of Philip II.* Vol. 1. New York: Harper and Collins.

———. 1982. *Wheels of Commerce.* London: Collins.

———. 1984. *The Perspective of the World.* London: Collins.

Brenner, R. 1985. *Betting on Ideas: Wars, Inventions, Inflation.* Chicago: University of Chicago Press.

Bruckmann, Gerhart. 1987. "Will There Be a Fifth Kondratieff?" In Tibor Vasko, ed., *The Long Wave Debate.* Berlin: Springer Verlag.

Bucher, Carl. 1907. *Industrial Evolution.* New York: Holt.

Cameron, Rondo. 1989. *A Concise Economic History of the World.* New York: Oxford University Press.

Cartier, Michel. 1991. "Aux origines de l'agriculture intensive du Bas Yangzi." *Annales ESC* (September–October): 1009–19.

Chan, Hok-lam. 1984. *Legitimation in Imperial China: Discussions under the Jurchen-Chin Dynasty 1115–1234.* Seattle: University of Washington Press.

Chandler, Tertius. 1987. *Four Thousand Years of Urban Growth.* Lewiston: St. David's University Press.

Chao, Kang. 1986. *Man and Land in Chinese History: An Economic Analysis.* Stanford: Stanford University Press.

Chase-Dunn, Christopher. 1989. *Global Formation: Structures of the World-Economy.* London: Blackwell.

Conybeare, J. A. C. 1990. "A Random Walk Down the Road to War: War Cycles, Prices and Causality." *Defense Economics* 1: 329–37.

Craig, P. P., and K. E. F. Watt. 1985. "The Kondratieff Cycle and War: How Close is the Connection?" *Futurist* 19: 25–28.

———. 1987. "Dynamic Programming of Socioeconomics and War: A Computer Experiment." In Tibor Vasko, ed., *The Long Wave Debate.* Berlin: Springer Verlag.

Davis, Howard T. 1941. *The Analysis of Economic Time Series.* Bloomington, Ind.: Principia Press.

Davis, Ralph. 1954. "English Foreign Trade, 1660–1700." *Economic History Review* 7: 150–64.

_____. 1973. *The Rise of the Atlantic Economies.* Ithaca, N.Y.: Cornell University Press.

Dickinson, F. G. 1934. "The Price of War." *Annals of the American Academy of Political and Social Science* 175: 166–74.

_____. 1940. "An Aftercost of the World War to the United States." *American Economic Review* 30, supplement, part 2: 326–39.

Doran, Charles F. 1983. "War and Power Dynamics: Economic Underpinnings." *International Studies Quarterly* 27: 419–41.

Dosi, Giovanni. 1983. "Technological Paradigms and Technological Trajectories: The Determinants and Directions of Technical Change and the Transformation of the Economy." In Christopher Freeman, ed., *Long Waves in the World Economy.* London: Frances Pinter.

_____. 1992. "The Research on Innovation Diffusion." In N. Nakicenovic and A. Gruebler, eds., *Diffusion of Technologies and Social Behaviour.* Springer: Verlag.

Duncan, T. Bentley. 1986. "Navigation Between Portugal and Asia in the Sixteenth and Seventeenth Centuries." In Cyriac K. Pullapilly and Edwin J. Van Kley, eds., *Asia and the West: Encounters and Exchanges from the Age of Explorations.* Notre Dame, Ind.: Cross Cultural Publications.

Dupuy, Ernst, and Trevor Dupuy. 1977. *The Encyclopedia of Military History.* Rev. ed. New York: Harper and Row.

Ebble, Ivana. 1986. *The Portuguese Trade with West Africa.* Ph.D. diss., University of Toronto.

Electronic Business. 1985. "Global Electronics: The Basis of Industry." 11:66–68.

Elliott, John H. 1970. *Imperial Spain, 1469–1716.* New York: Penguin.

Elster, Jon. 1989. *Nuts and Bolts for the Social Sciences.* London: Cambridge University Press.

Elvin, Mark. 1973. *The Pattern of the Chinese Past.* Stanford: Stanford University Press.

Eucken, Walter. 1951. *The Foundations of Economics.* Chicago: University of Chicago Press.

Fairbank, John K. 1992. *China: A New History.* Cambridge, Mass.: Belknap.

Ferguson, Charles H., and Charles R. Morris. 1993. *Computer Wars: How the West Can Win in a Post-IBM World.* New York: Random House.

Feuerwerker, Albert. 1992. "Questions about China's Early Modern Economic History That I Wish I Could Answer." *Journal of Asian Studies* 51: 757–69.

_____, ed. 1982. *Chinese Social and Economic History from the Song to 1900.* Ann Arbor: Michigan Monographs in Chinese Studies.

Fitzgerald, C. P. 1950. *China: A Short Cultural History.* London: Cresset.

Frank, Andre Gunder. 1978. *World Accumulation, 1492–1789.* New York: Monthly Review Press.

_____. 1990. "A Theoretical Introduction to 5000 Years of World System History." *Review* 13: 155–248.

Franke, Herbert. 1987. *Studien und Texte zur Kriegsgeschichte der Suedlichen Sung-zeit.* Wiesbaden: Otto Harassowitz.

Freeman, Christopher. 1987. "Technical Innovation, Diffusion, and Long Cycles of Economic Development." In Tibor Vasko, ed., *The Long Wave Debate.* Berlin: Springer Verlag.

_____, ed. 1983. *Long Waves in the World Economy.* London: Frances Pinter.

Freeman, Christopher, T. Clark, and Luc Soete. 1982. *Unemployment and Technical Innovation: A Study of Long Waves in Economic Development.* London: Frances Pinter.

Freeman, Christopher, and Carlotta Perez. 1988. "Structural Crisis of Adjustment." In Giovanni Dosi et al., eds., *Technical Change and Economic Theory.* London: Frances Pinter.

Gernet, Jacques. 1982. *A History of Chinese Civilization.* Cambridge: Cambridge University Press.

_____. 1962. *Daily Life in China on the Eve of the Mongol Invasion 1250–1276.* New York: Macmillan.

Gibbon, Edward. 1910. *The Decline and Fall of the Roman Empire.* New York: E. P. Dutton.

Gilpin, Robert. 1981. *War and Change in World Politics.* Cambridge: Cambridge University Press.

Godinho, V. M. 1963–1965. *Os Discobrimentos e a Economia Mundial.* Lisboa: Editorial Presencas.

Golas, Peter J. 1988. "The Sung Economy: How Big?" *Bulletin of Sung-Yuan Studies* 20: 90–94.

Goldstein, Joshua. 1985. "Kondratieff Waves as War Cycles." *International Studies Quarterly* 29: 411–44.

_____. 1987. "Long Waves in Production, War and Inflation: New Empirical Evidence. *Journal of Conflict Resolution* 31.

_____. 1988. *Long Cycles.* New Haven: Yale University Press.

_____. 1991a. "A War-Economy Theory of the Long Wave." In N. Thygesen, K. Velupillai, and S. Zambelli, eds., *Business Cycles: Theories, Evidence and Analysis.* New York: New York University Press.

_____. 1991b. "The Possibility of Cycles in International Relations." *International Studies Quarterly* 35: 477–80.

Grossman, Gene M., and Elhanan Helpman. 1994. "Endogenous Innovation in the Theory of Growth." *Journal of Economic Perspectives* 8: 23–44.

Hall, Peter. 1985. "The Geography of the Fifth Kondratieff." In Peter Hall and A. Markusen, eds., *Silicone Landscapes.* Boston: Allen and Unwin.

Hansen, A. H. 1932. *Economic Stabilization in An Unbalanced World.* New York: Harcourt, Brace.

_____. 1964. *Business Cycles and National Income.* Expanded ed. New York: W. W. Norton.

Hartwell, Robert M. 1966. "Markets, Technology, and the Structure of Enterprise in the Development of the Eleventh-Century Chinese Iron and Steel Industry." *Journal of Economic History* 26: 29–58.

———. 1967. "The Evolution of the Early Northern Sung Monetary System." *Journal of the American Oriental Society* 280–89.

———. 1982. "Demographic, Social and Economic Transformations in China 750–1550." *Harvard Journal of Asiatic Studies* 42: 365–442.

———. 1983. *Tribute Missions to China 960–1126.* Philadelphia, Pa.

———. 1988. "The Imperial Treasuries." *Bulletin of Sung-Yuan Studies* 20: 18–89.

———. 1989. "Foreign Trade, Monetary Policy, and Chinese 'Mercantilism.'" In T. Kinugawa, ed. *Collected Studies on Sung History.* Kyoto: Dohosha.

Haustein, H.-D., and E. Neuwirth. 1982. "Long Waves in World Industrial Production, Energy Consumption, Innovations, Inventions, Patents and Their Identification by Spectral Analysis." *Technological Forecasting and Social Change* 22: 53–89.

Henderson, Joseph B. 1984. *The Development and Decline of Chinese Cosmology.* New York: Columbia University Press.

Hicks, John. 1969. *A Theory of Economic History.* New York: Oxford University Press.

Ho, Ping-ti. 1956. "Early Ripening Rice in Chinese History." *Economic History Review* 200–18.

Hobsbawm, E. J. 1969. *Industry and Empire.* New York: Penguin Books.

Hopkins, Terry, Immanuel Wallerstein, and Associates. 1982. "Cyclical Rhythms and Secular Trends of the Capitalist World-Economy: Some Premises, Hypotheses and Questions." In Terry Hopkins and Immanuel Wallerstein, eds., *World-Systems Analysis: Theory and Methodology.* Beverly Hills, Calif.: Sage.

Huang, Ray. 1990. *China: A Macro History.* Armonk, N.Y.: M. E. Sharpe.

Imbert, G. 1959. *Des Mouvements de Longue Duree Kondratieff.* Aix-en-Provence: La Pensee Universitaire.

Inikori, Joseph E. 1987. "Slavery and the Development of Industrial Capitalism in England." In Barbara L. Solow and Stanley L. Engerman, eds., *British Capitalism and Caribbean Slavery: The Legacy of Eric Williams.* Cambridge: Cambridge University Press.

Israel, Jonathan. 1989. *Dutch Primacy in World Trade, 1585–1740.* Oxford: Clarendon Press.

Jones, E. L. 1988. *Growth Recurring: Economic Change in World History.* Oxford: Clarendon.

Kedar, B. Z. 1976. *Merchants in Crisis: Genoese and Venetian Men of Affairs and the Fourteenth-Century Depression.* New Haven, Conn.: Yale University Press.

Kennedy, Paul M. 1988. *The Rise and Fall of the Great Powers.* New York: Random.

Keynes, J. M. 1919/1971. *The Economic Consequences of Peace.* London: Macmillan.

Kinugawa, T., ed. 1989. *Collected Studies on Sung History Dedicated to Professor James T. C. Liu.* Kyoto: Dohosha.

Kondratieff, Nikolai D. 1935. "The Long Waves in Economic Life." *Review of Economic Statistics* 17: 105–15.

_____. 1984. *The Long Wave Cycle*. Trans. Guy Daniels. New York: Richardson and Snyder.

Kracke, E. A. 1953. *The Civil Service in Early Sung China 960–1067*. Cambridge: Harvard University Press.

Kurth, James K. 1979. "The Political Consequences of the Product Cycle." *International Organization* 33: 1–34.

Lamouroux, C. 1991. "Organization Territoriale et Monopole de The Dans la Chine des Song." *Annales ESC* 46: 977–1008.

Landes, David. 1969. *The Unbound Prometheus*. Cambridge: Cambridge University Press.

_____. 1983. *Revolution in Time*. Cambridge, Mass.: Belknap Press.

Lane, F. C. 1963. "The economic meaning of the invention of the compass." *American Historical Review* 63: 605–17.

_____. 1973. *Venice: The Maritime Republic*. Baltimore, Md.: Johns Hopkins University Press.

_____. 1987a. "Recent Studies in the Economic History of Venice." In B. G. Kohl and K. C. Mueller, eds., *Studies in Venetian Social and Economic History*. London: Variorum Reprints.

_____. 1987b. "Technology and Productivity in Seaborne Transportation." In B. G. Kohl and K. C. Mueller, eds., *Studies in Venetian Social and Economic History*. London: Variorum Reprints.

Lebadie, John Richard. 1981. "Rulers and Soldiers: Perception and Management of the Military in Northern Sung China 960–ca. 1060." Ph.D. diss., University of Washington.

Lewis, Archibald R. 1988. *Nomads and Crusaders, A.D. 1000–1368*. Bloomington: Indiana University Press.

Liska, G. 1990. *The Ways of Power*. Cambridge, Mass.: Blackwell.

Little, Daniel. 1991. *Varieties of Social Explanation*. Boulder, Colo.: Westview.

Liu, James T. C., and Peter J. Golas, eds. 1969. *Change in Sung China: Innovation or Renovation?* Lexington: D. C. Heath.

Lo, Jung-pang. 1955. "China as a Sea-power." *Far Eastern Quarterly* 14: 489–503.

_____. 1969. "Maritime Commerce and its Relation to the Sung Navy." *Journal of the Social and Economic History of the Orient* 12: 57–101.

Lopez, Robert. 1987. "The Trade of Medieval Europe: The South." In M. M. Postan and E. Miller, eds., *The Cambridge Economic History of Europe: Trade and Industry in the Middle Ages*. 2d ed. Cambridge: Cambridge University Press.

Lopez, Robert, and Harry A. Miskimin. 1962. "The Economic Depression of the Renaissance." *The Economic History Review* 2nd ser. 14: 408–26.

Lopez, Robert, and Irving W. Raymond. 1955. *Medieval Trade in the Mediterranean World*. New York: Columbia University Press.

Lopez, Robert, and A. L. Udovitch. 1970. "England to Egypt, 1350–1500: Long-term Trends and Long-distance Trade." In M. A. Cook, ed., *Studies in the Economic History of the Middle East*. London: Oxford University Press.

Luzzato, Gino. 1961. *An Economic History of Italy*. Trans. P. Jones. London: Routledge and Kegan Paul.

Ma, Lawrence. 1971. *Commercial Development and Urban Change in Sung China (960–1279)*. Ann Arbor: University of Michigan, Department of Geography.

Macfie, A. L. 1938. "The Outbreak of War and the Trade Cycle." *Economic History* 3: 89–97.

Malerba, Francis. 1985. *The Semiconductor Business: The Economics of Rapid Growth and Decline*. Madison: University of Wisconsin Press.

Mansfield, Edward D. 1988. "The Distribution of Wars Over Time." *World Politics* 41: 21–51.

Markoff, John. 1994. "Toys Now, Computers Tomorrow?" *New York Times* 20 April, C1, 13.

Mathew, K. S. 1983. *Portuguese Trade with India in the Sixteenth Century*. New Delhi: Manchar.

McCusker, John J., and Russell R. Menard. 1985. *The Economy of British America, 1607–1789*. Chapel Hill: University of North Carolina Press.

McEvedy, Colin, and Richard Jones. 1978. *Atlas of World Population History*. New York: Penguin Books.

McNeill, William. 1963. *The Rise of the West*. Chicago: University of Chicago Press.

———. 1974. *Venice: The Hinge of Europe, 1081–1797*. Chicago: University of Chicago Press.

———. 1982. *The Pursuit of Power*. Chicago: University of Chicago Press.

Mensch, Gerhard. 1979. *Stalemate in Technology: Innovations Overcome the Depression*. Cambridge: Ballinger.

Meskill, John, ed. 1965. *The Pattern of Chinese History: Cycles, Development, or Stagnation*. Lexington: D. C. Heath.

Mintz, Sidney W. 1985. *Sweetness and Power: The Place of Sugar in Modern History*. New York: Penguin Books.

Miskimin, Harry A. 1975. *The Economy of Early Renaissance Europe, 1300–1460*. Cambridge: Cambridge University Press.

Mitchell, Brian. 1980. *European Historical Statistics, 1750–1975*. 2d rev. ed. New York: Facts on File.

———. 1982. *International Historical Statistics, Africa and Asia*. New York: New York University Press.

———. 1988. *British Historical Statistics*. Cambridge: Cambridge University Press.

Miyakawa, Hisayuki. 1955. "An Outline of the Naito Hypothesis and its Effects on Japanese Studies of China." *Far Eastern Quarterly* 14: 532–52.

Mjoset, Lars. 1990. "The Turn of the Two Centuries: A Comparison of British and U.S. Hegemonies." In David Rapkin, ed., *World Leadership and Hegemony*. Boulder: Lynne Rienner.

Modelski, George. 1978. "The Long Cycle of Global Politics and the Nation-State." *Comparative Studies in Society and History* 20: 214–35.

_____. 1981. "Long Cycles, Kondratieffs and Alternating Innovations." In Charles W. Kegley and Pat McGowan, eds., *The Political Economy of Foreign Policy Behavior.* Beverly Hills: Sage.

_____. 1982. "Long Cycles and the Strategy of U.S. International Economic Policy." In William A. Avery and David P. Rapkin, eds., *America in a Changing World Political Economy.* New York: Longman.

_____. 1987. *Long Cycles in World Politics.* London: Macmillan.

_____. 1990. "Is World Politics Evolutionary Learning?" *International Organization* 44: 1–24.

_____. 1991. *Long Cycles in World Politics.* Japanese language edition. Tokyo: Koyo Shobo.

_____. 1992. "World System Evolution: A Learning Model." Paper presented at the Annual Meeting of the International Studies Association, Vancouver, Canada, April 1991, revised.

_____. 1995. "From Leadership to Organization: The Evolution of Global Politics." *Journal of World Systems Research* 1.

Modelski, George, and Sylvia Modelski, eds. 1988. *Documenting Global Leadership.* London: Macmillan.

Modelski, George, and Patrick Morgan. 1985. "Understanding Global War." *Journal of Conflict Resolution* 29: 391–417.

Modelski, George, and William R. Thompson. 1988. *Seapower in Global Politics 1494–1993.* London: Macmillan.

Mokyr, J. 1990. *The Lever of Riches: Technological Creativity and Economic Progress.* Oxford: Oxford University Press.

Motor Vehicle Manufacturers Association. 1981. *World Motor Vehicle Data.* Detroit.

Needham, John. 1969. *The Great Titration: Science and Society in East and West.* Toronto: Toronto University Press.

Needham, John, et al. 1986. "Military Technology: the Gunpowder Epic." Vol. 5, pt. 7 of *Science and Civilization in China.* Cambridge: Cambridge University Press.

Negri, Teofilo Ossian. 1974. *Storia di Genoa.* Milan: Aldo Martello.

Nelson, Richard, and Sidney Winter. 1982. *An Evolutionary Theory of Economic Change.* New York: Columbia University Press.

North, Douglass. 1968. "Economic History." *International Encyclopedia of the Social Sciences.* Vol. 5. New York: Macmillan.

_____. 1990. *Institutions, Institutional Change and Economic Performance.* New York: Cambridge University Press.

Norwich, John J. 1982. *A History of Venice.* New York: Penguin.

O'Brien, Patrick. 1982. "European Economic Development: The Contribution of the Periphery." *The Economic History Review* 35: 1–18.

Ohmae, Kenichi. 1990. *The Borderless World: Management Lessons in the New Logic of the Global Marketplace.* New York: Harper Business.

Olson, Mancur. 1982. *The Rise and Decline of Nations.* New Haven: Yale University Press.

Organski, A. F. K., and Jacek Kugler. 1980. *The War Ledger.* Chicago: University of Chicago Press.

Pack, Howard. 1994. "Endogenous Growth Theory: Intellectual Appeal and Empirical Shortcomings." *Journal of Economic Perspectives* 8: 55–72.

Peterson, Charles A. 1975. "First Sung Reactions to the Mongol Invasion of the North, 1211–17." In J. W. Haeger, ed., *Crisis and Prosperity in Sung China.* Tucson: University of Arizona Press.

———. 1983. "Old Illusions and New Realities." In Morris Rossabi, ed., *China Among Equals.* Berkeley: University of California Press.

Phillips, Carla R. 1990. "The Growth and Composition of Trade in the Iberian Empires, 1450–1750." In James D. Tracy, ed., *The Rise of Merchant Empires: Long-Distance Trade in the Early Modern World, 1350–1750.* Cambridge: Cambridge University Press.

Phillips, J. R. S. 1988. *The Medieval Expansion of Europe.* New York: Oxford University Press.

Pirenne, Henri. 1937. *Economic and Social History of Medieval Europe.* New York: Harcourt Brace.

Porter, Michael E. 1990. *The Competitive Advantage of Nations.* New York: Free Press.

Price, Jacob M. 1973. *France and the Chesapeake.* Vol. 2. Ann Arbor: University of Michigan Press.

Rasler, Karen, and William R. Thompson. 1989. *War and Statemaking: The Shaping of the Global Powers.* Boston: Unwin and Hyman.

———. 1991. "Technological Innovation, Capability Positional Shifts, and Systemic War." *Journal of Conflict Resolution* 35: 412–42.

———. 1992. "Assessing the Costs of War: A Preliminary Cut." In G. Ausenda, ed., *Effects of War on Society.* Republic of San Marino: Center for Interdisciplinary Research on Social Stress.

———. 1994. *The Great Powers and Global Struggle, 1490–1990.* Lexington: University Press of Kentucky.

Rawley, James A. 1981. *The Transatlantic Slave Trade.* New York: W. W. Norton.

Ray, George F. 1983. "Innovation and Long-term Economic Growth." In Christopher Freeman, ed., *Long Waves in the World Economy.* London: Frances Pinter.

Research Working Group. 1979. "Cyclical Rhythms and Secular Trends of the Capitalist World-Economy: Some Premises, Hypotheses and Questions." *Review* 2: 483–500.

Reischauer, E. O., and John Fairbank. 1960. *East Asia: The Great Tradition.* Boston: Houghton Mifflin.

Richardson, David. 1987. "The Slave Trade, Sugar, and British Economic Growth, 1748–1776." In Barbara L. Solow and Stanley L. Engerman, eds., *British Capitalism and Caribbean Slavery: The Legacy of Eric Williams.* Cambridge: Cambridge University Press.

Romer, Paul M. 1990. "Endogenous Technological Change." *Journal of Political Economy* 98, pt. 2: 71–102.

_____. 1994. "The Origins of Endogenous Growth." *Journal of Economic Perspectives* 8: 3–22.

Rose, A. 1941. "Wars, Innovations and Long Cycles: A Brief Comment." *American Economic Review* 31: 105–7.

Rossabi, Morris, ed. 1983. *China Among Equals: the Middle Kingdom and its Neighbors, 10th–14th Centuries.* Berkeley: University of California Press.

Rostow, Walt W. 1978. *The World Economy.* Austin: University of Texas Press.

_____. 1980. *Why the Poor Get Richer and the Rich Slow Down.* Austin: University of Texas Press.

_____. 1990. *Theorists of Economic Growth from David Hume to the Present.* New York: Oxford University Press.

Russett, Bruce. 1983. "Prosperity and Peace." *International Studies Quarterly* 27: 381–87.

Samuelson, Paul A. 1980. *Economics.* 11th ed. New York: McGraw Hill.

Sansom, G. B. 1978. *Japan: A Short Cultural History.* Stanford: Stanford University Press.

Sayrs, Lois W. 1993. "The Long Cycle in International Relations: A Markov Specification." *International Studies Quarterly* 37: 215–37.

Scammell, G. V. 1981. *The World Encompassed: The First European Maritime Empires, ca. 800–1650.* Berkeley: University of California Press.

_____. 1989. *The First Imperial Age: European Overseas Expansion, circa 1400–1715.* London: Unwin Hyman.

Schumpeter, Elizabeth B. 1960. *English Overseas Trade Statistics, 1697–1808.* Oxford: Clarendon.

Schumpeter, Joseph. 1934. *Theory of Economic Development.* Cambridge, Mass.: Harvard University Press.

_____. 1939. *Business Cycles.* New York: McGraw Hill.

_____. 1954. *History of Economic Analysis.* New York: Oxford University Press.

Semiconductor Industry Association. Multiple volumes. *Semiconductor Industry Association Yearbook and Directory.* San Francisco.

Shiba, Yoshinobu. 1970. *Commerce and Society in Sung China.* Trans. Mark Elvin. Ann Arbor: University of Michigan Center for Chinese Studies.

_____. 1983. "Sung Foreign Trade: its Scope and Organization." In Morris Rossabi, ed. *China Among Equals.* Berkeley: University of California Press.

Shapiro, Helen. 1993. "Automobiles: From Import Substitution to Export Promotion in Brazil and Mexico." In David B. Yoffie, ed., *Beyond Free Trade: Firms, Governments, and Global Competition.* Boston: Harvard Business School Press.

Shuman, J. B., and D. Rosenau. 1972. *The Kondratieff Wave: The Future of America Until 1984 and Beyond.* New York: Dell.

Silberling, N. J. 1943. *The Dynamics of Business.* New York: McGraw Hill.

Sitwell, N. H. H. 1986. *Outside the Empire: The World the Romans Knew.* London: Collins.

Sleigh, Dan. 1980. *Jan Compagnie: The World of the Dutch East India Company.* Cape Town, Union of South Africa: Tafelberg Publishers.

Slomovic, Anna. 1991. *An Analysis of Military and Commercial Microelectronics: Has DOD's R & D Funding Had the Desired Effect?* Santa Monica, Calif.: Rand Graduate School Dissertation.

Soderstrom, H. T. 1982. "Comment on Christopher Freeman's Innovation as an Engine of Growth: Retrospect and Prospects." In H. Giersch, ed., *Emerging Technologies: Consequences for Economic Growth, Structural Change and Employment.* Tubingen: Mohr.

Solow, Barbara L. 1987. "Capitalism and Slavery in the Exceedingly Long Run." In Barbara L. Solow and Stanley L. Engerman, eds., *British Capitalism and Caribbean Slavery: The Legacy of Eric Williams.* Cambridge: Cambridge University Press.

Solow, Barbara L., and Stanley L. Engerman. 1987. "British Capitalism and Caribbean Slavery: The Legacy of Eric Williams: An Introduction." In Barbara L. Solow and Stanley L. Engerman, eds., *British Capitalism and Caribbean Slavery: The Legacy of Eric Williams.* Cambridge: Cambridge University Press.

Solow, Robert H. 1957. "Technical Change and the Aggregate Production Function." *Review of Economics and Statistics* 39: 312–20.

_____. 1994. "Perspectives on Growth Theory." *Journal of Economic Perspectives* 8: 45–54.

Sombart, Werner. 1902/1924. *Der Moderne Kapitalismus.* Vol. 1. Munich: Duncker and Humboldt.

Steensgaard, Nels. 1970. "European Shipping to Asia, 1497–1700." *Scandinavian Economic History Review* 18: 1–11.

_____. 1990. "The Growth and Composition of the Long Distance Trade of England and the Dutch Republic Before 1750." In James D. Tracy, ed., *The Rise of Merchant Empires.* Cambridge: Cambridge University Press.

Strogatz, Steven, and Ian Stewart. 1993. "Coupled Oscillators and Biological Synchronization." *Scientific American* 269: 102–9.

Subrahmanyam, Sanjay. 1993. *The Portuguese Empire in Asia, 1500–1700: A Political and Economic History.* London: Longman.

Tarascio, V. J. 1989. "Economic and War Cycles." *History of Political Economy* 21: 91–101.

Tenenti, Alberto, and Corrado Vivanti. 1961. "Le Film d'un Grand Systeme de Navigation: Les Galeres Marchandes Venitiennes, XIV–XVI Siecles." *Annales* 16: 83–86.

Thompson, James W. 1921. "The Aftermath of the Black Death and the Aftermath of the Great War." *American Journal of Sociology* 26: 565–72.

Thompson, William R. 1982. "Phases of the Business Cycle and the Outbreak of War." *International Studies Quarterly* 26: 301–11.

_____. 1985. "Cycles of General, Hegemonic and Global War and the Periodicity Question." In Urs Luterbacher and Michael Ward, eds., *Dynamic Models of International Conflict.* Boulder, Colo.: Lynne Rienner.

_____. 1988. *On Global War.* Columbia: University of South Carolina Press.

_____. 1990. "Long Waves, Innovation and Decline." *International Organization* 44: 201–34.

_____. 1992a. "Systemic Leadership and Growth Waves in the Long Run." *International Studies Quarterly* 36: 25–48

_____. 1992b. "Long Cycles and the Geohistorical Context of Structural Transitions." *World Politics* 43: 127–52.

Thompson, William R., and Karen A. Rasler. 1988. "War and Systemic Capability Reconcentration." *Journal of Conflict Resolution* 32: 355–66.

Thompson, William R., and Lawrence Vescera. 1992. "Growth Waves, Systemic Openness and Protectionism." *International Organization* 46: 492–533.

Thompson, William R., and Gary Zuk. 1982. "War, Inflation and Kondratieff's Long Waves." *Journal of Conflict Resolution* 26: 621–44.

Tilly, Charles. 1990. *Coercion, Capital and European States, A.D. 990–1990.* Cambridge, Mass.: Blackwell.

Tinbergen, Jan. 1983. "Kondratiev Cycles and So-Called Long Waves: The Early Research." In Christopher Freeman, ed., *Long Waves in the World Economy.* London: Frances Pinter.

Todd, Daniel. 1990. *The World Electronics Industry.* London: Routledge.

Toynbee, Arnold. 1954. *A Study of History.* Vol. 9. New York: Oxford University Press.

Trotsky, L. 1923/1973. "The Curve of Capitalist Development." In L. Trotsky, ed., *Problems of Everyday Life.* New York: Monad Press.

Truman, Harry S. 1961. *The Public Papers of Harry S Truman.* Washington, D.C.: U.S. GPO.

Tsien, Tsuen-hsuin. 1985. "Paper and Printing." In Joseph Needham, ed., *Science and Civilization in China.* Vol. 5, pt. 5. Cambridge: Cambridge University Press.

Tyson, Laura D'Andrea. 1992. *Who's Bashing Whom? Trade Conflict in High-Technology Industries.* Washington, D.C.: Institute for International Economics.

Tyson, Laura D'Andrea, and David B. Yoffie. 1993. "Semiconductors: From Manipulated to Managed Trade." In David B. Yoffie, ed., *Beyond Free Trade: Firms, Governments, and Global Competition.* Boston: Harvard Business School Press.

U.S. Department of Commerce. 1975. *Historical Statistics of the United States: Colonial Times to 1970.* Washington, D.C.: U.S. GPO.

U.S. Office of the President. Multiple volumes. *Economic Report of the President.* Washington, D.C.: U.S. GPO.

U.S. Office of Technology Assessment. 1991. *Competing Economies.* Washington, D.C.: U.S. GPO.

Van der Wee, Herman. 1990. "Structural Changes in European Long-Distance Trade, and Particularly in the Re-export Trade from South to North, 1350–1750." In J. D.

Tracy, ed., *The Rise of Merchant Empires: Long-Distance Trade in the Early Modern World, 1350–1750.* Cambridge: Cambridge University Press.

van Duijn, J. J. 1983. *The Long Wave in Economic Life.* London: George Allen and Unwin.

Vasko, Tibor, ed. 1987. *The Long Wave Debate.* Berlin: Springer.

Vayrynen, Raimo. 1983. "Economic Cycles, Power Transitions, Political Management and Wars Between Major Powers." *International Studies Quarterly* 27: 389–413.

Verseth, Michael. 1990. *Mountains of Death: Crisis and Change in Renaissance Florence, Victorian Britain and Post-war America.* New York: Oxford University Press.

Vescera, Larry. 1994. *A Long Wave Theory of Protectionism.* Ph.D. diss., Claremont Graduate School.

Wake, C. H. H. 1979. "The Changing Pattern of Europe's Pepper and Spice Imports, ca. 1400–1700." *Journal of European Economic History* 8: 361–403.

———. 1986. "The Volume of European Spice Trade at the Beginning and the End of the Fifteenth Century." *Journal of European Economic History* 15: 621–35.

Wallerstein, Immanuel. 1984. *The Politics of the World-Economy.* Cambridge: Cambridge University Press.

———. 1989. *The Modern World-Economy.* Vol. 3. San Diego, Calif.: Academic Press.

Wang, Gangwu. 1963. *The Structure of Power in North China During the Five Dynasties.* Kuala Lumpur: University of Malaya Press.

Watts, David. 1987. *The West Indies: Patterns of Development, Culture and Environmental Change Since 1492.* Cambridge: Cambridge University Press.

Williams, John T. 1993. "Dynamic Change, Specification Uncertainty and Bayesian Vector Autoregression Analysis." *Political Analysis* 4: 97–125.

Williams, John T., Michael D. McGinnis, and John C. Thomas. 1992. "Breaking the War-Economy Link." Paper presented at the Annual Meeting of the International Studies Association, Atlanta, Ga.

Wittfogel, Karl, and Feng Chia-sheng. 1949. *History of Chinese Society: The Liao.* Philadelphia, Pa.: American Philosophical Society.

World Intellectual Property Organization. Multiple volumes. *World Industrial Property Rights Statistics.* Geneva: World Intellectual Property Organization.

Worsley, Peter. 1984. *The Three Worlds: Culture and World Development.* London: Weidenfeld and Nicolson.

Worthy, Edmund H. 1975. "Regional Control in the Southern Sung Salt Administration." In J. W. Haeger, ed., *Crisis and Prosperity in Sung China.* Tucson: University of Arizona Press.

Wright, Quincy. 1942/1965. *A Study of War.* Chicago: University of Chicago Press.

Yakovets, Yu. V. 1987. "Scientific and Technological Cycles: Program and Aim-Oriented Planning." In Tibor Vasko, ed., *The Long Wave Debate.* Berlin: Springer Verlag.

Yang, Lien-sheng. 1961. *Studies in Chinese Institutional History.* Cambridge, Mass.: Harvard University Press.

INDEX